THE UNMAKING OF AMERICANS

How Multiculturalism Has Undermined the Assimilation Ethic

JOHN J. MILLER

THE FREE PRESS

New York   London   Toronto   Sydney   Singapore

THE FREE PRESS
A Division of Simon & Schuster Inc.
1230 Avenue of the Americas
New York, NY 10020

THE FREE PRESS and colophon are trademarks
of Simon & Schuster Inc.

Designed by Carla Bolte

Manufactured in the United States of America

10   9   8   7   6   5   4   3   2   1

Library of Congress Cataloging-in-Publication Data

Miller, John J., 1970-
    The unmaking of Americans : how multiculturalism has undermined
the assimilation ethic / John J. Miller.
        p.   cm.
    Includes bibliographical references and index.
    ISBN 0–684–83622–X
    1. Multiculturalism—United States.   2. Americanization.
I. Title
E184.A1M527   1998
306.4'0973—dc21   97-38208
                                                            CIP

For my grandmother

KATHERINE GAGNE

CONTENTS

INTRODUCTION

My grandmother came to the United States in 1911 as a four-year-old girl from Austria-Hungary. Although she was young, she remembers cruising into New York Harbor, spotting the Statue of Liberty, and making her way through Ellis Island. During the course of writing this book, I went to the National Archives in Washington, D.C., to track down the ship's manifest for the *Crown Princess Cecilia*, the boat that carried my grandmother and her family to America. I never found it, but what struck me most about the experience was how so many people were at the same place trying to do the same thing on a cold night in January. Just ask one of the archivists. Looking for information about immigrant ancestors is one of the most popular research projects people bring to them. My search helped me understand as I never had before that immigration is one of America's great national stories, our country's creation myth.

Just as the story of creation takes up only the first 2 of 50 chapters in Genesis, immigration is only a small part of the American saga. There is much more to our national origin than the mere arrival of huddled masses from abroad. The *Americanization* of our immigrant forebears is what makes us able to take pride in our national motto, *E pluribus unum*, and rightly call ourselves a nation of immigrants. My grandmother's family did not migrate to Cincinnati and replicate life in the old country, although they lived in an ethnic neighborhood and kept many of their old ways. They struggled to learn about their new home, to speak its language, and to live by its rules. They also became citizens. My great-grandfather even had to take the citizenship test twice. After moving his family to Detroit, he passed the test there only because a kindly judge took pity on an old man who did not speak English very well but who wanted more than anything else to die an American. My grandmother eventually married a man from Michigan's copper country whose parents hailed from Quebec. They spoke better French than English.

My family's Americanization is not a unique tale. Most Americans can tell some version of it. Yet I wonder what would happen today. What if my grandmother were a little girl crossing the border from Mexico with her family, drawn by their dreams of creating a better life in the United States? Would she have the same experience of Americanization? Or would she be segregated into a public school where the teachers deliberately inhibited her from learning to speak, read, and write in English because they view her "native language maintenance" as more important? Would our culture of racial politics encourage her to think of herself as the member of some racial or ethnic category before she thought of herself as an American? Would she lack a clear, coherent picture of what it means to be an American in the first place?

My grandmother never had to worry about such things. In her day, it was widely accepted that immigrants should work hard, learn English (especially if they were kids), and become American citizens. Americans viewed these activities as positive actions that would benefit both individual immigrants and the country as a whole. In truth, the United States has not always welcomed every immigrant who wanted to come here, and often the logic of restriction has been based on regrettably racialist reasoning. And yet in more than two centuries of nationhood, America has forged a remarkably strong record of generosity by allowing and encouraging the immigration of people from all parts of the globe, and then accepting them, in fairly quick order, as full members of the national community.

Today, however, we face a significant threat to America's tradition of assimilation. This threat does not come from immigrants, but is best understood by listening to the public debate surrounding them. The vital questions are not about how many foreign-born people to let in or whom they should be, although these tend to dominate political discussions about immigrants. Instead, they are about how to treat immigrants and what we should expect of them once they arrive here. In a remarkably short time, the United States has gone from being a country that could confidently lay out a few principles to which immigrants and the native-born could adhere to being a nation unsure of what it should ask of these newcomers.

The need for Americanization is as great as ever, and yet we seem unwilling even to use a word like *Americanization* because it appears chauvinistic, judgmental, or just plain rude. Many Americans are strikingly hesitant to believe that their country is the greatest the world has ever known. They would never say such a thing in mixed company without making all the necessary qualifications about how it was wrong to steal land from the Indians, enslave blacks, deny women the vote, and so on. The chief purpose of retelling our history these days is to issue apologies. Sharing America's greatness with immigrants hardly seems like an option when it appears as though there was never much greatness to go around in the first place. The result is a sad reluctance to put forward a distinctly American national vision, for fear of offending someone again.

The consequences of this national self-doubt have created a mishmash of harmful public policies that actively inhibit the Americanization of immigrants. We allow our public schools to engage in the charade of bilingual education that rarely teaches children to speak, read, and write in English as well as they could. Often it leaves them illiterate in two languages and fluent in none. We allow our government to classify people by their skin color and treat them as members of groups rather than as individuals. We flirt with lowering the standards of naturalization so far that the only requirement for full membership in our political community could become filling out an application form, as if citizenship were nothing more than a driver's license. Roll it all together, and we seem to have forgotten what it means to be American and no longer know how to express or share the ideals that ultimately bind us together. The United States used to be quite good at making Americans. Today, when we are at our worst, we are unmaking them.

The struggle to understand and transmit American national culture to immigrants never has been an easy one. *E pluribus unum* is as much a riddle as a motto.[1] There is no reason why Americanization should be easy today. Yet the need for it perhaps has never been greater than right now for the simple reason that the idea of Americanization has fallen on such hard times. Restoring its good name should become a national priority. In doing so, we serve today's immigrants and ourselves.

The goal of this book is to revive Americanization. I hope to unite people on all sides of the immigration debate, from those who favor generous levels of immigration to those of a more restrictionist bent, in common cause. Understanding the importance of assimilation does not require agreement on the right number of immigrants to admit to the United States. Few or many, we should hope that every stranger in our land becomes a patriotic American. By building a new Americanization movement for the turn of the 21st century, we come closer to accomplishing this important goal.

The Unmaking of Americans is divided into two parts. Part One provides the history of Americanization as an idea, starting with an overview of its current state of disrepute and then going back in time to show how it fell to such low levels. Americanization's fall was hardly inevitable, and our history shows how we can do much better. Part Two provides an in-depth examination of our contemporary predicament, in which some of our most important public institutions engage in activity blatantly hostile to the unifying idea of Americanization. It concludes with a manifesto outlining a pro-Americanization political agenda that may not solve all of our problems but goes a long way toward alleviating some of them.

PART ONE

THE IDEA OF AMERICANIZATION

Chapter 1

AMERICANIZATION AND ITS ENEMIES

On an October morning in 1994, the largest political demonstration in Los Angeles history surged downtown. An estimated seventy thousand marchers walked west on Cesar E. Chavez Avenue, each step taking them closer to City Hall. They gathered at the city's center to rally against Proposition 187, a statewide ballot initiative to deny a range of public services, including education and nonemergency medical care, to illegal aliens. Just three weeks later voters approved the measure by a 3-to-2 margin. The courts eventually struck down its key provisions, but on this day nobody knew what would happen. Proposition 187 assumed a white-hot urgency. It was another ugly example of nativism, said the protesters, another sad attempt by privileged Anglos to make a panicky statement against the dusky hordes of Mexico. Traditional civil rights groups such as the Southern Christian Leadership Conference, founded by Martin Luther King, Jr., participated in the march. Their presence lent a powerful symbolism to the assembly.

Another kind of symbolism also entered the picture: Mexican flags were everywhere. And they did more than summon ethnic pride. They made a strong us-versus-them political statement about one of the most contentious issues California voters ever faced. The red, white, and green banners became the chief emblem of the movement to defeat Proposition 187. They made appearances in hundreds of smaller rallies around the state in later weeks. And they served as uncomfortable reminders to everyone that this issue—technically about the legal entitlements of people living in the United States without the public's consent—had mutated into a question of U.S. national identity. Some of the demonstrators offered unsettling answers. When a protester in San Marcos tried to stop one of his fellow demonstrators from torching an American flag a few days before the election, an angry mob chased and beat him.[1]

"This is just the opening salvo. It is our Fort Sumter!" declared one of the L.A. activists from a podium before the crowd.[2] His allusion to the first engagement of the Civil War—the bloodiest war in American history—was hardly comforting. In the state that attracted about 40 percent of the country's immigrants and in a city that saw balkanized race rioting just two years earlier, a reference to Fort Sumter spoke volumes. As Californians tuned into their local news that evening and thought over the merits of Proposition 187 in the following weeks, they saw these images: Mexican flags flying. American flags burning. Fort Sumter.

Regardless of whether the protesters had legitimate gripes to make about Proposition 187, they had changed the subject. Rather than focusing on the merits of a ballot initiative, their confrontational rally represented the emblematic rejection of American national identity. It signaled a profound violation of the assimilation ethic that has allowed the United States to become a nation of immigrants, a country whose people can trace their ancestry to all parts of the globe but who nonetheless share a sense of peoplehood that springs out of their common citizenship.

Not surprisingly, the L.A. protest wound up poisoning its own cause. In early October, support for the initiative had slipped, though it still appeared to command a majority in public opinion surveys. Overnight tracking polls following the march, however, showed that the demonstrators had not fired the first shot at Fort Sumter. Instead, they had met their Waterloo. Support for Proposition 187 soared. "If those people had used American flags instead of Mexican ones, we might have won this thing," said Frank Sharry, head of the National

Immigration Forum and an anti-187 organizer, after the election. Maybe. But by then it was too late. The whole anti-187 escapade— from the mass march in L.A. down to the tiniest high-school walkout in Van Nuys—forced a troubling conclusion into the minds of many Californians: The immigrants of today aren't like the immigrants of yesterday. They don't want to be Americans.

MELTING POT OR BOILING POINT?

Anxiety over the current wave of immigration is not confined to California. In a *Newsweek* poll, 60 percent of all Americans said that immigration is a "bad thing" for the country today. By way of comparison, 59 percent said that it was a "good thing" in the past.[3] Social scientist Rita Simon has shown that almost always a plurality and often a majority of Americans have wanted cuts in immigration levels since 1946, when the first reliable poll of this nature was taken.[4] In the 1990s, the discontent appears to have peaked. More than 60 percent of Americans today regularly say that they want immigration reduced.[5]

Americans are concerned about immigrants for many reasons; by far the most significant one—underscored by the L.A. protest—is the *against* sense that the United States is losing or has lost its national sense of purpose. "The historic idea of a unifying American identity is now in peril in many arenas," wrote historian Arthur M. Schlesinger, Jr., in *The Disuniting of America.* "If separatist tendencies go on unchecked, the result can only be the fragmentation, resegregation, and tribalization of American life."[6] In a 1993 poll, only 20 percent of all Americans believed that their country was "still a melting pot." Nearly two-thirds said that immigrants now "maintain their identity more strongly than in the past."[7] According to another survey, 86 percent of Americans think that "there was a time when people in this country felt they had more in common and shared more values than Americans do today." More shocking, about 30 percent do not think the United States will "still exist as one nation" in 100 years.[8]

In the three decades since 1965, the United States has admitted nearly 20 million immigrants. Since 1990, the annual average has been about seven hundred fifty thousand. Roughly 85 percent of these most recent newcomers hail from Asia, the Caribbean, and Latin America—

places that accounted for less than 20 percent of all immigrants during the 1950s, and only 5 percent in the first 10 years of the 20th century.[9] Could today's immigrants, coming from seemingly exotic locales, really subvert American national unity? The only way is if they do not become Americans, if they remain permanently apart from the American national identity as outsiders, people who might eventually break the country to pieces because they have no sense of belonging to it.

The challenge of assimilating the foreign-born is as old as the republic itself. Americans can take some solace from the fact that their country has a powerful record of helping immigrants successfully adapt to the American way of life. National unity has withstood more than 60 million immigrant arrivals since 1820, the year the government started counting them.[10] These masses did not tear the country to shreds. They even may have helped keep it together—an estimated 25 percent of federal troops during the Civil War were foreign-born.[11] These immigrants became Americans. Today, immigrants make up a smaller percentage of the U.S. population than they did at any point between the Civil War and the 1920s. According to the Census Bureau, about 9.3 percent of all Americans in 1996 were foreign-born, compared to the historic high of almost 15 percent in 1910.[12] In other words, the immigrants are more outnumbered right now than they have been throughout much of the past. Consequently, they face an intense amount of pressure to assimilate. Finally—and most important—is the strong historical tradition in the United States of *Americanizing* immigrants. Those 60 million arrivals did not reproduce their homelands in the new world. They and their descendants altered their identity and adopted a new way of life.

The United States can welcome immigrants and transform them into Americans because it is a "proposition country." American identity has more to do with beliefs than bloodlines. American citizenship is rooted in dedication to a set of political principles that involve commitments to the Constitution; the rule of law; and the individual rights of life, liberty, and the pursuit of happiness. Its origins are found in political principles, as opposed to racial or ethnic ties. Citizenship also includes a few cultural corollaries, such as the ability to speak English (or at least broken English). Because this definition of American citizenship does not make reference to biological ancestry—as the citizenship of most other nations implicitly does—it has allowed people born out-side the United States to arrive on its shores and over time to become American citizens. The struggle to become American is the process of assimilation, and assimilation is a vital part of keeping this nation of immigrants whole. The motto on the United States seal is *E pluribus unum*—Latin for "out of many, one." Without assimilation, the *pluribus* threatens to drown out the *unum,* imperiling the very concept of American nationhood.

For all the vitality of this tradition, however, it does not run on au-topilot. Our positive, historical record of immigrant assimilation is not enough. Americanization needs modern-day advocates willing to assert the importance of a strong national identity grounded in political prin-ciples. Unfortunately, such advocates are in short supply today. Elite opinion leaders regularly reverse the age-old pattern of urging immi-grants to adapt to the United States. Now the United States must adapt to them, they say. Martha Farnsworth Riche, head of the Census Bu-reau, heralds a marked change in how the United States confronts im-migrants: "Without fully realizing it, we have left the time when the nonwhite, non-Western part of our population could be expected to as-similate to the dominant majority," she wrote in *American Demograph-ics.* "In the future, the white Western majority will have to do some assimilation of its own," she claimed.[13] Doris Meissner, commissioner of the Immigration and Naturalization Service (INS), agreed. "We are being transformed," she remarked.[14] One gets the sense that this pair is not just talking about adding salsa to the menu—something that any Americanizer with a healthy pallet would encourage. Instead, they infer something deeper, a change in the very way that America functions as a country.

Although this need not be the case, Americanization unfortunately has become a dirty word. So has assimilation. "There are some people who have such a concern about assimilation. . . . Some of them are coming at it from a perspective of racism," said New York City school board member Luis Reyes.[15] Stephen Small calls assimilation a tool of subjugation: "Cultural assimilation, cultural acculturation . . . or cul-tural assassination!" he proclaims.[16] The value of Americanization probably hit rock-bottom in former Senator Paul Simon's 1980 book, *The Tongue-Tied American.* Two lengthy quotations serve as epigraphs to the presumptively titled first chapter, "Americanization Has Its Weaknesses." The first was spoken by a New York City school commissioner in 1896. In part, it reads: "I consider it the paramount duty of public schools, apart from the educational knowledge to be instilled into our pupils, to form American citizens of them." The commissioner goes on to emphasize the importance of suppressing traits that are inimical to citizenship. The second excerpt is from *Mein Kampf,* in which its author Adolf Hitler attacks the idea of learning a foreign language. The New York educator's quotation is perhaps a bit harsh in tone when it later speaks of "obliterating" the "foreign characteristics" that he deems "irritating." But it is hardly Hitleresque. The commissioner illustrates the important principle that there is a distinct American identity into which immigrants can and must fit. The juxtaposition of this pro-Americanization quote with the thoughts of one of history's monsters speaks volumes about the low standing of Americanization with elite opinion leaders, a standing so low that it apparently warrants equivalence with genocide.[17]

The constant clatter of derision aimed at the idea of Americanization has had harmful consequences. It has undermined public confidence in the country's ability to assert itself in the vigorous way necessary to make assimilation work. The fallout has included a series of public policies hostile to the Americanization of immigrants. Racial preferences encourage immigrants to think of themselves as members of groups rather than as individuals. Multicultural education does the same thing to students with its nonstop cheerleading of racial and ethnic entitlements. Bilingual education prevents thousands of children, especially Hispanics, from learning the language they will need to know to commit themselves fully to the American way of life, let alone to compete effectively in the American marketplace. Foreign-language voting ballots are throwing one of the most important institutions of American democracy, the voting booth, into linguistic disarray. The federal government harasses employers who want to ensure that their workers speak English on the job. The INS continues to toy with the idea of watering down the naturalization process by removing important standards that gauge citizenship applicants' understanding of U.S. history and government. Even though some of these policies were originally well-intended, today they present obstacles to Americanization.

Many immigrants will assimilate with great success, no matter how forcefully the Department of Education pushes for bilingual education or the Department of Justice insists on foreign-language voting ballots. But others may not do so well because government programs can retard, stymie, and prevent Americanization. Imagine a five-year-old child of immigrants from El Salvador. She spends her early years in a home in which Spanish is the dominant tongue. Her parents expect her to learn English in the public schools. In fact, they hope and pray that English will become her first language because they, of all people, understand the direct link between English fluency and quality of life in the United States. On her first day of kindergarten, however, their daughter is placed in a so-called bilingual program to develop her Spanish-speaking ability in the place of English acquisition. Her parents may or may not realize this. Without their consent, a school official has decided that their child needs to be taught in Spanish to improve her self-esteem. She will probably learn English—it is very difficult for children to remain completely shut off from the wider society—but perhaps not well enough to enroll in the honors courses she will need later on to go to college. Americanization will work on her, but not with the success that it might if English-language instruction were widely accepted by the education bureaucracy as critical for immigrant children. And she will never realize her full potential as a productive citizen contributing to the American economy.

Policies such as these are so common nowadays that it should come as no surprise that many people wonder whether immigrants have much interest in becoming Americans at all. But this is not the right conclusion. It is important to make a distinction between what, if any, special assistance the immigrants have asked for from the government and what they have had given to them by the political establishment. Immigrants were not clamoring for bilingual education, foreign-language voting ballots, racial preferences, and similar policies, when these were being enacted in the 1960s and 1970s. A Democratic senator from Texas—a native-born, non-Hispanic white—is widely regarded as the father of bilingual education, for instance. The advent of foreign-language voting ballots and racial preferences might be attributed to individual members of Congress, or at least to judicial decisions or the regulatory agencies charged with enforcing their implementation. Immigrants certainly are not the authors of such anti-Americanization public policies. And even if immigrants had fought for them from the start, it would not have mattered. Immigrants represent one of the least influential political constituencies in this country because they are fractured along lines of national origin. Even if they were united—a trick that interest groups have tried to pull from time to time without much luck—so many immigrants are noncitizens, and thus ineligible to vote, that their political clout is negligible.

The upshot is this: When immigrants seem slow to Americanize, and when the reason for their delay can be traced either to a specific government program or to an elitist animus toward assimilation, immigrants are not at fault. The real culprits are American institutions that advanced the interests of Americanization in the past either by teaching English in the public schools or broadly encouraging the foreign-born to orient themselves toward the American way of life and the political principles supporting it, but no longer do so today. Immigrants do not control these institutions, even as they are served by them. The elite political class—politicians, interest groups, and bureaucrats—retains control. Far too often in recent years it has ignored its historical duty to help newcomers assimilate.

At a time when large numbers of immigrants are arriving on American shores, the United States should not be shy about advocating Americanization. Yet hardly a word is said on its behalf. Just as the debate over immigration policy (the question of whom to admit) is trapped in a stale argument between let-them-in libertarians and keep-them-out protectionists, discussions of immigrant policy (how to treat newcomers once they are here) are split between left-wing multiculturalists and right-wing nativists. Neither side has much faith in assimilation. The multiculturalists say that immigrants should not have to assimilate. The nativists say that immigrants cannot assimilate. The two sides disagree on the power of assimilation. The multiculturalists consider its attraction strong and want to lessen it, the nativists consider its attraction weak and want to abandon any hope for it. Both sides agree that Americanization is not the answer, either because it asks too much of the foreign-born or because it deludes the native-born into thinking that immigrants really can become American. In making these claims, both camps rely on particularism, even racial or ethnic essentialism, and take a stand against the urgency of an immigrant policy that makes Americanization its explicit goal.

THE GLOBAL VILLAGE PEOPLE

The multiculturalists' greatest fear about assimilation is that it will happen. They view Americanization as a kinder, gentler form of ethnic cleansing. To them, it is nothing more than a gussied-up variety of nativism, a regrettable way of thinking from a morally inferior time. As the architects of anti-Americanization public policies such as bilingual education, they are intent on using state power to preserve native cultures, native languages, and group solidarity. Social philosopher Michael Walzer has said that multiculturalists are perhaps best understood as "local nationalists."[18] They support the idea that the United States is not a land of free individuals but a conglomeration of discrete nation-states. These nation-states are not imagined as regional (as in New England or Texas, each with its own cultural peculiarities), but as racial or ethnic. In a sense, they want to fracture the American identity and turn the United States into a small global village, like Epcot Center's World Showcase attraction. One fine day, multiculturists hope, the United States will look just like the United Nations.

The global village people tend to occupy the rarefied air of the university, although their influence has had a trickle-down effect on American popular culture, like the slow leak that rots a building. One of the hottest ideas in the academic world—at least in the bizarre corner of it that variously goes by the name Ethnic Studies or American Studies— involves so-called transnational identities. A transnational identity is a sense of ethnic kinship that knows no borders. This sentiment obviously has a place in the immigrant experience. The global village people, however, are eager to use it as a weapon to combat the transformative attractions of Americanization. Like curators in a natural history museum, they want to preserve immigrants' native cultures in perpetuity. Their preservation efforts ultimately represent attempts at solitary confinement—isolation from American values that they find repulsive.

A conference sponsored by the University of California at San Diego in May 1996 revealed the dim view of Americanization held by many academics. The conference was called Rethinking "Americanization," but very little rethinking actually took place. Speaker after speaker bashed the idea of Americanization as an oppressive tool of white supremacy. "Americanization must either be completely reworked or abandoned as a premise of American identity," announced Juan F. Perea, a law professor at the University of Florida. He criticized the notion that immigrants ought to learn English, suggesting that their very lives are at stake. Too many of them, he said, suffer from "death by English." Perea never defined this term with any specificity, but this did not stop him from advancing a sweeping complaint in its name: "For Latinos, illness by English of varying degree, even death by English, is a common affliction without a known cure. In my opinion, deaths by English in the United States are on the rise, increasing to epidemic or pandemic proportions. A principal, undiagnosed cause of death by English is the Americanization idea."

Perea was hardly the most radical anti-Americanizer on hand in San Diego. University of Michigan anthropologist Roger Rouse listed, in a rapid and almost feverish tone, a series of goals that he and his fellow travelers ought to pursue. Goal 1: "To attack the hypocrisies of the idea of the United States as a society of equality of opportunity, and emphasize its internal divisions along class, racial, and gender lines, and then to say because migrants enter into a hierarchicalized system and often into the bottom levels of it, one cannot apply the standards of a white middle class to the ways in which they act in addressing whether they are adapting adequately to their new context or not." In other words, call the immigrant dream of success in the United States a hoax, agitate Americans along class, race, and gender lines, and make no attempt to help newcomers assimilate because bourgeois ideals tarnish their heritage.

It gets worse. Goal 2: "You've got to break the national object. You've got to start with a supernational perspective. And secondly, of course, that when you see the United States in those terms [described as goal 1], you see it not simply embedded in a core-periphery relationship, but as a core that instead of reproducing an emancipatory force in the world is actually reproducing inequality." That's a jargonist's way of beseeching his listeners to attack the idea of a coherent American identity in favor of a transnational multiculturalism that does not recognize established political boundaries. Assimilation into American society is a threat to this goal.

More than a dozen academics presented papers at this conference, and almost every one of them attacked the idea of Americanization. They constantly harped on the claims that the United States is irredeemably racist, that racial attitudes have not changed significantly since the founding, and that immigrant assimilation is nothing more than the capitalist exploitation of a foreign-born proletariat. Even naturalization—the process by which immigrants become full members of the American political community and assume all of its rights and responsibilities—took a beating. According to Lisa Lowe, a professor of literature at UCSD, the notion of citizenship tricks Americans into thinking that everybody has equal access to the benefits of citizenship. In her mind, it is not a generous principle that reflects the very best and truest American ideals. Instead, she noted, it is nothing more than a fraud that masks the intractable inequalities of race, gender, and class.

These academics may seem like extremists, but on campus their unquestioning, negative view of Americanization is in the mainstream. Sociologist Nathan Glazer tells of asking a group of Harvard students taking a course on race and ethnicity in the United States what they thought about assimilation. "The large majority had a negative reaction to it," he writes.[19] Today, small groups of students claim to speak for all students of the same racial or ethnic background and routinely make demands for campus perks. Their requests fall on willing ears. Race-based dorms, study centers, academic departments, convocations, graduations, even yearbooks—these are what make today's American college campus a cauldron of anti-Americanization sentiment.

The global village people affect more than just colleges and universities. Their views influence important public debates about the meaning of American nationhood. On the question of Puerto Rican statehood—whether the United States should admit Puerto Rico, currently a U.S. commonwealth territory, as the 51st state—political commentator Juan M. Garcia-Passalacqua has said that Americans have no right to make cultural demands on islanders as it considers their status. Asking Puerto Rico to make English its official language before it becomes a state, for example, would demonstrate a fear of the "barbarians at the gates" and the "brown hordes." Moreover, according to Garcia-Passalacqua, linguistic assimilation is "ethnocentric."[20] There may be a close link between being Hispanic and speaking Spanish, but this does not mean that every Hispanic must necessarily speak Spanish. Indeed, English-speaking Hispanics often resent it when people tell them they speak English well, on the assumption that they are not native to the United States.[21] By tossing around accusations meant to boost America's sense of guilt and deflect its hope for linguistic assimilation before statehood, Garcia-Passalacqua apparently wants to carve out a place for Puerto Rico in the Union that does not make any kind of Americanizing demand at all. This leaves open the question of why Puerto Ricans would want statehood when they also could have complete political independence, but that is perhaps another issue. The point is that, on these grounds, the global village people in theory could offer statehood to every country in the world, and disallow Americans from objecting because they might think a little Americanization is in order first.

Economist John Isbister makes an especially bizarre case for turning the United States into a mishmash of nation-states. He believes that immigration threatens both the American economy and the environment, because so many newcomers are unskilled and all of them deplete natural resources. These beliefs would normally serve as arguments for restricting immigration. Isbister, however, would like his country to suffer this punishment to teach the world a lesson about multiculturalism: "The United States is on the road to becoming a dynamic multicultural society in which representatives of all the world's peoples will interact in ways that are peaceful and respectful and that have the effect of enriching all the parties to the interactions."[22] The debate over Proposition 187 seems to suggest otherwise. Despite this, Isbister carries on. Notice his emphasis on groups rather than individuals. If individual immigrants were to assimilate, of course, the United States could not promote the ideal of multicultural harmony that Isbister so desires. The United States apparently should not advocate Americanization because "the world needs a model of cultural respect."[23]

The hostility to Americanization displayed by Isbister, Garcia-Passalacqua, and the UCSD conference-goers is perhaps best understood as hostility to an American identity grounded in a set of basic political principles, as well as the notion that this identity is something that our civic institutions both can and ought to teach in the ways they have done so well in the past. In *Anti-Americanism*, political scientist Paul

Hollander notes, "It is quite likely that never before in history have such large numbers of people, comfortable and privileged to various degrees, come to the conclusion that their society was severely flawed or thoroughly immoral."[24] He cites dozens of downbeat assessments of the United States, from education writer Jonathan Kozol referring to America's "murderous" social order to novelist Kurt Vonnegut declaring that "[We are] the most hated nation on earth."[25] Criticizing American institutions is not the same thing as being anti-American, of course, and Hollander understands the difference. The problem is that the global village people appear not to. The "seemingly endless eruptions and wishful fantasies of the social critics for whom everything ends and begins with the unsurpassed corruptions of America" have done great damage to the assimilationist cause.[26] Because they think America is corrupt, by definition Americanization is corrupting. And so, in reckless minds, it even begins to look like Nazi ideology.

Interestingly, the immigrants seem to have few qualms about this so-called corruption. They vote with their feet, and each new arrival is a strong endorsement of American life and culture. It is the native-born—often ensconced in comfortably endowed university chairs—who say there is something rotten in the United States. And their cynicism has had the unfortunate effect of making the country doubt itself to the point where it often lacks the confidence necessary to assert itself in the forceful way that Americanization requires. There is so much confusion about who we are as a nation that not even Vice-President Al Gore can get his story straight. In a 1994 speech, Gore inverted the meaning of *E pluribus unum,* which he translated for his Milwaukee audience as "out of one, many," rather than the other way around.[27] He carelessly turned the United States's most-prized slogan for Americanization into its exact opposite, a statement encouraging dissimilation.

THE NEO-NOTHINGS

For all the failures of the multicultural left, conservatives sadly have not been much better at advancing the cause of Americanization. A few isolated voices have spoken out against public policies gripped by anti-Americanization ideologies, but far too many conservatives have abdicated their advantaged position in favor of nativism. During the 1850s, a political party popularly called the Know Nothings reached a sort of third-party significance. Then the rise of Abraham Lincoln and coming of the Civil War forced a fundamental political realignment, squelching the Know-Nothings' nativist agenda and consigning their party to the ash heap of history. Taking a cue from conservatism's fondness for prefixes, today's nativists might best be called the neo-nothings.

The neo-nothings' greatest fear about assimilation is that it cannot happen. Their particularist view of American culture believes that outsiders cannot become insiders. To become an insider, a person must undergo a long-term and complex process of socialization that should begin at birth. Americans are a people not because they are dedicated to a proposition, as Abraham Lincoln said at Gettysburg, but because they share in a distinct national culture that is ultimately rooted in an assortment of commonalities. These commonalities are based on kinship, religion, territory, language, or other characteristics. Forget all the high-flying rhetoric Americans hear on the Fourth of July. The source of national identity resides closer to the ground. "For many of us America constitutes not an idea but a quite tangible land and tradition which we like to consider not everybody's and anybody's but ours," writes historian Clyde Wilson.[28] There is nothing special about this sentiment. It is the basis on which virtually all nations are constructed. This union is a members-only club, and immigrants cannot gain membership. Even if the club wanted to give it to them, the immigrants would not fit in, try as they might. They would fail to assimilate. And so Americanization is futile.

"Immigration is a failure because assimilation, contrary to national myth, never really occurred," argues Chilton Williamson, Jr., in *The Immigration Mystique*.[29] Williamson is not simply referring to recent problems of adjustment among new arrivals. His assessment sweeps backward 150 years to the Irish immigrants of the 1840s. By his telling, they seem never to have become American. "The case of the Kennedys," he writes, "goes to show how imperfectly the assimilation of the potato-famine immigrants, as measured by their resentment of the Anglo-Protestant majority, had proceeded since the middle of the nineteenth century."[30] One need not be a fan of the Kennedy clan to take issue with Williamson when he tars all Americans descended from the Irish with the brush of Chappaquiddick: "And surely it says much about the 'progress' of the Commonwealth of Massachusetts between 1850 and 1995 that the man who best embodies the worst qualities (except Popery) attributed to the Irish immigrants by the Boston Brahmins should be today, as for the past thirty-three years, its most popular and irremovable politician," he writes.[31]

Other nefarious immigrant influences, according to Williamson, include "the songs, music, plays, and films that have become the popular classics of America in the twentieth century." Instead of representations of America, they are "a commercial vulgarization and ideological exploitation of them." To be sure he has made clear his complete disdain for virtually everything that has happened to the United States since about 1820, Williamson notes that "In the final decades of the nineteenth century and the early ones of the twentieth, it was immigrants and the sons of immigrants who fabricated the national preference for a kind of song never heard in America before, or anywhere else for that matter: music that had no roots, certainly, in American folk ballads and expressive lyrics."[32] He actually names Irving Berlin, Frank Capra, and George Gershwin as villains. Better not watch *It's a Wonderful Life* next holiday season.

It is tempting to write off Williamson as a crank from the nut-wing of the conservative movement, except that he is not an obscure hack. His book was printed by a major New York publishing house, he is a former literary editor of *National Review,* and his ideas are warmly endorsed on the book jacket by William F. Buckley, Jr.—the man most responsible for making the conservative movement mainstream (and expelling its racists, anti-Semites, and conspiracy kooks). Williamson rightly takes issue with INS Commissioner Meissner's proclamation that "we are being transformed." But his message runs much deeper. He says, in effect, that we already have been transformed—and for the worse. "*E pluribus unum* was pregnant with danger from the start, though that danger required a century or so to make itself apparent," argues Williamson.[33]

Most of the current neo-nothing critiques of immigration do not try to repeal the Ellis Island generation of newcomers. In *Alien Nation,* Peter Brimelow remarks that "the American experience with immigration has been a triumphant success" in the past precisely because immigrants traditionally have assimilated.[34] If the neo-nothings fail to agree on the immigrants of yesteryear, they do come together in trying to roll back most of the immigration that has taken place since 1965, when new laws made it possible for large numbers of Asians and Hispanics to migrate to the United States. In doing so, they recycle many of the complaints once hurled at the immigrants who passed through Ellis Island. Brimelow, for example, doubts whether today's immigrants can assimilate because so many of them are not white. Their skin color is problematic, in Brimelow's mind, because "the American nation has always had a specific ethnic core. And that core has been white."[35] Of course, skeptics said much the same thing about the immigrants from eastern and southern Europe in the first part of the 20th century. Greeks, Italians, Poles, and others were often considered to be members of separate races. They were not instantly welcomed on American shores because they shared in some secret white brotherhood with the people already here. Instead, they were the objects of enormous contention. According to many of the day's racial theorists, the trouble with immigrants was that they were not Nordic. Despite these concerns, by Brimelow's own admission, assimilation worked on them. Why should it fail now? Apart from tossing a few invectives in the general direction of multiculturalism, Brimelow does not supply an answer. Instead, he pleads for a scheme of race-based social engineering. "It is simply common sense that Americans have a legitimate interest in their country's racial balance," he writes. In short, he wants it "shifted back"—but back to where, he does not say.[36] If Williamson were at the controls, it might go back pretty far.

Williamson, in fact, echoes Brimelow: "The United States has a right, not to mention a duty, to attempt at least to manage the increase of its population, to determine the ethnic and racial composition of the people a half-century hence, and to ensure the stability of its social and political institutions in the foreseeable future."[37] Put aside the first part of this triumvirate. The matters of population growth and population control are beyond the scope of this book. But point two, on the importance of controlling the country's racial and ethnic makeup, is a red flag. It is especially unsettling in light of point three, which is really the crucial point. If the United States attends to the future stability of its social and political institutions (and it must), why should today's

Americans worry about their country's racial and ethnic composition in the year 2050 any more than Abraham Lincoln should have worried about the Italian immigrants who arrived in 1910? The answer—the only answer possible for Brimelow, Williamson, and the other neo-nothings—is that racial and ethnic characteristics are essential, and beyond the reach of assimilation. In this view, the hope that the United States will transform the immigrant becomes a fear that the immigrant will transform the United States. And this fear, grounded in racial and ethnic essentialism, is what drives the neo-nothings' hostility toward Americanization.

At bottom, the neo-nothing message is nothing can overcome race, not even Americanization. Ironically, conservatives' support of colorblind law and hostility toward affirmative action lean heavily on the notion that certain things must overcome race, such as a commitment to individual rights. The neo-nothings, however, completely upend this belief. And none match the racial paranoia of former *Washington Times* columnist Samuel Francis. In an article for the newsletter *American Renaissance,* he describes the threat to the United States posed by nonwhite immigrants. "The threat of white extinction is due to nonwhite immigration and high fertility coupled with low white fertility," writes Francis.[38] The United States is a white creation, he argues, and in addition to suggesting the wholesale deportation of illegal immigrants (and perhaps many recent legal immigrants), Francis urges whites to "formulate a white racial consciousness that identifies racial and biological endowments as important and relevant to social behavior, and their own racial endowments as essential to the continuing existence of Euro-American civilization." Immigrant assimilation is not an option "because these endowments are largely unique to whites, the behavior they make possible cannot be replicated by most nonwhites."[39]

The vast majority of conservatives, of course, do not buy into Francis's way of thinking. When they look at people, they see individuals rather than collectives. Conservatives grimace when President Bill Clinton announces that he wants a cabinet that "looks like America." This is not because they hope for an all-white cabinet, but rather because they think looks do not count for much. The neo-nothings, on the other hand, seem to say that looks are what the

United States is all about. And where does this lead politically? For Chilton Williamson, Jr., it leads to the not-so-very-uplifting hope that "the Right will eventually . . . recover the nativist tradition."[40] And so the neo-nothings try to drive a stake into the heart of Americanization. They have not succeeded, but they have distracted mainstream conservatives from taking up a cause that could reverse the assimilation crisis.

RESTORING THE SPIRIT OF AMERICANIZATION

Americanization offers a third way to handle the assimilation dilemma by navigating between the dead-end politics of the global village people and the neo-nothings and rejecting the hostility to assimilation that underlies each of them. It invites the participation of both patriotic liberals and freedom-loving conservatives in a conscious effort to help immigrants assume the American way of life, and ultimately keep this nation of immigrants bound by the idea of common citizenship. This strategy has worked in the past—the vast majority of Americans rightly think that assimilation has been a remarkable success. It can work again.

A new Americanization movement would take advantage of the fact that negative attitudes toward assimilation represent the opinion of elitist intellectuals, not the public at large. Ordinary Americans clearly want Americanization to take place. Indeed, there is a great yearning for it, a hope and desire that becoming American is still something worth doing. This yearning in itself may have little to do with immigrants, yet it is in the immigration debate that the sentiment most clearly manifests itself. Anxiety over immigrants is in reality directed more at the policies preventing Americanization than at immigrants themselves.[41] One survey found 61 percent of Americans agreeing with the statement: "Anyone from any country in the world should be free to come to America if they are financially able to provide for themselves and their family."[42] This is hardly a mandate for restriction. It suggests that Americans like immigrants once they have achieved a certain comfort level with them. Indeed, it is hard to imagine that the same Americans who tell pollsters that they want immigration reduced also harbor an intense dislike for the individual immigrants they know personally, the ones whose lives intersect with their own in dozens of ways and places.

In the past, when large numbers of immigrants came to the United States, the native-born made their Americanizing motives explicit. Between the turn of the 20th century and the First World War, a vigorous Americanization movement grew up around the idea that immigrants could become full members of the American community, but that they often needed the help and encouragement of the people who were already here. For a variety of reasons, these efforts fell into disrepute in the 1920s and have only partially recovered. Even so, the millions of immigrants who arrived during those years, as well as the millions who arrived in the 19th century, became Americans in word and deed. Apart from a few rumblings of support—the U.S. Commission on Immigration Reform, formerly chaired by the late Barbara Jordan, has called for the "effective Americanization of new immigrants"[43]—not much has been said recently in favor of Americanization. More important, nobody has supplied a sustained examination of what a renewed Americanization would involve. It is time to do that, to revive the spirit of Americanization for today's immigrants.

For all the turmoil generated by Proposition 187, there remains an abiding sense among many people that immigrants themselves are not the problem. Five months before the vote on Proposition 187, a poll found that 64 percent of Californians thought that immigrants could become just as good citizens as people born in the United States. Thirteen percent actually thought that they made "better" citizens.[44] That's not a bad set of marks—and it suggests that a remnant faith in Americanization, once rejuvenated, can revolutionize the way the United States thinks about and deals with immigrants. Perhaps more important, it can change the way America thinks about itself.

Chapter 2

THE AMERICAN IDEA

When Pilgrims aboard the *Mayflower* first spotted the highlands of Cape Cod in 1620, most thought that the worst lay behind them. Bad planning and treacherous financiers had delayed their departure from England for months. Two false starts had eaten up even more time. Their supplies dwindled. The *Mayflower's* smaller companion, the *Speedwell,* proved itself unseaworthy and had to be abandoned. The Pilgrims crowded 100 passengers onto a ship built for fewer and pushed ahead, trusting Providence. Storms thrashed at them, forcing the ship's captain at one point to pull in the sails and leave the *Mayflower* adrift. They spent a total of 67 miserable days crossing the Atlantic, far more time than most thought they would need. As William Bradford, one of the Pilgrim leaders, relates in his history of Plymouth Colony, "they were not a little joyful" finally to see land at daybreak on November 19.[1]

But the voyage took its toll. Murmurs of rebellion drifted through the *Mayflower's* hold, and these grumblings occasionally turned into "discontented and mutinous speeches," according to Bradford.[2] The Pilgrims were outnumbered by and dependent on people they called strangers—non-Pilgrims either hired to sail the *Mayflower* or to work as servants in the new settlement. When the strangers realized that they had sighted Cape Cod instead of Virginia, their intended destination, many argued that the Pilgrims had no right to the land before them, that disembarking there would put them outside the jurisdiction of any known legal authority, and that they would "use their liberty" once they reached shore. Most aboard the *Mayflower* were by ancestry English, but religious and social differences prevented the Pilgrims and strangers from sharing a deep-rooted sense of kinship. They did not fully trust each other. Anarchy nearly broke loose before any of them set foot on Plymouth Rock.

Then came an archetypal moment in American history—a moment in which these early Americans did something quintessentially American. They chose to create a political identity that would bind them as a community in an unexpected place. They invested wholly in a string of words on a piece of paper, the Mayflower Compact. A simple statement of principles that promised self-government and unity, it called for "a Civil Body Politic." Forty-one men signed it—virtually every adult male. In doing so, the Pilgrims and their shipmates adopted the essential institutions of democracy and forged a political allegiance among themselves. What's more, they allowed a document and the ideas within it to bridge their deep internal divisions. John Quincy Adams later called the Mayflower Compact "perhaps the only instance, in human history, of that positive, original social compact, which speculative philosophers have imagined as the only legitimate source of government."[3] It is easy to overstate the historical importance of the Compact—many scholars doubt that it had much bearing on Plymouth Colony's later development—but none can deny that it serves as an ur-text of American nationhood, a prototype of the American tradition of written constitutions.

BIRTH OF A UNIVERSAL NATION

"America began with an idea," writes historian Diane Ravitch, referring to the Compact.[4] America continued with an idea, too. It became—and remains today—a nation dedicated to the proposition that all men are created equal. This extraordinary notion animates the American people, whose very sense of peoplehood derives not from a common lineage but from their adherence to a set of core principles about equality, liberty, and self-government. These ideas, recognized at the founding of the United States, are universal. They apply to all humankind. They know no racial or ethnic limits. They are not bound by time or history. And they lie at the center of American nationhood. Because of this, these ideas uphold an identity into which immigrants from all over the world can assimilate, so long as they, too, dedicate themselves to the proposition.

Before the founding of the United States, kinship—or at least the perception of kinship—was the most important element in nation building. Bloodlines united nations. Most people lived and died within a few miles of their birthplaces. They knew only a small world and treated outsiders with suspicion. Unlike the Pilgrims—who originally fled England for Holland to escape religious persecution, and then sailed to the New World to separate themselves forever from what they considered a decadent Europe—the vast majority of humanity could not pull itself free of one society and restart in another. Everywhere people accepted their patrimony because they had no alternatives. Indeed, most of them had no need for alternatives. Their traditions and customs, handed down from a mythical and mysterious past, interpreted their existence and imbued their lives with meaning. Their sense of peoplehood was both familiar and familial, and it provided them with comfort in a complex and unknowable world.

Facing an unexplored continent, the early Americans knew little of this comfort. Although some of the colonies imposed restrictions on the kinds of people they would admit into their society—in 1637, for instance, Massachusetts made it extremely difficult for anyone but Puritans to settle within its boundaries—the urgent demands of a young capitalist economy expanding westward cried out for all sorts of settlers, not just those of a particular variety. This essentially ruled out the kinds of religious, social, ethnic, and racial parochialisms that had come to define the nations of Europe. Most Americans in the 17th and 18th centuries were still white, English, and Protestant—but not all of them. Diversity set in early. At least seven hundred thousand immigrants, including Africans held in bondage, had reached mainland British North America by 1760.[5] Of these, between one hundred thousand and one hundred fifty thousand were Scotch-Irish—Presbyterians of Scottish ancestry transplanted to Ulster and suffering from civil disabilities for dissenting from the Anglican church. Another seventy-five thousand immigrants spoke German and hailed from the Rhineland or Switzerland. Roughly 10 percent of the pre-Revolutionary colonial population was German speaking.[6] In Pennsylvania, the Germans were almost as numerous as the English.[7] The residents of New Amsterdam, the 17th-century Dutch settlement that became New York City, shared as many as 18 different languages.[8] Later, the colonies of New York and New Jersey both harbored large Dutch populations. By 1790 the first U.S. Census recorded that roughly 40 percent of the white population was non-English. Many of these people traced their roots to other parts of the British Isles, but more than one of every seven white people in the United States was of continental European stock. Half again as many are of unknown ancestry. This contrasted sharply with the New World colonies of France and Spain, where virtually all of the European settlers came from the same mother country. According to historian Roger Daniels, "the colonies that became the United States seem polyglot" in comparison.[9]

Many early Americans remarked on the difference. "Europe, and not England, is the parent country of America," wrote Thomas Paine in *Common Sense*. "This new world hath been the asylum for the persecuted lovers of civil and religious liberty from every part of Europe," he continued.[10] In a letter to a group of Irish immigrants, George Washington said that "The bosom of America is open to receive not only the opulent and respectable stranger, but the oppressed and persecuted of all Nations and Religions."[11] On the eve of the American Revolution, French-born J. Hector St. John de Crèvecoeur asked a famous question in his *Letters from an American Farmer:* "What, then, is the American, this new man? He is neither an European nor the descendant of an European; hence that strange mixture of blood, which you will find in no other country. I could point out to you a family whose grandfather was an Englishman, whose wife was Dutch, whose son married a French woman, and whose present four sons have now four wives of different nations." The Americans are a "promiscuous breed" creating a place where "all nations are melted into a new race of men," he wrote.[12]

Crèvecoeur might have let his French romanticism get the better of him in these passages—he would have been hard-pressed in the 1770s to locate more than a handful of families like the one he described—but surely he, Paine, and Washington were on to something. Together, they eloquently pointed to a fundamental characteristic of American nationhood: its nonsectarian and nonethnic nature. The developing American nation might have had an English taproot, but its other roots spread widely and drank from many different sources. This diversity eventually found itself acknowledged in the motto inscribed on the great seal of the United States: *E pluribus unum.* The effort to adopt an image to accompany this motto took longer than expected. Between 1776 and 1782, Congress wrangled over a variety of proposals. It finally approved the familiar image (seen on the one dollar bill) of an eagle clutching a bundle of 13 arrows. As a result, *E pluribus unum* often is taken as a reference to the 13 colonies forming one union. And although this a proper interpretation, it has been eclipsed by the meaning Americans today most commonly ascribe to the motto: out of racial and ethnic diversity comes one nation. One of the earliest proposals, submitted by Thomas Jefferson in 1776, would have made this connection explicit. He suggested that a shield with six fields occupy the center of the seal. Each of the six fields would contain an emblem representing one of the European countries sending immigrants to America. Jefferson assigned three of the fields to the British Isles: England, Scotland, and Ireland. The other three went to continental Europe: France, Germany, and Holland. Although John Adams and Benjamin Franklin supported Jefferson's idea, Congress could not make up its mind and the search for a seal continued.[13]

If England, Scotland, Ireland, France, Germany, and Holland provided most of the *pluribus* in colonial America, then English institutions provided the *unum*. The dominant language and literature, the common law, a form of representative democracy, and the folkways of community and family life all derived, in large part, from an English patrimony. After 1776 and a hard war, however, Americans' sense of nationhood no longer rested on a broad cultural identification with the English. Americans explained and vindicated their split with the mother country by identifying and defining the principles that made them a separate and distinct nation. They developed their own ideas and institutions. Most important was the tradition of written constitutions and the independent practice of self-government. Their endeavors ran along peculiarly nonethnic lines. Other revolutionaries from various times and places have not encountered this problem. When Haiti rebelled from France around the turn of the 19th century, for instance, the Haitians (virtually all of them black slaves) could justify their desire for independence by making an irrefutable point: "We are not French," they could say. Despite their diversity, the early Americans did not have the same option. Most of them were, in fact, English. They needed some other kind of reason for having fired on the redcoats at Concord.

What they arrived at was more than a simple excuse. It was a fundamental break from old ties. With the Declaration of Independence, Americans did not constitute themselves a provisional government. Rather, they constituted themselves as a permanent people. Moreover, they constituted themselves in a way that no other group of people had done before. They eschewed the common links of ancestry, religion, and historical experience. As G. K. Chesterton has noted, "America is the only nation in the world that is founded on a creed. That creed is set forth with dogmatic and even theological lucidity in the Declaration of Independence."[14] The Americans appealed to the natural rights of mankind—the self-evident truths that "all men are created equal and that they are endowed by their Creator with certain unalienable rights, [and] that among these are life, liberty, and the pursuit of happiness." They did not have to do this. There had been other revolutions in British history in which the rebels had appealed to the longstanding rights of Englishmen and had won assurances from the monarchy that these rights would be honored. The American revolution, however, was different. It refused to look to the British conscience for sympathy and good will. It declared to a candid world that the British king and Parliament had violated not only their own constitutional laws but also the universal standard of equal rights by which all governments must be judged. In flunking that test, the political bands that had connected the crown and the colonies were dissolved. The American people were on their own, and they were dedicated to a proposition.[15]

This proposition settled the potential problem of *pluribus*. The Americans were one people, the Declaration said, and as one people they accepted the idea that they were comprised of individuals with equal rights. Significantly, the Declaration did not say that all people were *treated* as equals. They were created that way. When the treatment lagged behind the creation, as in the case of slavery, they had injustice. In practice, the American identity still contained racial limits. But it included few ethnic ones. This is an important point, because even though it deliberately excluded many people who were already living on American soil, it consciously included many who might have been left out—the *pluribus* from the seal. The universal principles of nationhood also primed the American identity for more *pluribus* in the future. The Founders may not have fully understood the implications of this universalism and how immigration would, over many years, introduce non-Protestant, non-European, nonwhite peoples into the national fold. But they certainly understood what their universalism meant in an abstract sense.

Race remained a problem—a big problem, with blacks still in bondage and abolition an unfulfilled hope fiercely resisted by southern interests. Thus, the founding documents were better than the political society that gave birth to them because they allowed for evolution, for the grim reality of slavery to catch up with the shining ideal that all men are created equal. In the words of constitutional scholar Robert A. Goldwin, "The founders left in their text no obstacles to the profound improvements that have come about," especially in the area of race.[16] In the long run, the principles of American nationhood would not sustain racial or ethnic particularism. More to the point, the universal ideas at the center of this nationhood pried open the doors of the American identity.

This became increasingly clear thanks to immigrants, whose presence forced the United States to face basic questions about what kind of nation it wanted to be. Indeed, immigrants repeatedly brought into sharp focus America's universalist ideals, as well as the need for them. Americans did not have to descend from the Founders, only live up to the principles they set forth. Four score and two years after the signing of the Declaration of Independence, Abraham Lincoln returned to this founding document, as he did so many times, in making his case against slavery. No orator has described the universal reach of the American identity in such powerful fashion. How was it that new immigrants, separated from the founding generation of Americans by time and ancestry, are made a part of America? At an 1858 campaign speech in Chicago, shortly before the famous Lincoln-Douglas debates, Lincoln explained how:

> We have . . . among us perhaps half our people who are not descendants at all of these men [the Founders], they are men who have come from Europe—German, Irish, French, and Scandinavian—men that have come from Europe themselves, or whose ancestors have come hither and settled here, finding themselves our equals in all things. If they look back through this history to trace their connection with those days by blood, they find they have none, they cannot carry themselves back into that glorious epoch and make themselves feel that they are part of us, but when they look through that old Declaration of Independence, they find that those old men say that 'We hold these truths to be self-evident, that all men are created equal,' and then they feel that that moral sentiment taught in that day evidences their relation to those men, that it is the father of all moral principle in them, and that they have a right to claim it as though they were blood of the blood, and flesh of the flesh, of the men who wrote that Declaration, and so they are.[17]

Lincoln's audience greeted these remarks with a loud and continued applause. This Illinois crowd agreed that the lifeblood of America does not course through the veins of its people, as much as through the healthy body politic of the United States. And joining that body politic was something that all immigrants, with some effort, could do.

Modern-day opponents of the America-as-an-Idea theory try to rebut Lincoln. "It is commonly said that America is more than a nation; it is an idea," writes the *National Review*'s John O'Sullivan. "My thesis is the precise opposite: America is more than an idea; it is a nation."[18] No country that bases its national identity on a set of abstract principles can remain coherent for very long, says O'Sullivan. "Almost all the ideological nations have collapsed, generally in acrimony," he writes, pointing to the Soviet Union and Yugoslavia as examples. "And when they have done so, they have broken down into historic nations with roots in common sentiments and a common heritage." Thus, the idea-state of the Soviet Union split into Russia, Ukraine, and more than a dozen other breakaway republics. Yugoslavia cracks violently into Bosnia, Croatia, Macedonia, Serbia, and Slovenia. The failure of idea-nations "should make a conservative suspicious of this theory of nationhood," argues O'Sullivan.[19] And since the United States is not on the brink of collapse, something more than a set of ideas must link its people, he writes.

To an extent, O'Sullivan has a point. Immigrants do not transform into Americans merely by setting foot on American soil, and our nation cannot survive on ideas alone. American exceptionalism has its limits. But O'Sullivan ignores its unlimited possibilities. America is not a nation like any other. It has none of the elements that comprise traditional nations, such as a common bloodline, a uniform religion, and a long-established territorial claim. We have discussed the diversity of the people who populated the American colonies—a diversity that has only grown with waves of immigrants from Ireland in the 1840s; from eastern and southern Europe in the decades framing the turn of the 20th century; and from Asia, the Caribbean, and Latin America in the late 20th century. Religion in the early republic varied from the moral puritanism of Massachusetts to the vague deism of Jefferson in Virginia. Today it includes Protestants, Catholics, Jews, and an array of smaller faiths, to say nothing of secular humanism. Rather than occupying a land tilled for generations and cluttered by the graves of ancestors, the American countryside at the founding was new and forever reaching westward. The west may have closed since then, but Americans remain a remarkably mobile people who live in a country that spans a continent. While some of their number may feel tied to a particular patch of soil, many others bounce from city to city or state to state. The notion of an ancestral home is almost an oxymoron in the United States. In short, America lacks the varieties of particularism that define other nations. It replaces these with a particularism of ideas that anybody can share.

This does not mean that the United States fails to have the strengths commonly ascribed to more typical nations. It can generate strong visceral attachments to country. Americans have adopted a series of national habits and rituals that range from singing the Star-Spangled Banner before sporting events to the annual celebration of Independence Day to the omnipresence of American flags. Is there another country that so conspicuously displays its banner on the porch, in the classroom, at the auto dealer's lot? None of these habits and rituals seem, on the surface, to have much to do with the American idea. Yet they serve a necessary purpose. As C. S. Lewis writes, "In battle it is not syllogisms that will keep the reluctant nerves and muscles to their post in the third hour of the bombardment."[20] And, indeed, the United States can stir fiery patriotism as well as any country.

Behind all of the symbols, however, does lie the syllogism, the American idea. To forget that America is "built like a church on a rock of dogmatic affirmations" is, as British writer D. W. Brogan put it, "not to be a realist but to be a romantic."[21] The American idea may not leap to mind as bombs fall from the sky, but it does reveal itself in more contemplative moments. The U.S. Constitution is a perfect example. It is a sort of sacred text to Americans, with an original copy displayed in almost religious reverence at the National Archives in Washington, D.C. Tourists play the part of pilgrims as they amble by. Few of them actually stop to read the words. And yet the words are there, however faded, and they imbue the Constitution with much more than symbolic power. In other settings, Americans ruminate on this symbol's substantial meaning. "In the two centuries of its existence," writes historian Bernard Bailyn, "it has become the subject of more elaborate and detailed scrutiny and commentary than has been given to any document except the Bible."[22] If the Bible is the most important cultural text produced by western civilization, then the U.S. Constitution is the most important one produced by Americans. Its ideas animate American culture. The values inscribed therein are, in effect, the DNA of American civilization. They pass down from generation to generation, experiencing occasional modification or correction but never transformation.

The Constitution picks up where the Declaration of Independence leaves off. The Declaration, after all, does not create a government. It simply says that to secure the universal rights of mankind, a government must be "institute[d]" among men, who must, in turn, "organiz[e] its powers in such form as to them shall seem most likely to effect their safety and happiness." In other words, human choice determines the means by which people guarantee their unalienable rights. And depending on how people choose, loyalty to their form of government may not be the only form of loyalty to the principle of human equality. It may not even be the best imaginable or possible. But it is a necessary loyalty. Securing the universal rights of humankind requires supporting a nation that is dedicated to them. The American citizen, then, is committed to the principles of the Declaration as well as to the particular institutions of American constitutional government.[23]

The universalism of the American identity grants the United States another exceptional quality: the ability to assimilate immigrants. The idea-based definition of American nationhood is the United States' most important and abiding institution of Americanization. It probes the American conscience, asking basic questions about what Americans think of themselves, their country, and their sense of what ought to constitute membership in it. The answers to these questions are not always precise or harmonious. Yet in more than two centuries of actual nationhood, Americans have revealed again and again an astounding confidence in their own ability to turn newcomers into Americans, to remake the foreign in their own image. There always have been doubters, and sometimes their doubts have shaped majority opinion. In the main, however, Americans have agreed with George Washington, who welcomed immigrants "to a participation of all our rights and privileges if, by decency and propriety of conduct, they appear to merit the enjoyment."[24] This invitation, with its origins in the distinctly propositional nature of American nationhood, has prepared the way for millions of immigrants from all parts of the world to settle in the United States and call it home. It also has given Americans the confidence to fend off the manic xenophobia that grips ethnic nations when they are confronted by even a small number of immigrants. And while Americans sometimes have looked on immigrants with mixed emotions, they generally have risen to the occasion and forthrightly declared their faith in Americanization. As author and physician Oliver Wendell Holmes once wrote, "We are the Romans of the modern world—the great assimilating people."[25]

FROM IMMIGRANTS TO AMERICANS

Nothing better demonstrates the propositional nature of American nationhood or the spirit of Americanization than the evolution of U.S. naturalization law. The simple fact that the United States allows foreigners to become citizens—indeed, has a centuries-old tradition of it—speaks directly to the question of how the country thinks of itself. If the United States were an ethnic nation, it would not have offered complete social and political membership to millions of immigrants with unfamiliar origins. It might allow foreigners to visit, work, or reside here, but almost certainly it would not grant them citizenship. As an idea nation, however, the United States can establish rules of membership that focus on attachments to the principles of the founding. This ability marks an extraordinary optimism about the transformative qualities of America, a firm belief in the country's Americanizing potential. Perhaps more than anything else, this faith has allowed the United States to meet the full promise of its universal principles.

The Founders' main concern regarding immigration was not ancestry, but whether newcomers would rid themselves of any undemocratic principles that they might have learned in an unfree land. They wanted to make sure that immigrants would assimilate successfully into American political culture.[26] A free society requires a certain set of principles to maintain it. Would America's openness ultimately import people with opposing values? "To admit foreigners indiscriminately to the rights of citizens, the moment they put foot in our country," wrote Alexander Hamilton, "would be nothing less than to admit the Grecian horse into the citadel of our liberty and sovereignty." The solution, according to Hamilton, was to draw immigrants gradually into civil society, "to enable aliens to get rid of foreign and acquire American attachments; to learn the principles and imbibe the spirit of our government; and to admit of a philosophy at least, of their feeling a real interest in our affairs."[27] This ideological commitment would connect people from different backgrounds. The Grecian horse would not plunder a city, but help build the city on a hill. The challenge was to create a legal device that would unite all Americans, no matter where they were born, in a common civic enterprise. Naturalization thus became a key mechanism in the process of Americanization.

Full citizenship in most countries springs from one of two sources: parental inheritance or place of birth. The first principle, known as *jus sanguinis* or "the right of blood," comes from Roman law and allows citizenship to pass automatically from parent to child. The second principle, known as *jus soli* or "the right of soil," has a feudal origin and intends to create a bond between person and parcel. Both found their way into American law. *Jus sanguinis* functions mainly to bestow citizenship on children born abroad to U.S. citizens.[28] *Jus soli* is the stronger principle, cited in the first sentence of the 14th Amendment: "All persons born or naturalized in the United States and subject to the jurisdiction thereof, are citizens of the United States and of the State wherein they reside."[29] This provision, ratified in 1868, intended originally to award citizenship to black Americans. More recently, it has been interpreted to grant citizenship to anybody born in the United States, including the children of illegal immigrants.[30]

Although the United States relies on both of these principles, it has developed a third: naturalization, or the practice of gaining citizenship by legal petition. This concept actually predates Columbus's voyage to the New World. It was firmly established in English law by the start of the 15th century, and its roots may reach as deep as 1365.[31] The word *naturalization* made its English-language debut in 1559, when an English historian referred to "naturalized" French men.[32] Shakespeare used the verb *naturalize* in his comedy *All's Well That Ends Well*, a play probably written in the early 17th century.[33] Naturalization did not become a good avenue to citizenship for some time, however. Before 1844, naturalization in England required a special Act of Parliament. Even then it came with certain disabilities. Naturalized citizens could not become Privy Councilors or members of Parliament, hold political office, or receive from the crown a grant of land in Great Britain or Ireland.[34]

The idea of naturalization grew to maturity in the New World. As a third path to citizenship, it found a natural home in colonial America. Naturalization became an incentive for settlement in a land of wide-open spaces and enormous economic potential. Thanks to bureaucratic hassles from England, however, the naturalization of foreigners was an extremely difficult process during the 18th century. Non-English subjects who aspired to citizenship in the colonies were not exempt from seeking parliamentary approval. And they could not simply petition their local governments for action. Naturalization typically meant a trip to London, which many settlers tried to accomplish before sailing across the ocean. Those aliens without the benefit of such foresight suffered from restrictions on their property rights and commercial activity. Catholics were barred from citizenship entirely while Jews and Quakers were eligible. These rules against naturalization were most honored in the breach, but they nonetheless existed and many colonists resented them.

Colonial governments sidestepped this inconvenience by offering to naturalize aliens as colonial subjects, if not full-fledged imperial ones. Parliament limited their ability to do even this on several occasions, but in 1740 it finally allowed foreigners to naturalize locally as English subjects if they could prove seven years of continual residence in British territory. During the 1760s, however, naturalization became caught up in a broader power struggle between the colonies and the crown, as London tried to gain more administrative control over North America. In 1764, the imperial government declared that foreigners not naturalized under the 1740 law had no property rights, a punitive measure in the minds of many colonists. In 1773, it banned the colonies from making their own naturalization laws altogether. By 1776, the colonists had had enough on this matter and many others. In the Declaration of Independence, they charged George III with a despotic attempt to "prevent the Population of these States; for that Purpose of obstructing the Laws for Naturalization of Foreigners."

After independence, state governments took control of naturalization laws. The particulars varied from place to place, but the states did share a set of common requirements whose remnants still exist today: a public oath of allegiance, a disavowal of foreign commitments, a period of residency, and a demonstration of good character.[35] Since membership in the emerging nation relied heavily on ideological criteria, the concept of American citizenship in later years would broaden to include people descended from every race on the planet.[36] The Constitution eventually vested the federal government with the responsibility of creating uniform rules for naturalization.[37] In 1790, Congress required that an applicant for citizenship be a "free white person" who had lived in the United States for two years. In 1795, Congress bumped up the residency requirement to five years. It also allowed any American court to grant citizenship. Combined with the open immigration policy of the time, this trait represented a generous formula of almost xenophilic inclusion and served as an impetus for incredible rates of population growth throughout the 19th century.

The infamous Alien and Sedition Acts that appeared in the summer of 1798 might seem to contradict this notion, since on the surface they look like emanations of xenophobic exclusion. Nothing could be further from the truth. For one thing, the sedition aspect of these laws applied to everyone, not just immigrants. Moreover, the alien side of them is best understood as the momentary product of partisan political conflict between Hamilton's Federalists and Jefferson's Republicans. Granted, they were somewhat extreme. They required each alien to file a declaration of intention to become a citizen at least five years before naturalization and also increased the period of residency to 14 years. The Aliens Act went even further, granting the president unlimited powers to deport any noncitizen "whom he shall judge dangerous to the peace and safety of the United States." This portion of the Alien and Sedition Acts grants the entire set a sort of nativist notoriety. Yet the Aliens Act was never used against anyone. After two years, it expired and was never reauthorized. Moreover, the Federalists did not approve the law out of anti-immigrant animus so much as political expediency. Most immigrants were joining the other party, and the Federalists simply wanted to hobble their partisan foes. Their ploy did not do them much good. With the election of Jefferson to the presidency in 1801, the minimum period of residency dropped back to five years, where it has remained ever since.[38]

The federal government did not take much of a role in controlling immigration during the first half of the 19th century. That job devolved to states and localities, which in practice meant busy port cities such as New York, where two-thirds of all immigrants landed between 1820 and 1860. They guarded against the admission of infirm and destitute immigrants, but very few people were actually kept out. This was, in every sense, an open immigration policy. As the century wore on, most states and territorial governments tried to push the door open even further. They actively recruited immigrants on the eastern seaboard and potential migrants in Europe to settle within their borders. To accomplish this, they published informational brochures in many languages on the glories of America. Minnesota declared that "It is well to exchange the tyrannies and thankless toil of the old world for the freedom and independence of the new." States regularly engaged in negative advertising against their neighbors, warning settlers about the hazardous number of blizzards, droughts, locusts, and Indian attacks that always seemed to lie just across the state line. Yet all of them shared a basic exuberance about the enormous opportunities afforded by the United States.[39]

Citizenship requirements for immigrants continued to decrease through much of the 19th century, and even the line between alien and citizen began to blur. The newest states wanted to attract settlers regardless of their citizenship. In 1846, Wisconsin extended the vote to aliens who declared their intention to naturalize and had lived in the state for at least one year. In 1850, Michigan allowed aliens to vote if they had two-and-a-half years of residency. By the 1880s, 18 states had granted voting rights to immigrants who declared their intent to become citizens.[40] Aliens in these states and elsewhere encountered few obstacles to holding property or engaging in business. The rules of naturalization themselves were lax. Sometimes courts simply would declare entire groups of people to be citizens without examining their eligibility. Fraud crept in, too. The Tammany Hall political machine in New York City would arrange regular citizenship ceremonies in front of friendly judges shortly before election day.[41] Between 1856 and 1867, for example, naturalizations during years with a presidential race increased by as much as 462 percent over the previous year.[42] "The difference between alien and citizen was small and almost indistinguishable," writes historian Reed Ueda.[43]

Opposition to this convergence found an early voice in the nativist and anti-Catholic Know-Nothing party, so named by hostile pundits because of its members' extreme secrecy. (When outsiders asked about the organization, members were to respond "I know nothing.")[44] The Know-Nothings tried to impose a 21-year residency requirement for naturalization, but their movement floundered in the 1840s and 1850s. The Civil War silenced political nativism for a time by uniting immigrants (who mostly settled in the urban north) and restrictionists in a common cause for union.[45] In 1864, Abraham Lincoln won re-election with this plank in his Republican party platform: "Foreign immigration which in the past has added so much to the wealth, resources, and increase of power to this nation—the asylum of the oppressed of all nations—should be fostered and encouraged by a liberal and just policy."[46] Like most Americans of the time, Lincoln believed that immigrants were a crucial part of the country's heritage. In declaring Thanksgiving a national holiday, Lincoln gave thanks to God for having "largely augmented our free population by emancipation and by immigration."[47]

The federal government gradually assumed greater authority over admissions policy after the Civil War, leading up to total federal control in 1891. During this period, patriotic immigrant boosterism continued to thrive. The country also refined and modified its sense of self in important ways. A controversy over individual versus group rights erupted in 1874 when Congress nearly reserved a huge tract of western land for Mennonites (a group of Anabaptists that includes the Amish) as a strategy to convince them to settle in the United States rather than Canada. Opponents of the measure prevailed when they declared that no group should be accorded preferential treatment on the basis of "a special right to compact themselves as an exclusive community."[48]

More important than this, however, was an expanded understanding of what it means to be an American. In 1870, Congress broadened the "free white person" principle to permit the naturalization of African immigrants. Many in Congress originally had tried to make naturalization available to all nonwhites. "It is 'all men' and not a race or color that are placed under the full protection of the Declaration, and such was the voice of our fathers," declared Senator Charles Sumner of Massachusetts. "The word 'white' wherever it occurs as a limitation of rights, must disappear. Only in this way can you be consistent with the Declaration."[49] Despite such rhetoric, Sumner won only half a victory. Western states opposed the naturalization of Asian immigrants, whose numbers were growing, and Congress chose to add only aliens of African descent or nativity to its list of potential citizens. The failure to make naturalization truly colorblind undoubtedly felt like a letdown to some, but the success of including blacks did carry the country closer to its founding proposition.

Asians would have to wait, and the prohibition on naturalization in 1870 foreshadowed the restrictive legislation that would affect them in years to come. Labor unions were particularly keen on preventing more immigration from Asia. In 1882, Congress passed the Chinese Exclusion Act, which suspended the entry of Chinese workers and created a new category of immigrant especially for the Chinese: "aliens ineligible for citizenship." Restrictions on the naturalization of Burmese, Malaysian, Filipino, Thai, Indian, and Korean immigrants followed. Even people with mixed-Asian backgrounds were excluded. In 1912, a federal court denied naturalization to a "half-breed German and Japanese." The 14th Amendment granted citizenship to the U.S.-born children of Asians, but the immigrants themselves could not become full members of American civil society.⁵⁰ Although each of these laws and court rulings had a significant effect on Asians and their descendants, they occurred at an incremental pace over the course of about five decades.

After more than a century, a sweeping revision to naturalization laws arrived in 1906 and took effect the next year. Confronted by mass immigration from eastern and southern Europe, Americans had debated immigrant assimilation for several years in ways that echoed the concerns of the Founders. Americans seemed to ask if the newcomers believed in our political foundations or wanted to subvert us. In response, the Naturalization Act of 1906 reaffirmed residency and racial requirements and added a few new rules. From that point on, candidates for naturalization would have to demonstrate the ability to speak English, answer questions about American history and civics, and find two witnesses to vouch for their moral character and commitment to constitutional principles. Anarchists and polygamists were banned entirely. On the state level, barriers between citizens and aliens reemerged. Alien suffrage started to fade away and disappeared completely by 1926.⁵¹

While the naturalization law remained immune to the effects of racialization, with the exception of Asians, admissions policy did not. The National Origins Quota Acts in the 1920s demanded that immigrants be not only white but also a certain kind of white person. Immigration from eastern and southern Europe was essentially shut down. Naturalization policy, however, avoided this fate. The Second World War generated new worries about national security and foreign entanglements, causing Congress to tighten naturalization laws and reinforce the Asian exclusion in 1940—but these were short-term measures. The quest for Allied unity inspired the beginnings of a reversal. In 1943, Congress repealed Chinese exclusion and allowed foreign-born Chinese to naturalize. Three years later, it extended the offer to Filipinos and Asian Indians. With the onset of the Cold War in 1950, Congress allowed present or past support for communism to justify a denial of naturalization. Clearly the United States was abandoning what racialist elements remained in its sense of national identity. Opening naturalization to certain Asian nationals marked a decline in the fear of foreign races. The denial of naturalization to communists, on the other hand, signaled an objection to ideological betrayal.

Naturalization laws abandoned their remaining racialist premises and fully embraced ideological nationhood in 1952, when Congress passed the McCarran-Walter Act and overrode a veto by President Harry S. Truman. Although heavily criticized at the time by Americans who wanted to make immigrant admissions colorblind, the act represented a significant step toward American universalism. It eliminated the "aliens ineligible for citizenship" category and barred the use of race, nationality, or sex in determining naturalization. In doing so, it abandoned the concept that some people made better American citizens than others because of who their parents were. It allowed that all immigrants represent the raw stuff out of which Americans can be made. Not every immigrant will become an American, of course. Some would not care to try and others would fail. A good many would not be allowed into the country in the first place. But after 1952, the United States walked away from the pernicious notion that immigrants' ancestry could in and of itself disqualify them from the possibility of citizenship. The only new requirement in 1952 was the expansion of an old one. Naturalization applicants had to be able not only to speak and understand English, which they had been doing since 1907, but also to read and write simple words and phrases in English.[52]

It is striking how little naturalization laws have changed since the founding of our country. Apart from a debate over residency requirements at the end of the 18th century and the 1907 reforms, the essentials of how the United States grants citizenship to immigrants has not changed much in more than 200 years. Since 1907, the principles of naturalization have remained extraordinarily stable. Citizenship study materials produced for immigrants in 1910 are remarkably similar to those published today. What has changed over the course of two centuries is the pool of eligibility. Whereas only certain kinds of foreign-born people could become citizens in 1790 (under what must still be considered a fairly generous and liberal rule relative to its time), by the 1950s the idea that all men are created equal expressed itself in the law of naturalization. Only a country dedicated to universal principles could evolve in such a way.

Everyone knows that Americans today owe an enormous debt to

English history. Yet the universal principles of American nationhood are something unto themselves. They have not confined themselves strictly to the tribe of St. George. As historian Daniel J. Boorstin has written, in North America "the civilization of Englishmen became something it never could have become within their little island."[53] Those who doubt that history have only to look at what happened in the first part of the 20th century, when millions of immigrants from strange places settled in the United States. Although this influx caused great concern, it inspired an even greater response: the Americanization movement.

Chapter 3

THE RISE OF
AMERICANIZATION

Without warning, a group of textile workers abandoned their stations on the morning of Friday, January 12, 1912. Angered by an industrywide pay cut, these Italian immigrants threw their fury at the American Woolen Company's equipment by cutting belts, jamming gears, and clubbing machines. Then the workers turned to other employees in the mill, ordered them to quit their jobs, and hurled threats at those who hesitated. After shutting down one operation, they moved on to another plant. It stopped production, too. Only an encounter with the police—who had to turn back a rushing mob—put an end to the day's disruption. By the following Monday, nearly 30,000 workers at 11 mills were on strike in Lawrence, Massachusetts. Roughly one of every three residents refused to go to work. Thus a center of American textile manufacturing came to a halt as it hosted a two-month showdown between workers who considered themselves exploited and employers who considered the workers' demands unreasonable. The famous "Bread and Roses" strike had begun.[1]

This was more than class warfare. Immigrants were at the center of the strike and the controversy surrounding it. According to historian Donald B. Cole, "the initial violence, the threats of blowing up the mill, and the prominence of the Italians [all] formed a picture the strike observers could not forget."[2] Almost half of Lawrence's population was foreign-born. Another 38 percent were the children of immigrants. "Immigration almost completely controlled the history of the city," writes Cole, from its original Irish settlers to the more recent waves of Italians, Lithuanians, Poles, and Syrians. In 1910, the immigrants living within one mile of the textile mills came from 51 countries and spoke 45 languages.[3] Lawrence was a place of opportunity to these newcomers, even as they labored for many hours and endured a high cost of living. The strike soon thrust a notorious reputation for its squalor and lawlessness on Lawrence. This reputation—and more important, the native reaction to it—had important ramifications for immigrants everywhere. Lawrence helped fuel the Americanization movement, a massive private-and-public effort to help immigrants assimilate. Before flaring out in the 1920s, this broad social movement influenced the lives of millions of immigrants in a mostly positive way.

The strike in Lawrence arose over a wage dispute caused by a new government regulation meant to improve workers' quality of life. At the start of 1912, Massachusetts limited the workweek to 54 hours. The textile mills complied and cut the number of hours they offered to their employees. Wages were not actually lowered, but suddenly less of them were available. In previous hour reductions, the mills had been careful to make sure that their employees maintained their weekly salaries. This time, however, the workers took home 20 to 30 cents less each week—a significant amount in many households. The workers in Lawrence were upset and, partly because the move came with little advance notice, willing to take action.

A young man named Angelo Rocco presided over a January 10 meeting of the Italian-immigrant branch of the International Workers of the World, a socialist union whose members were popularly known as the Wobblies. After the group voted for a strike, Rocco immediately sent a telegram to professional IWW strike organizers, most of them Italian, and invited them to Lawrence. Before long, workers of all nationalities were walking off the job, trashing machinery, fighting with police, and destroying city property. This was by no means the most violent strike in American history, but it grabbed the attention of the Boston and New York media like few others had. The situation turned especially ugly a few weeks into the standoff when police discovered several batches of dynamite in immigrant neighborhoods. Although these bombs were planted by scheming industrialists, the damage was done. Most of the public viewed the strike as an ugly clash between robber barons and foreign rabble-rousers. The sides reached a settlement after 63 days—with the workers winning steep pay hikes—but the conflict seemed unresolved and never-ending. The IWW continued to agitate. An anarchist May Day parade renewed resentments. Trials related to striker violence lasted into November.

In the minds of many, the Lawrence strike cast doubts on the ability and willingness of recent immigrants from eastern and southern Europe to assimilate. Would a well-adjusted, Americanized population really behave this way? Major figures in the strike had Italian last names like Giovannitti, Caruso, and Di Prato. Even Nicola Sacco and Bartolomeo Vanzetti, both of whom would be executed in 1927, were on the scene.[4] Other leaders were the Franco-Belgian Detollenaere and the Syrians Marad and Hajjar. Polish and Portuguese meeting halls became beehives of striker activism. So much foreign influence inspired fears of bolshevism. As ordinary Americans followed the news and read the tales of strikers organized along ethnic lines, cable cars plundered in street riots, speeches delivered in a dozen languages, verbal attacks launched at the native-born, musicians who played foreign national anthems, and immigrants arrested for carrying concealed weapons, they began to wonder what kind of people the United States had been importing in recent years. The public certainly did not sympathize with the mill owners, whose antistriker tactics occasionally seemed brutal and inhumane. (These tactics even became the subject of congressional hearings in early March 1912.) But neither was the public enamored with the mass of immigrant workers. These millions of southern and eastern Europeans were "dumb, easily lead, illiterate," in the words of one writer.[5] Even some of the people with long records of supporting free immigration began to have doubts after Lawrence. "What have we done that a pack of ignorant foreigners should hold us by the throat?" asked John Graham Brooks.[6] A local citizens group accused the immigrants of lacking the "real spirit of America."[7] A question and answer haltingly traveled through the public mind, writes the historian Cole: "[I]f this immigrant city were as slum-ridden, diseased, poverty-stricken, lawless, and un-American as people said, then were not all immigrant cities? If the picture of Lawrence in 1912 was accurate, then the millions of immigrants who came to America after 1845 had failed to find any semblance of security and had failed to become Americans."[8]

THE ONSET OF NATIVISM

Lawrence brought attention to a long-developing demographic trend. Between 1880 and 1920, at least 25 million immigrants arrived in the United States—two and one-half times the number that came during the 40-years from 1840 to 1880. About 9 million entered in the first decade of the 20th century. More than just the numbers had changed, however. Previous groups of newcomers had left northern and western European countries such as England and Germany. These more recent arrivals were the so-called new immigrants. They were born in seemingly exotic countries like Italy, Russia, Austria-Hungary, and Poland. Americans had heard of these places, but did not know much about them. Suddenly, people with almost no tradition of living in the United States could be found in virtually every American city. Most of them flocked to urban areas in the Northeast and Midwest, thanks to the frontier vanishing, farm land growing scarce, and urban industry expanding rapidly. A large proportion of these eastern and southern Europeans were peasants with no obvious skills to offer. To many Americans, this transformation threatened the nation's social fabric by diluting its racial and ethnic homogeneity. By the turn of the century, less than one-half of the entire population was both white and born of two native parents.[9] There were also economic concerns, especially in the trade unions, that these newcomers were a source of cheap labor for big business and that they drove down wages among natives. Right or wrong, these perceptions about people and pocketbooks left many Americans uncomfortable. A great debate started to brew.

Nativism already had established itself as a powerful anti-immigrant force in the United States well before this influx. It originally came forth with vigor in reaction to large-scale Irish immigration in the 1840s, when nativism also had a distinct anti-Catholic bias. Nativism subsided during the middle of the 19th century but started to crawl out of its hibernation in the 1880s. Congress banned the immigration of Chinese people in 1882, and a series of laws and court decisions over the next few decades restricted the entry and rights of other Asians as well. The only thing that concerned the new nativists more than race was radicalism and the role that some immigrants took in fomenting civil discord. Immigrant workers often were at the center of labor disputes. From 1881 to 1905, there were at least thirty-seven thousand strikes in the United States, many of them short and local but several of them long and more widespread.[10] German-language anarchist newspapers in Chicago printed instructions on how to make dynamite.[11] Fears of the foreigner focused on one flashpoint in particular. During a one-day, nationwide strike in 1886, a group of anarchists gathered in Chicago's Haymarket Square. When police tried to break up the meeting, a bomb burst amid a throng of demonstrators. The authorities never identified the bomber's identity, but sentenced seven people to death in connection with the explosion—six of them were immigrants. The Haymarket Affair, as it came to be called, whipped up nationalist anxiety. Editorialists screeched indignantly. "These people are not Americans, but the scum and offal of Europe," raged one. In many circles, immigrants came to be seen as lawless subversives with violent streaks.[12]

Anti-immigrant sentiment percolated during the 1890s, but it never reached a critical mass, even during a four-year economic slump. The fierce labor disputes of recent years began to subside. Strikes continued, but without the ugly tenor of Haymarket. Toward the end of the decade, a cheerful certainty seemed to rule the day. The 1896 campaign banners of presidential candidate William McKinley focused on a return to prosperity, and business boomed after his election. The Spanish-American War, waged in 1898 and 1899, fostered a sense of triumphalism—and none of the suspicions about foreign-born Americans that arise during wartime (partly because Spanish immigrants were so few). "All in all, as the nineteenth century came to a close, American civilization seemed to gain its second wind," writes historian John Higham. "Buoyed by unfolding opportunities, optimists now ridiculed the fear that the United States was overcrowded."[13]

Yet all the while, the pessimists remained a sizable minority. The human tide of migrants continued to roll in from Europe. As each new wave crashed on American shores, it eroded support for the immigrant. New arrivals raised new doubts. Their neighborhoods were concentrated in a handful of urban areas and visible to all. Their phenotype was no longer the familiar image of the Irish, German, or Scandinavian. Now it was the Jew, Magyar, and Slav. Even their whiteness came into question. According to Congressman Thomas Abercrombie of Alabama, "The color of thousands of them differs materially from that of the Anglo-Saxon."[14] The sheer volume of newcomers—more than a million a year in 1905, 1906, and 1907—continued to break down native confidence in America's ability to absorb so many entrants at once. General concerns spread about the immigrants' low skills, lack of education, and tendency to live in slums and amid poverty. Muckraking journalists such as Jacob Riis, for all their humane intentions, reinforced negative stereotypes. In his famous expose, *How the Other Half Lives,* Riis used both camera and pen to reveal the squalor and "galling bondage" of life in tenements overflowing with the new immigrants. "In the tenements all the influences make for evil," wrote Riis, "because they are the hotbeds of the epidemics that carry death to rich and poor alike; the nurseries of pauperism and crime that fill our jails and police courts . . . that maintain a standing army of ten thousand tramps with all that that implies; because, above all, they touch the family life with deadly moral contagion."[15] There were deeper questions, too, about whether foreign-born people from countries with despotic regimes would understand democratic principles, whether they could adapt to them, and whether they even were capable of committing to them.

Most of these worries boiled down to a single question: Would this new group of people assimilate successfully into American life? The answer was not at all clear, and some of the evidence was troubling. Between 1900 and 1910, the number of naturalized male adults grew by only 7 percent, while the number of noncitizen male adults grew by 73 percent. The percentage of aliens among foreign-born adult men expanded from 43 percent in 1900 to 55 percent in 1919.[16] Acquiring citizenship usually demands a certain amount of cultural assimilation. Since 1907, naturalization applicants have had to demonstrate the ability to speak English, for example. This growth in the noncitizen population suggested to some that the latest immigrants would live in castelike separateness from other Americans. Perhaps this was their destiny. In a 1910 report to the U.S. Immigration Commission, the Immigration Restriction League (IRL) warned against "the immigration of large numbers of aliens of low intelligence, poor physique, deficient in energy, ability, and thrift."[17] Their eventual absorption into mainstream society was doubtful, according to the IRL. They were permanent failures: "A considerable proportion of immigrants now coming are from races and countries, or parts of countries, which have not progressed, but have been backward, downtrodden, and relatively useless for centuries. If these immigrants 'have not had opportunities,' it is because their races have not made the opportunities; for they have had all the time that any other races have had; in fact, often come from older civilizations. There is no reason to suppose that a change of location will result in a change of inborn tendencies."[18]

Prescott F. Hall offered a disturbing interpretation of the new immigration in the January 1912 issue of the *North American Review,* a prominent monthly journal. In his article, Hall described "the difference between hostile and peaceful invasions in history" and argued that "it has usually been the peaceful migrations and not the conquering armies which have undermined and changed the institutions of peoples."[19] The Roman empire did not fall because barbarian hordes sacked Rome, he said, but because the invading Goths and Vandals absorbed the Roman people into their own, rather than the other way around. Hall saw in this tale a warning for an early-20th-century America confronting another peaceful migration. "[W]e are getting a great many immigrants who are below the mental, moral, and physical average of both our country and their own," he wrote.[20] "The 'barbarians' of the present time, however, do not come from the plateaus of central Asia or from the jungles of Africa; they are the defective and delinquent classes of Europe—the individuals who have not been able to keep pace at home and have fallen into the lower strata of its civilization."[21] Hall left his readers with a vexing thought: Despite America's best intentions, these new immigrants just might topple a young republic with Roman-sized ambitions.

THE AMERICANIZATION ALTERNATIVE

After the textile strike, Lawrence set about reviving its image. Local groups quickly issued a series of pamphlets to combat all of the negative publicity. "Lawrence—Here She Stands: For God and Country!" declared one of them. Another: "Lawrence As It Really Is, Not as Syndicalists, Anarchists, Socialists, Suffragists, Pseudo Philanthropists and Muckraking Yellow Journalists Have Painted It." City leaders tried to make the immigrants feel like valued members of the community, wholly capable of becoming—and encouraged to become—good American citizens. A big step in this direction came from Father James T. O'Reilly, Lawrence's leading Catholic priest. He organized a massive Columbus Day parade in the autumn of 1912 and attracted thirty-two thousand marchers of all nationalities. Many of them waved small American flags and carried "For God and Country" banners in an explicit rejection of the IWW slogan, "No God, No Country." "The vast numbers participating in this all-city affair represented and united its immigrant groups," writes Cole. "Immigrants who had come together in January to strike now joined to pledge their Americanism. The immigrant had been tested and was now demonstrating his loyalty."[22] Today, a plaque at the base of the flagpole in Lawrence's city common commemorates the parade. Nowhere in the city does a plaque commemorate anything else that happened that year.[23]

Other Lawrence residents went beyond pamphlets, parades, and plaques. Dozens of private groups and public institutions mobilized to take a hands-on approach to the problem of assimilation. They offered English-language classes for adults and sponsored social gatherings. Naturalization ceremonies became elaborate, flag-waving affairs. Over the next several years, the public schools developed an "American Plan for Education in Citizenship." Their labors resulted in a book published in 1918 to national acclaim. Its lessons in history taught "love and loyalty for America," civics focused on "devotion to the Community," and literature promoted things "which the American spirit holds dear." When the First World War arrived, immigrants hurried to volunteer for service, even though the noncitizens among them were not required by law to go to war on behalf of the United States. Lawrence celebrated their efforts by holding banquets for returning veterans and building memorials to the fallen. Four Liberty Loan drives collected $16 million in the city, much of it from immigrants. Lawrence's *Evening Tribune* took these signs as a "vindication of 1912." All was not sweetness and light for Lawrence. The textile mill workers struck again

in 1919, and residents worried off and on about the influence of bolshevism among their foreign-born neighbors. Even so, the city was able
to remake itself from a place torn by violent ethnic strife into a community of unquestioned patriotism.

Lawrence had become active in the Americanization movement—a
young but growing social crusade dedicated exclusively to the assimilation of foreign-born Americans. Its members placed their faith in the
ability of immigrants to adapt to life in the United States. The Americanizers looked at the same social, economic, and demographic evidence as those who reached pessimistic conclusions about the new
immigration, but they reacted in an entirely different way. Rather than
calling for an immediate end to immigration, they engaged newcomers
directly and encouraged their assimilation through a positive program
of education and guidance. The Americanizers were motivated partly
by altruism—a sincere desire to help their new neighbors make a home
in the United States and become contributing members of society. But
worries also affected them. What would happen if these new immigrants did not assimilate? Would they keep Lawrence and other commercial capitals stuck in an economic gridlock? Would they change the
country into something beyond recognition? Perhaps former President
Theodore Roosevelt put it best in 1915, when he struck a chord somewhere between moral fervor and self-interest in a speech to the Knights
of Columbus at Carnegie Hall in New York City: "We cannot afford to
continue to use hundreds of thousands of immigrants merely as industrial assets while they remain social outcasts and menaces any more
than 50 years ago we could afford to keep the black man merely as an
industrial asset and not as a human being."[24]

As an outgrowth of progressivism, the Americanization movement worried about the dehumanizing aspects of rapid industrializa-
tion. It also felt that social action could improve individual behavior
and pave the way for the immigrant's incorporation into American
life. Over the course of nearly two decades, it came to take its place
beside other broad-based movements that toiled for abolition, civil
service reform, and women's suffrage. Like these other causes, Americanization imbued its devotees with an urgent sense of national purpose. And it appealed to many groups, from those that favored free
immigration and wanted to guarantee its continuation, to restric-

tionists worried about whether the foreign-born would merge with the general population, to immigrants who approved of Americanization's upbeat demeanor. "To a nation charged with evangelical impulses, Americanization was a mission of redemption; to a country of salesmen, it offered an adventure in high pressure salesmanship," writes Higham.[25] The public came to support the Americanizers' vision of optimism and generosity as it outshined the bleak worldview of foreign-bashing fear mongers. The Americanizers' contagious sense of hope allowed immigrant uplift to prevail over immigrant exclusion, at least for a while.

The Americanizers believed that newcomers and natives would have to reach an accord if immigration were to succeed as both a social and economic phenomenon. Immigrants needed to become a part of American society, rather than mere sojourners in it. They had responsibilities to their new home. In a rough order of priority, these included living by its laws, working at jobs, learning English, and earning citizenship. The native-born population would reap some reward when immigrants performed any of these duties, ranging from simple matters like preservation of the peace to more complex benefits like economic gain, national cohesion, and domestic tranquillity. The immigrant would profit as well, went the thinking, since assimilation underwrote success in the United States. Success could come in a small step, such as gaining the know-how to outsmart a conniving landlord, or in a large one, such as breaking outside the confines of an unskilled mining job and into a supervisory position that required a command of English.

Americanization demanded much of immigrants, but it was not just a one-way street. Natives had to keep their part of the bargain. A popular if imperfect metaphor among the Americanizers put natives in the role of hosts and immigrants in the position of guests. The hosts felt compelled to help their guests make the transition to self-sufficiency. They wanted to help immigrants become good neighbors. To this end, the Americanizers encouraged a barrage of classes, lectures, and publications on the English language, naturalization, and American citizenship. They used a variety of private and public institutions as engines of assimilation, including corporations, schools, and naturalization offices. Their hope, ultimately, was the immigrant's full acceptance in and of American society, including the complete assumption of its rights and opportunities.

If the Americanizers had a weak point, it was in their vague definition of Americanization. The goals of their movement were not as clear as those of the abolitionists who struggled to end slavery or of the suffragettes who wanted the vote. Instead, the Americanizers often spoke ephemerally, their rhetoric making constant reference to "the American way of life," "patriotic Americans," "American ideals"—words and phrases that could mean different things to different people. At a basic level, they communicated nothing more than a desire to share and inspire. But what? One prominent crusader, Secretary of the Interior Franklin K. Lane, delivered this vacuous statement in 1919: "It has never seemed to me that it was difficult to define Americanization or Americanism: 'I appreciate something, I admire something, I love something; I want you, my friends, my neighbors, to appreciate and admire and love that thing, too. That something is America!"[26] It may have earned a cheer from the audience, but like so much of what Lane's colleagues said, it hardly enlightened.

Other Americanizers were more eloquent, if not totally illuminating. Rabbi Stephen S. Wise of New York, himself an immigrant, said that "Americanism is not a matter of birth but worth, not of descent but aspiration, not of inheritance but achievement. The supreme ideal of foreign-born Americans must be to lift themselves to the level of the best and highest through selfless service of the noblest republic history has known."[27] A series of books on "Americanization Studies," sponsored by the Carnegie Foundation and first published in 1920, printed this definition in the publisher's note to each of its ten volumes: "Americanization in these studies has been considered as the union of native and foreign born in all the most fundamental relationships and activities of our national life. For Americanization is the uniting of new with native-born Americans in fuller common understanding and appreciation to secure by means of individual and collective self-direction the highest welfare of all."[28]

Edward George Hartmann, the author of the most comprehensive history of the Americanization movement, argues that this lack of clarity means that people knew intuitively what phrases like "the American way of life" meant: belief and support of the ideas undergirding the

American founding, spelled out in the Declaration of Independence and the U.S. Constitution, and further revealed by statesmen like Washington, Jefferson, and Lincoln; representative democracy; individual equality under the rule of law; faith in public schools as agents of upward mobility; the value of a common language; and the benefits of capitalism and the rewards of thrift.[29] Peter Roberts, who headed a vigorous Americanization program for the YMCA, builds on this theme. In his 1920 how-to manual, *The Problem of Americanization,* he writes that Americanizers "must believe that these men who come from foreign countries have in them the stuff of which self-governing citizens are made."[30] The Americanizers clearly wanted to share the bounties of political freedom and economic opportunity with immigrants, but knew that these gifts were not simply there for the taking. To receive them, the foreign-born would have to comply with the habits of a nation that made them possible. They would have to join the republic both legally and psychologically.

One of the best attempts to explain Americanization in a few words came in a 1919 speech by Supreme Court Justice Louis D. Brandeis. "What is Americanization?" he asked at Faneuil Hall in Boston. His answer:

> It manifests itself, in a superficial way, when the immigrant adopts the clothes, the manners, and the customs generally prevailing here. Far more important is the manifestation presented when he substitutes for his mother tongue the English language as the common medium of speech. But the adoption of our language, manners, and customs is only a small part of the process. To become Americanized the change wrought must be fundamental. However great his outward conformity, the immigrant is not Americanized unless his interests and affections have become deeply rooted here. And we properly demand of the immigrant even more than this. He must be brought into complete harmony with our ideals and aspirations, and cooperate with us for their attainment. Only when this has been done will he possess the national consciousness of an American.[31]

Americanization, finally, meant adherence to the American idea.

This was an old problem, and the Americanizers were not the first to confront it. If a nation is to remain a nation, after all, something must bind its people together. Throughout history, nations have been able to rely on ethnic bonds and bloodlines to do the job. The United States, however, does not have this advantage. Its people can trace their ancestry to all parts of the globe—an observation that fascinated Alexis de Tocqueville in the 1830s. "How does it happen that in the United States, where the inhabitants have only recently immigrated to the land which they now occupy . . . where, in short, the instinctive love of country can scarcely exist; how does it happen that everyone takes as zealous an interest in the affairs of his township, his country, and the whole state as if they were his own?" he asked. His answer: the United States "make[s] them partakers in the government" by allowing them to assume political rights. In other words, Americans let immigrants participate in civic life, their activities ranging from marching in parades to naturalizing as citizens. They begin to appreciate the idea of American citizenship, which nourishes "rational" patriotism, as opposed to the "instinctive" passion that attaches itself to inherited cultural baggage. Rational, American-style patriotism "springs from knowledge; it is nurtured by the laws; it grows by the exercise of civil rights; and, in the end, it is confounded with the personal interests of the citizen," wrote Tocqueville. "A man comprehends the influence which the well-being of his country has upon his own; he is aware that the laws permit him to contribute to that prosperity, and he labors to promote it, first because it benefits him, and secondly because it is in part his own work."[32] Americanization pulls immigrants in, rather than keeping them out. And once they feel like they are on the same team as everyone else, they start cheering for the right side.

So these were the Americanizers' ideals. Yet perhaps the Americanization movement is best defined not by its goals or by its rhetoric, but by its actual accomplishments. Americanization, after all, was not simply an intellectual exercise. It encouraged individuals and groups to become active in a cause that called for hours of drudgery and a deep well of enthusiasm. And what it accomplished in the first part of the 20th century would hinge not on what people said it would do, but on what it actually did.

BIRTH OF A MOVEMENT

If the Americanization movement needs an exact date of birth, the year 1907 would be a good place to look for one (even though Americanization's roots stretch back a bit further). That year, three significant events jump-started the crusade. First, the New York chapter of the YMCA established evening classes for immigrants, where students took lessons on English, naturalization, and the U.S. government. By the following year, as many as six thousand immigrants enrolled in YMCA classes in one hundred thirty cities and towns around the country. Within five years, an estimated fifty-five thousand immigrants had received instruction at three hundred YMCA branches. Classes met mostly in the evening after workers completed their day shifts, but some went on during the middle of the day in factories and shops. There were even a handful of classes held at midnight. Public lectures covered even more topics, such as personal hygiene, sanitation, and industrial safety. Because of programs like these, the YMCA would become one of the driving forces behind private sector Americanization, and many other organizations would follow its lead.

The second significant event also happened in 1907. New Jersey passed the first legislation in any state supporting English-language and civics classes for immigrants. It allowed the boards of education of its school districts to set up evening classes for immigrants. The New Jersey State Board of Education laid out uniform rules for school management, inspection, and certification. It also offered a funding mechanism that channeled state monies to local districts that became active in this area. Other states would mimic this example, but New Jersey was the first state to show how public bodies could support the Americanization movement in meaningful ways.[33]

Third and finally, 1907 saw the founding of the North American Civic League for Immigrants, a group of philanthropists, social workers, writers, and industrialists who organized for "the civic betterment of the immigrant."[34] As its president D. Chauncy Brewer said in 1910, the league worried about the consequences of not helping immigrants assimilate. Community leaders "have been noting with uneasiness the changing character of our population," he wrote. "The majority of the immigrants entering the continent or who may become resident here, are well meaning, and may become useful citizens if they receive the attention to which they are not only entitled as a matter of humanity, but which prudence necessitates because of their relation to our economic and political affairs."[35] The league recruited members in nine states and distributed thousands of informative pamphlets to immigrants at ports of entry and railroad stations. It also helped new arrivals reach the homes to which they were destined, coordinated job placement, and protected women and girls from prostitution rackets.[36]

The league did not get involved directly in the business of English language training at first (it would within a few years), but instead tried to convince public school officials to offer more adult education services and helped them sign up students. It also sponsored a series of civics lectures, hosting 150 of them in 13 New England cities in 1911. Lectures were delivered in English and nine other languages, and they also were available in written form. Libraries around the country purchased thousands of copies. Titles included "The Need of Learning English and the Advantages of an Education," "The Story of the American People," "Abraham Lincoln," "George Washington," and "A Primer for the Alien Desirous of Becoming a Citizen." Prominent citizens associated themselves with the league and its work. Their ranks included Anne Morgan, the daughter of J. P. Morgan; Frank Trumbull, chairman of the Chesapeake and Ohio Rail Road; and Felix Warburg, an influential banker.[37]

Educators at the American International College in Springfield, Massachusetts, introduced a system of phonetics that claimed to give its non-English speakers a vocabulary of three thousand words after 36 weeks of study. All of the students at the college were themselves immigrants, and they pursued a curriculum that focused intensely on American history, government, and ideals. The hope was to create a generation of Americanized immigrant leaders who would return to their communities and promote Americanization among their neighbors. In 1910, the school had 100 students.[38]

The North American Civic League for Immigrants and other groups increasingly pressured state governments to become more involved in the Americanization drive. Their first big success came in New York, which established its Bureau of Industries and Immigration in 1910. When Frances A. Kellor assumed leadership of the bureau, she became the first woman in the country to head a state agency. Thanks in large part to Kellor's devotion, the bureau would serve as one of the most important organizations in the Americanization movement over the next 10 years by coordinating activities, helping similar groups get started, and conducting investigations into immigrant conditions. California, Massachusetts, and New Jersey soon followed suit. English-language and citizenship classes proliferated in these states and elsewhere as Americanization fever spread.[39]

In 1911, the Federal Immigration Commission gave a tremendous boost to the Americanizers. It had just concluded four years of research and issued an enormous 42-volume report. Its main recommendation—and its most controversial one—was to reduce immigration levels. Among the new immigrants, noted the report, "assimilation has been slow as compared to that of the earlier non-English-speaking races."[40] This finding highlighted the need for additional programs similar to those the YMCA, the North American Civic League for Immigrants, and the state agencies already were providing. Senator William P. Dillingham of Vermont, chairman of the commission, praised the Civic League in particular. "All these newcomers need help. They need to be interested in American institutions, and it can only be done through a society of this nature, and by cooperation of churches, societies, and individuals by team work," he said.[41]

Big business soon became aware of the Americanization movement. The captains of industry wanted to prevent foreign-born workers from agitating, especially after the strike in Lawrence. A series of committees and groups sponsored by corporate interests looked into the conditions of immigrant life in New England. They concluded that industry needed to engage in Americanization activities. Concern spread rapidly to the middle Atlantic states and then to the Midwest "until practically every chamber of commerce or similar organization of every municipality of significance containing an alien population had a special immigration committee taking a vigorous and active part on behalf of the Americanization of the immigrant," writes Hartmann.[42] Helping the foreign-born adjust to American society suddenly seemed not only an act of benevolent patriotism but also a business necessity.

By the spring of 1914, the Americanizers were so pleased with how their individual efforts at the state and local levels were proceeding that they decided to try to make their movement more national in scope. They created the Committee for Immigrants in America out of a successful local organization based in New York and New Jersey, and turned it into a clearinghouse for Americanization activities. The committee lobbied the federal government to become formally involved in the Americanization movement, and the Department of the Interior agreed to establish a Division of Immigrant Education within its Bureau of Education. Unfortunately for the Americanizers, there was no money available for staffing the new agency, let alone financing any type of program. The committee, however, responded by offering to staff and fund the division privately—a proposal that the Bureau of Education eagerly accepted.[43]

The Division of Immigrant Education's first major project was to help local communities interested in setting up English-language and citizenship classes. Many wanted to do this, but did not know how to go about sponsoring a successful program. The division helped remedy this problem with a steady stream of advice. Perhaps its main function, however, was to call attention to the need for Americanization. It became a virtual public relations machine for the Americanization movement, issuing press releases and newsletters in almost nonstop fashion. Until 1919, the Bureau of Education's Americanization activities were completely underwritten by the Committee for Immigrants in America.[44]

A NEW RACE OF MEN

As the Americanization movement gained momentum, the dramatist Israel Zangwill gave a name to one of the most powerful ideas ever to grip the American imagination. His 1908 play *The Melting-Pot* celebrated the intermarriage between people of different ethnic, racial, and religious backgrounds. Note that Americanization and intermarriage are not the same thing. Americanization is primarily concerned with the cultural and political assimilation of immigrants and their children. The melting pot, however, goes a step further. It advocates genetic assimilation, or the biological fusing of many peoples into one. And although it remains distinct from the concept of Americanization, many Americanizers saw it as the logical consequence of what they were trying to achieve. "Just as cross-fertilization is beneficial to plant life," noted the scientist W. J. McGee, "the intermingling of peoples in this country must produce the most beautiful, most intellectual, and most powerful race of the world . . . the American, even today, presents the highest type of beauty which ever adorned the earth." The journalist

Herbert N. Casson captured the spirit best when he rhapsodized, "It might even be said that the man of purest American blood is he who has the most cosmopolitan lineage."[45]

Although Zangwill is only a minor figure in American literature, he created one of its most enduring scenes. *The Melting-Pot* tells the story of David Quixano and Vera Revendal. Both are Russian immigrants, but David is Jewish and Vera is Christian. The two fall in love. They plan to wed, but relatives complain and other problems arise. In the play's melodramatic conclusion, David and Vera reconcile on a rooftop overlooking lower Manhattan and the Statue of Liberty. They hold hands and watch the sun set:

> VERA: Look! How beautiful the sunset is after the storm!
>
> DAVID: It is the fires of God round His Crucible. *(He drops her hand and points downward.)* There she lies, the great Melting-Pot—listen! Can't you hear the roaring and the bubbling? There gapes her mouth *(he points east)*—the harbour where a thousand mammoth feeders come from the ends of the world to pour in their human freight. Ah, what a stirring and a seething! Celt and Latin, Slav and Teuton, Greek and Syrian,—black and yellow—
>
> VERA *(softly, nestling to him):* Jew and Gentile—
>
> DAVID: Yes, East and West, and North and South, the palm and the pine, the pole and the equator, the crescent and the cross—how the great Alchemist melts and fuses them with his purging flame! Here shall they all unite to build the Republic of Man and the Kingdom of God. Ah, Vera, what is the glory of Rome and Jerusalem where all nations and races come to worship and look back, compared with the glory of America, where all races and nations come to labour and look forward![46]

The Melting-Pot was a smash hit. It played to full houses in dozens of cities around the United States and had a successful run in London. It remained in print for years. After seeing a performance in Washington, President Theodore Roosevelt wrote to Zangwill: "I do not know when I have seen a play that stirred me as much."[47] Later, he would say "We Americans are the children of the crucible."[48] In 1926, *Literary Digest* wrote that Zangwill "made a phrase that long postponed restricted immigration in America."[49] This vast overstatement speaks to the enthusiastic environment in which Zangwill's play was received. It is not a coincidence that melting-pot fever seized the country at the same time as the Americanization movement rose to prominence. Or that Roosevelt, a leading booster of the movement, praised the play's theme so fervently.

Indeed, the melting pot might best be understood as the ultimate form of Americanization. If Americanization's main goal was to incorporate immigrants into the general population and make them the equals of all Americans, there was every reason to believe that intermarriage between people of different racial and ethnic backgrounds would follow. It would not necessarily have to occur with the immigrant generation—many first-generation Americans arrived in the United States already married. Others would find an enormous amount of comfort from marrying within their own group. But some would not. And more important, the children of immigrants would have much less incentive to marry within their own group. Second-generation Americans would be more at ease within American society. They would probably reach adulthood as fluent English speakers comfortable with their place in the world. Looked at this way, the melting pot is simply Americanization working on a generational level.

For all of the promotional energy Zangwill and the Americanizers poured into the melting pot, they were hardly the first to celebrate intermarriage. Ralph Waldo Emerson had once compared America to a smelting pot and wrote that "the energy of Irish, Germans, Swedes, Poles, and Cossacks, and all the European tribes,—of the Africans, and of the Polynesians,—will construct a new race."[50] Before Emerson, the Frenchman J. Hector St. John de Crèvecoeur published the memoirs he wrote in the 1770s while living as a farmer in upstate New York. "What, then, is the American, this new man?" he asked. "He is neither an European nor the descendant of an European; hence that strange mixture of blood, which you will find in no other country . . . Here individuals of all nations are melted into a new race of men."[51] George Washington spoke of immigrants who "assimilated to our customs, measures, and laws: in a word, soon become one people" with the native-born.[52] Herman Melville wrote that "You can not spill a drop of American blood without spilling the blood of the whole world."[53] In his famous essay in 1893 on the closing of the American frontier, historian Frederick Jackson Turner wrote that "In the crucible of the frontier, the immigrants were Americanized, liberated, and fused into a mixed race, English in neither nationality nor characteristics."[54] Despite this long history, the idea of the melting pot flowered most fully under the Americanizers' watch.

Modern critics of the melting pot ethic say that it was fundamentally exclusionary because it included only whites, and left Asians, American Indians, and blacks out in the cold. Yet there is little merit to this claim. Certainly Emerson made mention of more than just the children of Europe. Zangwill also went the distance. To be sure, Crèvecoeur's statement—probably the most famous of the lot—addresses only whites. But consider the fact that he wrote before the American Revolution, when there were virtually no Asians in North America. American Indians and blacks are another matter, and we might wish that Crèvecoeur had included them in his list of ingredients for the new American race. That he did not is unfortunate, but hardly damnable. It is certainly not enough to invalidate his fundamental point that American identity is remarkably inclusive. Crèvecoeur's only sin is that it eventually would become more inclusive than he foresaw.

And here lies the sheer power of Zangwill's melting pot metaphor. It actually has its origins in England—Zangwill was an English Jew of Russian ancestry—where the melting pot was a popular symbol representing a complete transformation.[55] In some sense, Zangwill simply carried the image across the ocean rather than creating a homegrown version himself. What he did, however, is treat the melting pot in a way that gave it a unique meaning in the United States, where it now refers almost exclusively to racial and ethnic mixture. It even implicitly built on one of the nicer assumptions of some social Darwinists—the idea that racial mixture would yield a stronger alloy. This was, to say the least, a controversial proposition that had begun to lose favor as a result of the new immigration from eastern and southern Europe. Yet the implication remains compelling. The melting pot would admit all comers and produce something new and greater than the sum of its parts.

Race mixing was not accepted universally when Zangwill wrote. Many old-stock Americans thought that intermarriage with the new immigrants would be deracinating. This has been a matter of contention among blacks, too. In the United States, black-white miscegenation was fairly common before the Civil War, as was miscegenation between blacks and American Indians. There is no good estimate of how much white blood runs in the black gene pool, but some researchers have estimated that black Americans' ancestry is one-fifth white.[56] This is a controversial subject because so much of this mixing was the result of slaveholders raping slaves. Nevertheless, black Americans are truly a mixed-race people. The biggest hurdle to recognition of this fact is the infamous theory of race in which one drop of black blood makes a person black. (It is worth noting that black Americans would be a mixed people even if there were no black-white miscegenation. Most black Americans can trace their African ancestry to the west coast of Africa, a culturally and ethnically diverse region. In the United States, these many peoples amalgamated in their own segregated melting pot.) Regardless of this history, blacks have long debated the merits of intermarriage with whites. The former slave and abolitionist leader Frederick Douglass considered black-white marriages acceptable, and married a white woman late in life. An equally strong intellectual tradition among black nationalists, including Alexander Crummell and Marcus Garvey, has opposed this practice. In addition, marriages between blacks and whites were illegal in more than half the United States during the 1940s. In 1966, the year before the Supreme Court permanently banned such laws in a unanimous decision, 19 states still had them on the books.[57] To be sure, many Americanizers did not have blacks in mind when they spoke of the melting pot. Yet it was on many people's minds.

A compelling critique of intermarriage came from the immigrants themselves. What if the melting pot melts away identities that are worth preserving? The Jewish reaction to Zangwill was particularly severe. Zangwill was himself a militant Zionist, and his advocacy of the melting pot seemed like a blatant contradiction. Zangwill cannot have it both ways, said the critics. Either all races should fuse into a new American race, or some should preserve themselves within the United States. Zangwill lamely replied in 1914 that assimilation could occur without any "gamic interaction" between Jews and Gentiles. But his play gave no hint that this was an acceptable option, and he argued elsewhere that the melting pot would inevitably work on Jews in the United States.

In this sense, *The Melting-Pot* was not only prescriptive but also descriptive. Nobody actually forced people into the melting pot against their will. Yet lots of people, including Jews, found themselves jumping into it voluntarily. The melting pot simmered because Americans—even the newest ones—wanted it to, not because it was imposed upon the country by a hostile overclass, as modern critics have argued. Intermarriage had long been a reality in the United States, even though the data are quite scarce. (The data become reliable only in the second half of the 20th century—long after the fame of *The Melting-Pot* had peaked.)[58] There is absolutely no question it went on, only how rapidly and with whom. This notion came under attack 40 years after Zangwill's death in 1926. Politicians, academics, and ethnic activists denied that there ever was a melting pot. They were wrong—and theirs is a story told in chapter five.

For most Americanizers, the melting pot was not their first priority. They understood that the kind of national unity they encouraged among both native-born and foreign-born would probably lead toward something very like the melting pot, but that was years away. Their concerns were much more immediate. In 1914, as they were beginning to draw the federal government into the Americanization movement, they had no idea how immediate their concerns would become. The Americanization movement was growing increasingly wide in scope, but the onset of World War I in the second half of that year pushed it irresistibly into a rapid-growth phase—and also to its doom.

Chapter 4

THE FALL OF
AMERICANIZATION

"The greatest patriotic parade that New York ever saw will start at 8:30 this morning." So read the first sentence of a front-page *New York Times* story on the Fourth of July, 1918.[1] That day, more than seventy thousand marching immigrants swept up Fifth Avenue for 10 hours in "a demonstration of the loyalty of Americans of foreign birth to their adopted country."[2] Tens of thousands of others who wanted to participate were turned away to keep the event from growing too large. At least 40 national-origin groups took part, ranging from an 18-person Haitian entourage to the ten thousand-strong Italian and Jewish contingents. Every group showed its devotion to the United States. A troupe of Russian girls dressed in red, white, and blue. A Venezuelan band played the national anthem. The Chinese display featured a baseball team. Lithuanian immigrants carried a banner that read "Uncle Sam is Our Uncle." The *Times* reporter could hardly contain his enthusiasm: "And in this long, kaleidoscopic pageant, now bright with splendid costumes, now drab with long columns of civilians, marching with a solemnity of spirit that brought its meaning home impressively to those who looked on, there was slowly woven a picture of fighting America of today, a land of many bloods but one ideal."[3]

This was the high-water mark of the Americanization movement. The United States had gone through a period of mass immigration, and now was at war in Europe against some of the immigrants' birth countries. Americanization had made voluntary devotion to the United States an important goal, and it helped keep the country whole through this troubled period. American leaders hoped that even in these trying times everybody could live up to the motto set forth by the League of Foreign-Born Citizens in the New York march: "Americans of many peoples, but one nation."[4] A few months earlier, several groups of natives and immigrants had petitioned President Woodrow Wilson to declare July 4, 1918, a day for immigrants to declare their loyalty to the United States. Wilson agreed and eagerly took part in the festivities himself. He went to Mount Vernon and presided over a ceremony at Washington's tomb. "Foreign-born citizens of the United States of 35 nationalities who had placed wreaths of palms on the tomb in token of fealty to the principles laid down by the father of this country, cried their approval of his words in many languages and then stood with reverently bared heads while the voice of John McCormack soared over the hallowed ground in the notes of the 'Star-Spangled Banner,'" reported the *Washington Post*.[5] Dozens of similarly patriotic gatherings occurred around the country, each using the loyalty of foreign-born Americans as its theme.[6]

The parade in New York, the ceremony at Mt. Vernon, and all of the other events made an important political point: The United States may have many foreign-born people living in it, but these are also Americans who dedicate themselves to American interests. Problems loomed ahead, however. Starting in 1914, the First World War paradoxically drove the Americanization movement to its greatest heights and at the same time paved the way for its ultimate undoing.

WARTIME AMERICANIZATION

Before the war, Americanization was mainly a local phenomenon. Lots of people were thinking the same sorts of things, but their efforts were almost totally decentralized. The hypernationalism of war changed that, transformed the movement into a national crusade, and made it an important aspect of American security strategy. Its chief goal was to maintain industrial production by keeping immigrants on the job and off the picket line. And to the extent that it accomplished this with emphatic appeals, soaring rhetoric, and flag-waving rallies, it was a triumphant success.

Herein lay a nagging uncertainty: A first principle of Americanization holds that every immigrant is a potential citizen. This is a generous and sympathetic principle, because it not only wants to share the glory of being an American with people who are not yet American but also to recognize the personal difficulty of assimilating. In the new, nationalized version of Americanization, however, the fear of foreign subversion played a central role. In this view, Americanization was important not because it provided a humane response to the problem of accommodating a foreign-born population, but because it would keep that population in line. Americanization subsequently increased suspicions about immigrants. Would they remain loyal during a war?

When the first shots were fired in 1914, officially the United States was not taking sides in the conflict. Yet many people could see which countries would become their adversaries over the next few years. Moreover, about one of every three foreign-born Americans— a total of nearly 5 million—had been born a subject of the Central Powers. Half of these came from Germany, the rest from Austria-Hungary, Bulgaria, and Turkey. The possibility of fighting a war in Europe was bad enough. The threat of mutiny within U.S. borders was terrifying.

For a while the prospect of immigrant dissension was a relatively minor issue, and Americanizers took advantage of the charged atmosphere of nationalism to advance their own message of inclusion and assimilation. The success of wartime Americanization was due in large part to the yeoman efforts of the movement's founders. They offered a set of well-developed answers to a series of questions that much of the public was only starting to ask. All of a sudden, prominent figures involved themselves in the war effort by borrowing from the Americanizers' playbook. Secretary of State William Jennings Bryan and former President William H. Taft spoke on citizenship at a "New Voters' Day" celebration in Baltimore. The Bureau of Naturalization moved to make its ceremonies more lavish and more public in an attempt to show that the United States not only valued its immigrants but also expected them to become patriots devoted to the star-spangled banner, not the flags of foreign nations. As a part of this campaign, July 4, 1915, was dubbed National Americanization Day, and activities were planned in 150 cities across the country. In Pittsburgh, more than ten thousand adults—most of them immigrants—heard one thousand children sing patriotic songs as they formed a giant American flag. In Indianapolis, recently naturalized citizens gave speeches in 11 languages on the responsibilities of American citizenship. According to Frances A. Kellor, who played a key role in organizing the events, National Americanization Day inspired dozens of communities to become more involved in the Americanization movement. Detroit expanded its night school classes for immigrants, Boston offered new citizenship courses, and Wilmington, Delaware, started a naturalization school. Student registrations in these cities and elsewhere skyrocketed.

President Wilson did the most on that day to underline the importance and meaning of Americanization. He traveled to Philadelphia to deliver the main address to a group of new citizens. In his remarks, he spoke about both the contributions immigrants made to the United States and the duties they owed to it. First he extended an invitation, then a compliment. "You dreamed dreams of what America was to be, and I hope you have brought the dreams with you. No man who does not see high visions will ever realize any high hope or undertake any high enterprise, and just because you brought the dreams with you, America is more likely to realize the dream you brought. You are enriching us if you came expecting us to be better than we are," said Wilson. Next came a more cautionary tone.

> I certainly would not be one even to suggest that a man cease to love the home of his birth and the nation of his origin—these things are very sacred and ought not to be put out of our hearts—but it is one thing to love the place where you were born and it is another thing to dedicate yourself to the place to which you go. You cannot dedicate yourself to America unless you become in every respect and with every purpose of your will thorough Americans. You cannot become thorough Americans if you think of yourselves in groups. A man who thinks of himself as belonging to a particular national group in America has not yet become an American, and the man

who goes among you to trade upon your nationality is no worthy son to live under the Stars and Stripes.[7]

Americanization was now national. For the first time, people all over the country recognized its importance and agreed on several standard methods for advancing its goals. Philanthropic, business, civic, and educational organizations all took a keen interest. Women's groups such as the Daughters of the American Revolution became involved. Even though labor unions remained skeptical of Americanization because big business supported it, many of their leaders came to applaud its efforts to educate immigrant workers. By 1916, millions of posters, pamphlets, and curriculum guides on English, naturalization, and citizenship were in circulation. As the First World War continued to grind away in Europe—and as direct American involvement in the fight appeared more certain—private groups as well as federal, state, and municipal governments extended their support of Americanization. The movement grew so strong that "practically every hamlet in the United States which contained an immigrant populace felt the full impact of the crusade," writes Edward George Hartmann.[8]

When the United States formally entered the war in 1917, many immigrants put their own lives on the line. Even though the foreign-born comprised less than 15 percent of the general population and noncitizens had easy access to draft exemptions, immigrants made up 18 percent of the soldiers enlisted in the U.S. Army. Both ethnic leaders and the federal government made much of these immigrant soldiers. A Victory Liberty Loan poster painted by the well-known illustrator Howard Chandler Christy made use of Americanization themes. It featured an Honor Roll of ethnic-sounding names below a caption declaring them "Americans All!"[9] Americanization's primary goal was still to keep the economy humming with productivity. But as the army's muster rolls show, it continued to advance the broader interests of genuine devotion that motivated veteran Americanizers.

A DEVIL'S BARGAIN

Yet this remarkable accomplishment contained a devil's bargain, since it also prepared the way for Americanization's fall. The original, cosmopolitan nature of Americanization was starting to fade. The war years pushed the movement's chief motivation away from sympathy for new Americans and toward fear of foreign subversion. Americanization was presumably a part of national security strategy because immigrants posed a risk to national security. So why have immigrants at all? Why not remove the threat by removing the immigrants—or at least stopping more from coming?

These seeds of doubt did not fall on fallow fields. For years nativism had lain dormant. Its inherent pessimism could not overcome the optimism that nourished the mission of Americanization. It lamely watched the United States absorb a continuous shower of immigrants whose annual rate of admission between 1903 and 1914 never sank below seven hundred fifty thousand and six times soared above 1 million. The nativists were not quiet so much as powerless. Their political victories in the years leading up to the war were small, even trivial. In 1909, a handful of states enacted punitive measures aimed at restricting the rights of aliens. Michigan denied barber licenses to noncitizens. New York made aliens pay 20 times as much as citizens for hunting permits. Two Massachusetts counties even made it illegal for noncitizens to pick wild berries or flowers from property they did not own.[10] These odd laws were mere slaps on the wrist and probably more ignored than enforced. They could even be interpreted as enticements to citizenship, although true Americanizers generally preferred positive recruitment to negative reinforcement.

The upbeat tenor of progressivism muzzled many of the racial anxieties nurtured by nativism, but it hardly eliminated them. In the south and west, especially, the forces of restriction found an audience. Growing concern about the Yellow Peril of unhalted Japanese immigration sometimes spilled into resentments directed at the exponentially more numerous immigrants from eastern and southern Europe. Senator F. M. Simmons of North Carolina even accused the newcomers from Europe of being "nothing more than the degenerate progeny of the Asiatic hoards [sic] which, long centuries ago, overran the shores of the Mediterranean."[11] But these were mainly regional controversies. On the national level, politicians suppressed nativism. Rather than promote fear mongering, they scrambled for immigrant votes. The three-way presidential race of 1912 saw the Bull Moose insurgent Theodore

Roosevelt, the incumbent President William H. Taft, and the successful Democratic challenger Woodrow Wilson battle with each other
over everything from promising to veto restrictive legislation to bribing
foreign-language newspaper editors not to accept advertisements from
other candidates.[12]

Just because the nativists did not have a national champion does not
mean that they had no impact. During the recession of 1913–14, popular clamor to cut back on immigration rose in volume. If these complaints did not catch the attention of business leaders or lawmakers in
the Northeast and Midwest, nativism began to cut a swath across the
landscape that reached from the Deep South to the Pacific Northwest.
Frustrations that could not vent through political channels often bil-
lowed out in personal ways. In one tragic incident, the Jewish manager
of an Atlanta pencil factory found himself the defendant in a rape-and-
murder trial. The prosecution's case against Leo Frank was extraordinarily thin, but anti-Semitic and anti-immigrant sentiments conspired
to convict him. When the governor of Georgia commuted his death
sentence to life imprisonment, southern lynch law seized control of the
situation. Frank was abducted from jail and butchered. At the time,
Tom Watson, a well-known anti-Catholic troublemaker and one of
Frank's chief detractors, had this to say about Jewish immigration:
"From all over the world, the Children of Israel are flocking to this
country, and plans are on foot to move them from Europe *en masse* . . .
to empty upon our shores the very scum and dregs of the *Parasite
Race.*"[13] The Frank episode was spectacular and unique, but it was not
an isolated example of anti-Semitism. It was the sinister outgrowth of a
broader social movement whose energies were temporarily contained
by the benign mission of Americanization. But the clock was ticking,
and events outside anyone's control would set off the explosive intensity of a nativism suddenly at full-strength. The First World War was
coming.

From the start, the war placed a high premium on national loyalty,
and any trace of dissension from the common cause stirred fiery emotions. It was positively un-American. Yet suspicion gradually overtook
sympathy as the driving force behind Americanization. Instead of deliberate attempts to include new people in the American franchise, and
thereby win their devotion to it, a greater emphasis was to be placed on

exclusion and rooting out suspect people, often for cursory or irrational reasons. This was generally accomplished with calls for national unity and appeals to patriotism. Indeed, nativism did not displace Americanization so much as co-opt it.

The nativist revival would first direct its fury at German Americans. For years the Germans were considered a hard-working, law-abiding group of model immigrants. Even though hundreds of thousands of them streamed through Ellis Island alongside the disfavored eastern and southern Europeans, they were immune to many of the charges leveled at their fellow travelers. This had the ironic effect of making the Germans remarkably unprepared for what was about to happen. Unlike other immigrant groups, they had never faced much overt hostility. Their leaders had not been prodded into political meekness by native suspicion, at least not to the same extent as other groups. When the war in Europe erupted, so did German-American emotions. Rather than suppressing the words and deeds that would grate against the country's essentially pro-British sympathies—something that a less coddled group might have done—they boldly cheered on the Fatherland.

For a time, pro-German activity simply raised eyebrows. But as tensions in Europe escalated, these sentiments were soon deemed a threat. In late 1914, German-American groups started to lobby aggressively for an embargo on the export of war supplies, an act that would have proved detrimental to British interests. The Germans promoted their initiative as keeping in line with U.S. neutrality, though its real-world effects were not lost on a public that increasingly came to see German Americans as pawns of the Kaiser. On January 30, 1915, representatives from every significant German-American organization intensified anxieties by assembling in Washington in a brash political show of force. Their timing could not have been worse. Just a few days later, the German government declared submarine warfare on Great Britain. It would not be long before German torpedoes were killing American citizens on the open seas.[14] In July, a U.S. Secret Service agent uncovered German plots to bomb a steamship bound for France, disrupt production at U.S. munitions plants, and encourage American steel workers to strike. German spies had even purchased a New York daily newspaper, *The Mail,* for propaganda purposes.[15]

Public reaction to this news was not charitable. In a climate of amplified nationalism—and the United States was quickly reaching this point, even though it was not yet fighting—divided loyalties constitute the gravest offense imaginable. Organized German-Americanism became almost synonymous with treason. In an editorial, the *New York Times* railed at German-American groups: "Never since the foundation of the Republic has any body of men assembled here who were more completely subservient to foreign influence and a foreign power and none ever proclaimed the un-American spirit more openly."[16]

The nativist impulse had found an outlet and an imprimatur. It could focus its energies on a newly down-and-out immigrant group and also receive sanction under the wartime cover of patriotic duty. On the whole, the United States was much more generous to its German-born population than other warring countries, but anti-German sentiments frequently surfaced with a sweeping vindictiveness.[17] In a pamphlet titled *The Tentacles of the German Octopus in America,* author Earl E. Sperry announced that "overwhelming proof is afforded that large numbers of German-Americans are disloyal citizens."[18] Hundreds of school systems stopped teaching the German language. Stores owned by German Americans were stoned, breaking windows and causing other damage. German opera was boycotted and symphonies avoided playing Beethoven and Mozart. Raw fear kept German-American groups from holding public meetings. Towns, businesses, and individuals with German names changed them. Restaurant menus stopped listing "German-fried" potatoes and sauerkraut and started listing "America-fried" potatoes and "liberty cabbage." In a few places hamburgers became "liberty steaks." In Cincinnati, pretzels were banned from lunch counters. There were, of course, disloyal Germans living in the United States. Yet complete innocents bore the brunt of what amounted to a rhetorical, political, and often physical carpet-bomb attack on an entire group of people.

Nativism now zeroed in on the German population, rather than other immigrant groups. Anti-Catholicism, which had animated nativist sentiment for most of the 19th century, fell from favor. It was perceived as a tool of the enemy, a threat to national unity. With such an intense focus on Germans, many immigrant groups that had previously encountered adversity found new opportunities to proclaim their Americanness. This was due in no small part to an Americanization movement that buttressed its traditional concerns with wartime activities like patriotic parades and bond drives. Even as a massive campaign of culture-crushing conformity bombarded German immigrants, the original Americanizers continued their liberal mission of inclusiveness. "To a remarkable degree the psychic climate of war gave the average alien not only protection but also a sense of participation and belonging," writes Higham.[19]

Despite this, the war allowed nativists to get involved in the Americanization movement on the grounds that they were preserving national security. Americanization subsequently gained a harder edge. Rather than being an inclusive method of persuading immigrants to adopt the American way of life, wartime Americanization repeatedly tried to exclude certain immigrants because they allegedly threatened America. In 1917, Congress approved a literacy test for immigrants, requiring that newcomers demonstrate literacy, but not necessarily in English. This was hailed as a restrictive measure, even though it ironically did almost nothing to lower admission levels. Tax rates doubled among certain immigrants. The Department of Justice also received new authority to arrest, detain, and deport alien radicals.[20] Much of this legislation was passed in the name of Americanization—or at least *Americanism,* a term that was coming to mean much the same thing. One result was an apparent change in the purpose of Americanization. The founding Americanizers kept up their regular program of teaching English and encouraging citizenship. Yet with growing frequency, immigrants were seen not as potential patriots, but as genuine risks. "Reckon each [American born in enemy territory] as a pound of dynamite," wrote Samuel Hopkins Adams at the tail end of the fighting in Europe. "Not all these enemy aliens are hostile. Not all dynamite explodes."[21] Americanization's irreversible distortion had begun.

THE DRIVE FOR CONFORMITY

When the war ended in November 1918, so did the German threat. Anti-German nativism evaporated almost overnight. New anxieties arose as the government canceled war orders, runaway inflation gripped the country, and the dollar lost half its value. In 1919, more than 4 million workers participated in three thousand six hundred strikes. Peace was supposed to bring prosperity and calm the uneasiness over immigrant loyalty. All it seemed to do, however, was exacerbate fears. Americanization had become so widespread by this point that it included devotees who did not always have the immigrants' best interests in mind. A great deal of damage had been done to the public's perception of immigrants. As Kellor noted in a 1919 essay, "Much of the propaganda essential to winning the war has made the ground look like a battlefield after a tank has passed over it—ploughed deep but unfit for culture for some time to come."[22] Several anthropologists have identified the immediate postwar period as an ideal breeding ground for what they call revitalization movements, or severe cultural reactions to profound social stress.[23] Whatever the cause, nativism continued to thrive, assuming new forms that further clawed at the Americanization movement.

Nativism's initial target was ideological, rather than religious, ethnic, or racial. The rise of bolshevism in Russia had invigorated radical political groups in the United States that were formerly inhibited by wartime regulations. Far-left socialists were fingered as the chief agitators in several large labor strikes. Scores of communist and anarchist periodicals hit the presses. The new radicalism was inherently confrontational and occasionally turned to violence. A rash of anarchist bombings struck at public officials in Philadelphia and elsewhere. The number of Americans who were members of organizations that preached revolution is unknown, but probably was quite small. Yet here was conclusive evidence that subversion still threatened the United States, even though the war had ended. Moreover, it was plain to everyone that the vast majority of the radicals were immigrants. "Fully 90 percent of Communist and anarchist agitation is traceable to aliens," wrote Attorney General A. Mitchell Palmer.[24] This intersection allowed old nativist prejudices to merge with new ideological concerns. Each played off the other and together they led to the Red Scare.

Palmer and his cohorts arrested hundreds of alleged radicals during the infamous Palmer Raids of 1919 and 1920. Although some of the people they detained were genuine revolutionaries and threats to public safety, many had only attended a meeting. They were deemed guilty by association. The Department of Justice created a General Intelligence Division to monitor radical literature and keep the federal government apprised of potential trouble. (J. Edgar Hoover led this effort in his first major law enforcement job.) A good deal of Palmer's activity was public grandstanding inspired by his high political aspirations. But the Red Scare had ramifications beyond his personal career. It was conducted under the guise of Americanism and promoted the goal of rooting out un-American influences. The confidence and optimism that had breathed life into Americanization for so long was fast dissipating. It was now coming to be seen as little more than a tool to weed out people with undesirable political views. Doubts about the foreign-born mounted. An American Legion publication made this clear: The new immigrants "were not of our sort . . . could not speak English, [and] were hostile to American institutions."[25]

Many longtime advocates of immigrant assimilation were taken aback by this trend. In Boston, Judge George W. Anderson railed at the ringleaders of the Red Scare: "Talk about Americanization! What we need is the Americanization of the people who carry out such proceedings as these."[26] Despite this, deviant Americanizers were full of passionate intensity. The Red Scare eventually became a casualty of its own excesses (and Palmer became a laughingstock, his political ambitions dashed), but it left scars on the public's perceptions of the foreign-born population and immigrants' ability to join a union of American citizens.

During this period, the original Americanizers toiled to keep their movement alive. The Bureau of Naturalization signed an agreement with the Boy Scouts of America in which the boys served as ushers at citizenship ceremonies and promoted school attendance by writing tens of thousands of letters to immigrants. Schools, businesses, and state governments continued to channel funds to Americanization activities. Connecticut even established its own Department of Americanization, which set up a speakers bureau, published posters and circulars, and produced a special moving picture on Americanization. Yet these were temporary accomplishments. A stronger, countervailing trend saw dozens of states pass coercive laws aimed at the foreign-born. The helping hand of assimilation had mutated into an iron fist of conformity. In 1919, 15 states barred foreign-language instruction from their schools, even private ones. Idaho and Utah mandated Americanization classes for aliens who did not speak English. Oregon ordered foreign-language newspapers to print English translations of their entire contents. It would later insist that all children attend public rather than private elementary schools, although the Supreme Court struck down this measure.[27]

A desire for American cohesion had been transformed into a colorless lust for national conformity. Many of the newest Americanizers believed that for immigrants to assimilate fully, they would have to stamp out every last flicker of foreign culture in the United States. At the school Henry Ford set up for his immigrant employees to learn English, students took part in a pantomime that symbolized Americanization's new turn with spectacular flair. In the performance, a giant melting pot occupied center stage. Students dressed in outlandish, foreign garb and carrying signs proclaiming their homelands marched into the pot from backstage. At the same time, another group of students emerged from each side of the pot. They wore identical suits of clothes and carried small American flags.[28] Americanization was no longer about welcoming the foreign-born and encouraging them to become full members of American society. The voluntary nature of Americanization faded away. Immigrants now were expected to march into a crude and impersonal assimilation assembly line. "There can be no Americanization from the top down," warned Kellor.[29] But the deafening machines of compulsive conformity drowned out her pleas.

The economy took a nosedive in 1920, prompting many industrialists who had financed Americanization activities among their employees to pull out. Although Americanization had promised them a better workforce, now productivity sagged, labor shortages became rare, and unemployment rose. The economic necessity of Americanization all but vanished, in their view. Several prominent business groups took forthright stands against the ways in which the Red Scare blindly tarred all immigrant workers, but theirs was a rear guard action. The demand for Americanization was as great as ever, however, thanks to surging levels of immigration. By September 1920, five thousand newcomers were passing through Ellis Island each day. In 1921, admissions rose to more than eight hundred five thousand. They had returned to prewar levels. Yet these new immigrants were met with worries over jobs and wages, not a program of inclusion and uplift. The Americanization movement was heading for the exit door.

AMERICANIZATION IS AN UGLY WORD

Perhaps nothing drove it there so swiftly as the revival of racial nativism. A kind of intellectual tribalism came back into vogue, and writers such as Prescott F. Hall, who had attacked eastern and southern Europeans with such fervor before the war, found themselves sitting in the glow of a new popularity. Much of this resurgence grew out of *The Passing of the Great Race* written by Madison Grant, a wealthy Manhattan socialite with a dilettante's interest in natural science. The book was published to little notice in 1916 and by the early 1920s, had sold a modest 16,000 copies. Even though Grant never became a household name, his work deeply influenced opinion leaders at publications such as the *New York Times* and the *Saturday Evening Post* and had a substantial trickle-down effect with the general public.[30] Grant advanced the idea that European whites were not all created equal. Different racial and ethnic types inhabited one of three castes. On top were the Nordic types, or northern Europeans who came from chilly climates. In the middle were the Alpines, who hailed from central Europe. And at the bottom were the Mediterraneans, whose roots stretched to eastern and southern Europe and who, not coincidentally, made up most of the new immigrant population in the 1920s. Grant said that America was founded by Nordic whites, and that everything must be done to prevent the mongrelization of this legacy. Certain immigrant groups particularly repelled Grant, such as Polish Jews, "whose dwarf stature, peculiar mentality and ruthless concentration on self-interest are being grafted upon the stock of the nation."[31] Virtually all non-Nordic people attracted Grant's animus. In the introduction to the 1921 edition of his book, Grant wrote that "Neither the black, nor the brown, nor the yellow, nor the red will conquer the white in battle. But if the valuable elements in the Nordic race mix with inferior strains or die out through race suicide, then the citadel of civilization will fall for mere lack of defenders."[32]

Americans were rapidly losing faith in the original mission of Americanization. The ability of immigrants to assume the mantle of responsible citizenship was probably more open to question now than at any point in the previous two or three decades. Predictably, the idea of the melting pot came under attack. One of Grant's disciples, Kenneth

Roberts, warned that a continuing flood of Alpine and Mediterranean immigrants would produce "a hybrid race of people as worthless and futile as the good-for-nothing mongrels of Central America and Southeastern Europe."[33] Anti-Semitic fears of international Jewish conspiracies also flourished, as did eugenics theory. Birth control advocate Margaret Sanger spoke openly of the need for "more children from the fit, less from the unfit," with the latter category defined as "all non-Aryan people."[34] Madison Grant proposed the mandatory sterilization of the "weak and unfit."[35]

The controversy Grant stirred up provided a backdrop to the rebirth of the Ku Klux Klan (KKK). The organization founded by ex-Confederates after the Civil War had long since vanished. Two months after the Leo Frank lynching in 1915, however, William J. Simmons decided to revive the KKK with the mob of Georgians involved in that incident. Even though the new Klan was as interested as its predecessor in ruthlessly harassing blacks, there was an important difference, too. Simmons consciously cloaked his group in patriotic rhetoric. This was a flag-waving organization deeply suspicious of immigrants. Whereas the first KKK accepted any white male as a Klansman, the new outfit would take only native-born Protestant whites. For a time, the KKK was inconsequential. During the First World War, its hooded members would occasionally march through southern towns, bellow warnings to spies (although probably nobody within earshot actually was one), and encourage people to buy war bonds. With their strange garb, they made a peculiar sight. But they were not wholly different from any of the hundreds of wartime organizations that tried to promote American interests on the homefront.

In the early 1920s, however, Klan leadership turned over and its membership exploded. By 1923, the group could claim almost 3 million dues-paying adherents, most of them living in southern rural areas. Top Klansmen supported the race theories of Madison Grant and his followers, and immigration restriction became a priority among them. The KKK essentially denied the possibility of immigrant Americanization. Instead, immigrants appeared to be agents of de-Americanization. "We demand a return of power into the hands of the everyday, not highly cultured, not overly intellectualized but entirely unspoiled and not de-Americanized average citizens of the old stock," said Imperial Wizard

Hiram Wesley Evans, who had succeeded Simmons.[36] The true mission of Americanization, according to these white-robed Americanizers, was to keep out the delinquent classes of Alpine and Mediterranean newcomers. Americanization's original meaning had been twisted out of shape and rendered unrecognizable. An Italian writer summed up the transformation concisely: "Americanization is an ugly word," he wrote.[37]

In 1921 and 1924, Congress passed laws that effectively closed the door to further immigration from eastern and southern Europe. The KKK was not solely, or even largely, responsible for this. The Klan's nativist sentiments, however, were a manifestation of deep political and social currents running through the country. Madison Grant's race theory was in the mainstream. For the first time in recent memory, an important figure in presidential politics balked at lenient immigration policies. In a 1921 article for *Good Housekeeping* magazine, Vice-President Calvin Coolidge lent his name to Nordic racialism under the headline "Whose Country Is This?" Although he stressed the importance of Americanization and its goal of inculcating good citizenship, his tone was mainly negative. "Biological laws tell us that certain divergent people will not mix or blend. The Nordics propagate themselves successfully. With other races, the outcome shows deterioration on both sides," he wrote. These alleged differences must be inscribed in American law: "Quality of mind and body suggests that observance of ethnic law is as great a necessity to a nation as immigration law."[38]

Ethnic law and immigration law soon merged. An uneasy coalition of labor leaders, anti-bolshevik crusaders, and ordinary Americans ultimately came together to win restrictive legislation in Congress. Big business was skeptical, but technological developments combined with the black migration to the urban north appeared to lessen industry's dependence on foreign-born workers. "Machinery," wrote one business editor, "does not go out on strike, it cannot decide to go to Europe, or take a job in the next town."[39] Everything was in line for restrictive legislation: intensity among its advocates, withering enthusiasm among its detractors, and general support among the public.

The result was the national origins quota system, signed into law in 1924 by President Calvin Coolidge. The Johnson-Reed Act essentially made U.S. immigration law reflect the racial and ethnic makeup of the United States according to the 1890 census. In this calculus, some people were more fit to become Americans than others. Northwestern Europeans were six to seven times more likely to gain admission than eastern and southern Europeans. About three-quarters of the 154,000 available immigration visas went to people from Britain, Germany, Ireland, and Scandinavia. The Poles were allotted 6,524 spots, the Italians received 5,802, Russians were assigned 2,712, Hungarians were given 869, the Lithuanians had 386, and the Greeks were allowed 307.[40] The golden door was closing. Nativism had triumphed.

After the law's passage, many restrictionists pressed for further gains. But they fell victim to the completeness of their own victory. In the coming years, new arrivals from abroad plummeted. The United States admitted nearly 3 million immigrants from 1920 to 1924. About 1.5 million came from 1925 to 1929, and only half a million during all of the 1930s.[41] With the immigrant population so drastically downsized, and with its makeup notably more Nordic than it had been in the past, nativism lost much of its rationale. But only because it had succeeded.

THE GRANDFATHER OF MULTICULTURALISM

As the great era of immigration from eastern and southern Europe was coming to a close in 1924, a Jewish immigrant who had lived in the United States since the age of five published a collection of essays called *Culture and Democracy in the United States*. Although the ideas contained within it had little impact at the time, they became enormously influential later in the century. Horace M. Kallen was the first multiculturalist.

Kallen, the son of a German rabbi, had been scolding the Americanizers for years. He was displeased with more than merely the perverted final stages of a dying social movement. He was deeply opposed to assimilation, and he did not like the idea of Americanization almost from the start. In one of his less guarded moments, Kallen even conflated the benign activities of the YMCA with the vicious ones of the KKK.[42] His theories were originally presented to a class of Harvard students that he taught in 1906 or 1907.[43] They made their formal debut in a 1915 essay for *The Nation* entitled "Democracy versus the Melting Pot."[44] Only intellectuals in the Northeast seemed to pay much attention to them at the time, and even there they received, at best, a quiet reception. Yet Kallen's argument for a culture of cultures had staying power. Whereas nativism posed the most significant challenge to the concept of Americanization when Kallen wrote at the start of the century, multiculturalism became its most threatening adversary toward the end.

In place of Americanization, Kallen suggested that the United States embrace something he called cultural pluralism. America did not have a single national culture, wrote Kallen. Rather, it had many different cultures: "the peculiarity of our nationalism is its internationalism."[45] This fact required something other than the vigorous advocacy of assimilation. Indeed, welcoming ethnic diversity and its apparent immutability would keep with the country's founding ideals. "Democracy involves, not the elimination of differences, but the perfection and conservation of differences," wrote Kallen. "It aims, through Union, not at uniformity, but at variety, at a one out of many, as the dollars say in Latin, and a many in one."[46] (The dollars, of course, said no such thing. This is Kallen bowdlerizing the national motto.) Thanks to immigration, "the United States are in the process of becoming a federal state not merely as a union of geographical and administrative unities, but also as a cooperation of cultural diversities, as a federation or commonwealth of national cultures."[47]

This is proto-multiculturalism. Kallen called for more than the simple toleration of ethnic difference. He wanted the social affirmation of it. People could not simply be plain-old Americans, just as somebody cannot merely be a member of a family—people are either fathers, mothers, brothers, sisters, sons, daughters, or some combination of these things, he said. The Americanizers practically proved the point themselves. They were really a bunch of hypocrites, thought Kallen. They would say that "hyphenated Americanism" is a threat because it promotes divided loyalties, yet at the same time they demanded the hyphen for blacks: "In the case of the negro, the hyphenation is insisted on, and it is doubtful whether even the late Mr. Roosevelt could have brought himself to consent to a son of his marrying a negress."[48] According to Kallen, Americanizers suffered from "invincible egotism"— or what today might be called ethnocentrism.[49] They frowned on everybody's ethnic pride but their own. When they spoke endearingly of Anglo-Saxon institutions as the bulwark of American freedom, Kallen asked: "If this is not ethnic nationality returned to consciousness, what is it?"[50] These institutions were not expansive, as the Americanizers claimed, but parochial: "they were the institutions [of American life] in so far and only in so far as they served to maintain the privileged classes in America secure in their privileges."[51] Immigrants remained weak and exploited by what Kallen peevishly called the British-American establishment.

As historian Philip Gleason notes, Kallen's concept of cultural pluralism "has always been more a vision than a rigorous theory."[52] It relied heavily on metaphor, rather than clear-cut exposition. Yet Kallen offered his vision with both heartfelt passion and literary flourish. The United States faced a crucial choice about its own nationhood: "At the present time there seems to be no dominant American mind other than the industrial and theological. The spirit of the land is inarticulate, not a voice but a chorus of many voices each singing a rather different tune . . . What must, what can, what *shall* this cacophony become—a unison or a harmony?"[53]

Unison was what the Americanizers were striving for, a sort of nonmusical drone of sameness that could be enforced only through the tyranny of conformity. A much wiser choice would have been harmony—a cultural pluralism that respects group rights: "Thus 'American civilization' may come to mean the perfection of the cooperative harmonies of 'European civilization'—the waste, the squalor and the distress of Europe being eliminated—a multiplicity in a unity, an orchestration of mankind. As in an orchestra every type of instrument has its specific timbre and tonality, founded in its substance and form, as every type has its appropriate theme and melody in the whole symphony, so in society, each ethnic group may be the natural instrument, its temper and culture may be its theme and melody and the harmony and dissonances and discords of them all may make the symphony of civilization."[54]

There were two problems with what Kallen was proposing. First, it needed a political superstructure—or, in keeping with the musical metaphor, Kallen's symphony of ethnic difference lacked an orchestra conductor. How would the musicians maintain rhythm? What would keep them from falling into cacophony, despite their best intentions? Kallen was silent on this point, except for a few vague gestures in the direction of group loyalty to the United States. He apparently trusted the goodwill of men (or groups) to overcome everything in their way. The institutions that had secured American freedom and prosperity apparently were not necessary for cultural pluralism. In a letter to Kallen shortly after the essay in *The Nation* appeared, his friend and admirer John Dewey said that cultural pluralism "means the English tradition [must be] reduced to a strain along with the others."[55] To the extent that the English tradition had to be reduced for the United States to develop its own sense of nationhood, however, the American Revolution had taken care of that. What remained was an independent country that owed a tremendous debt to English life and thought. Even the most impassioned rebels in 1776 would have admitted as much. The English tradition, in this sense, is not just one among many in the United States. It was present at the creation. Americans made it their own, to be sure, and they universalized many of its qualities. Whereas in England the rights of Englishmen were basically restricted to Englishmen, in America they were made available to all kinds of people— including the newcomers from eastern and southern Europe. The chief task of the Americanization movement was to allow immigrants to share in life, liberty, and the pursuit of happiness. If American political and cultural institutions, grounded by English tradition, were "reduced to a strain along with others," then the whole point of American nationhood would collapse.

This leads into the second problem. Kallen believed ethnic identity was insular and strangely removed from external forces. Even if a conductor were leading an orchestra of ethnic groups, it is not certain from Kallen's perspective that the musicians would look for his lead. According to Kallen, the individual could never escape from "the inwardness of his nativity."[56] This is what made cultural pluralism the logical outgrowth of the recent immigration. Yet it provided virtually no grounds for believing that cultural pluralism would result in any sort of social cohesion. Citing biological grounds, Kallen even questioned whether something like a melting-pot society was possible. "In historic times so far as is known no new ethnic types have originated, and from what is known of breeding there comes no assurance that the old types will disappear in favor of the new," he wrote.[57] He explicitly agreed with the Anglo-Saxon supremacist writer Edward A. Ross—"One of the most race-conscious of American social scientists," according to Higham—

that the development of a new American ethnic category is "as mystically optimistic as it is ignorant."[58]

As these passages demonstrate, racialism was fundamental to Kallen's notion of cultural pluralism. Kallen did not make a clear distinction between cultural and genetic heritage. At one point, his 1915 essay veers toward environmental explanations of group differences, only to switch back later with an emphasis on biology. He ultimately linked race and nationality rather tightly. All human associations, wrote Kallen, "have constituted communities tending to preserve and to sustain the continuity of the physical stock. Empirically, race is nothing more than this continuity confirmed and enchanneled in basic social inheritances. It is hardly distinguishable from nationality."[59] Group identity would have real substance even in the absence of cultural expression. This fact, in the end, is what makes cultural pluralism both fitting and desirable, thought Kallen. "Taking for its point of departure the existing ethnic and cultural groups [a democracy] would seek to provide conditions under which each might attain the cultural perfection that is *proper to its kind*," he wrote.[60] The next logical question is neither asked nor answered: How is what's proper for German Americans different from what's proper for Dutch Americans, Italian Americans, or Polish Americans? Despite this, Kallen appears to think that every group must have its place, which is hardly a liberal idea.

Contemporary reviewers took note. Kallen obviously had kinder sympathies than Madison Grant, but how were they different? Writing in the *New York Times,* Nicholas Roosevelt warned that Kallen's cultural pluralism would "result in the Balkanization of these United States." The influential critic Brander Matthews compared cultural pluralism to "a Racial Crazy Quilt." Although many Zionists sided with Kallen, Jewish educators in New York City tended to distance themselves from his work. They wanted Jewish children not only to attend public schools to benefit from their Americanizing influences but also to receive a supplemental Hebrew education after school. They had no time for a federation of ethnicities.[61] The very fact that Jewish Zionists and mainstream Jewish educators disagreed about Kallen shows how pluralism can operate within a single ethnic category— something that Kallen did not appreciate.

Kallen had a remarkably long and wide-ranging career as a writer and thinker. The vast number of intellectual pursuits that occupied him until his death at the age of 91 in 1974 pulled him away from the debate over immigration and cultural pluralism at the very moment he might have fleshed out his ideas. Because he never did, cultural pluralism came to mean many things. Many people completely overlooked the racialism that underlies Kallen's entire argument. In the 1930s, some people equated the term *cultural pluralism* with the liberal Americanization that Kallen originally reacted against. The real meaning of Kallen's writings, however, became apparent many years later with the rise of multiculturalism.

THE LEGACY OF AMERICANIZATION

Like most Americans, the residents of Lawrence, Massachusetts, did not pay much attention to Horace Kallen. They did not become preoccupied with the immigration debate leading up to the Johnson-Reed Act of 1924, either. The legislation aroused no major controversy in the community—a fact that "demonstrate[s] how Americanized the city had become," writes Cole. Indeed, the story of the Americanization movement in Lawrence "suggests that immigrants all over the United States were better off and more easily assimilated than generations of writers would admit."[62] Even so, there is no way to judge with any precision the effect that the Americanization movement had on immigrant assimilation, or what would have happened in its absence. There can be little doubt, however, that millions of immigrants in Lawrence and elsewhere wound up doing more or less what the original Americanizers encouraged them to do: live by the law, learn English, and become citizens. Few people today worry about the assimilation of the grandchildren of Italian and Jewish immigrants who arrived 80 years ago.

Most striking about this period is the massive mobilization of private and public resources to help immigrants become Americans. A consensus formed around the spirit of Americanization and the need for native-born Americans to reach out and help their newest neighbors adjust to life in the United States. They felt a sense of responsibility. Many people thought that if the case for assimilation were made compassionately and logically, immigrants would do what they must to win full membership in U.S. society. "Americanization is a process of education, of winning the mind and heart through instruction and enlightenment," said P. P. Claxton, the commissioner of education. He also stressed its voluntary nature. "It must depend . . . on the attractive power and the sweet reasonableness of the thing itself," he said.[63] The Americanizers made this case again and again. Hundreds of pamphlets, newspapers, and books printed their advice with startling regularity. Thousands of immigrants rushed into classrooms after work to learn English, and they often posted near-perfect attendance records.[64] Millions of them naturalized. And the peaceful invasion that so panicked Prescott F. Hall in 1912 failed to undermine the national integrity of the United States.

Perhaps the Americanization movement is best measured in small, personal ways. In *The American Kaleidoscope,* political scientist Lawrence H. Fuchs tells the story of Salvatore DeMeo, an Italian immigrant whose belongings Fuchs discovered in an old Corona cigar box. DeMeo worked at one of the mills in Waltham, Massachusetts, as a day laborer. Judging from his passport, he had earned enough money to travel back and forth between the United States and Italy several times. After his last trip, however, he settled down and took courses on the English language and American citizenship for three years, receiving hundreds of hours of instruction. DeMeo kept a 67-page manual on American history and government—a typical product of the Americanization movement. In this well-worn booklet, DeMeo learned that being 100 percent American did not depend on where his grandfather came from but on obeying the laws of the United States. "All residents of America should become citizens of America . . . America needs all the wisdom of all the people who live under her flag," he read. Underlined was the statement that a naturalized citizen should vote at every opportunity, "not just when he feels like it." He should learn about the candidates and "vote for what I believe in my own heart is right, and for the best man, no matter what his race or creed or ancestry." Fuchs found one more item in the cigar box: DeMeo's naturalization papers.[65] We may never be able to tell from this little time capsule whether or not DeMeo became a patriotic flag-waver. But we do know that he led a productive life, worked very hard to learn about his new home, and eventually became an American citizen. And that would have been enough to make any Americanizer proud.

Chapter 5

AMERICANIZATION'S RESURGENCE AND UNDOING

During the Second World War, Maggie Gee, the descendant of Chinese immigrants, became a WASP. She joined the Women Airforce Service Pilots after dropping out of the University of California at Berkeley to help with the American war effort. One of only two Chinese Americans to serve in the WASPs, Gee transported airplanes from base to base and flew training missions with men who would later fight overseas. Gee knew firsthand the sorts of difficulties Chinese Americans faced on the domestic front. Her mother, An Yoke Gee, was native-born and thus a U.S. citizen. But she lost her citizenship when she married a Chinese immigrant. Under the Cable Act of 1922, women who married "aliens ineligible for citizenship"— a category that included most Asian immigrants—forfeited what their husbands could never gain.[1] Yet as historian K. Scott Wong has shown, the Second World War became a turning point in the lives of Chinese Americans. Many used the occasion to demonstrate their profound patriotism. Moreover, it inspired the federal government to begin removing the various civil disabilities it previously had placed on Chinese immigrants. In 1943, for example, Congress repealed the Chinese Exclusion Act, making a small amount of Chinese immigra-

tion possible for the first time since 1882, and also permitted Chinese immigrants to naturalize. In a sense, the midcentury American experience allowed the process of Americanization to continue, and not just for Chinese
Americans.

After the turbulent period between the First World War and immigration restriction, the country was ripe for a change in the way it perceived immigrants. The public had never been entirely comfortable
with the brutal forms that Americanization had assumed in the early
1920s, and had become more at ease with the foreign-born people who
had come to America before the restriction. The spirit of Americanization was about to make a long-term comeback. As a social movement,
it was dead. As an idea, however, it lived on. Indeed, it had never been
defeated intellectually, even though it was briefly smothered by nativist
emotions. The ideological basis of American nationhood remained re-
silient. It still had a tremendous appeal. Over the next 40 years, a variety of circumstances and thinkers would revive this old concept,
culminating in the 1965 repeal of the national origins legislation that
allowed individuality to outweigh group membership and relied heavily on the propositional basis of American nationhood.

Like the Army of the Potomac at Antietam, the spirit of Americanization had won a tactical victory in 1965 only to see the potential for
a strategic triumph slip away. During the 1960s and 1970s, leading intellectuals would reject the assimilationist creed and undo much of
Americanization's 20th-century accomplishments. The Chinese-American activist William Wei shows how badly things went wrong. In his
1993 book *The Asian American Movement*, he traces the development
of "a common Asian American identity rooted in a past history of oppression and a present struggle for liberation."[2] This is a curious tale,
because Asian Americans are frequently recognized as one of the great
success stories of modern assimilation. The Korean grocery store owner
and the Vietnamese valedictorian have become popular symbols of
how the American dream is still a reality. Wei, however, rejects these
images. "For Asian Americans and other people of color," he writes,
"equality has been difficult to attain because they have had to cope with
one of the most oppressive systems of racial prejudice and class domination that has ever existed in any democratic country."[3] According to
Wei, the Asian-American struggle to overcome begins in the 1960s,

when a nascent Yellow Power movement "discover[ed] that the U.S. Constitution applied only to white Americans."[4] Since then, he writes, Asian Americans have encountered raw hatred, ruthless resistance, and even sheer violence as they have toiled to make a life for themselves in the United States.

Whereas Maggie Gee showed grit in the face of adversity, William Wei shows disdain in the face of acceptance. What happened in the roughly 50 years between Gee's entry into the WASPs and Wei's bitter complaint? How did the idea of Americanization slide off track and careen into today's assimilation crisis? What went right and how did it go wrong?

THE RETURN OF AMERICANIZATION

Nativism peaked during the 1920s, but anxieties over the foreign-born lessened among the general public as immigrant arrivals declined. Entry rates in the 1930s plunged to levels not seen in a century. Since the native-born population had grown by a factor of 10 between 1830 and 1930, new immigrants as a percentage of the population during this decade were at their lowest point in American history. For four consecutive years, 1932–35, emigrants actually outnumbered immigrants. Counting both inflow and outflow, the country netted an annual average of only six thousand nine hundred foreign-born people during the 1930s—or about as many as arrived every two days during 1914.[5] Moreover, Americanization did seem to be working. It was not the formal product of an organized movement, but the informal outcome of a widely shared attitude about the importance of assimilation. To the relief of many people, the foreigners were becoming less foreign and more American. Perhaps the frantic worries of 1924 and the national origins quota system had been somewhat misplaced.

As economic depression set in following the stock market crash of 1929, bread-and-butter issues dominated American thinking. The gross national product shrank by more than 50 percent, millions of working Americans lost their jobs, and millions of others saw their wages reduced. If something similar had happened just 10 years earlier, anti-immigrant sentiment probably would have risen to unimaginable levels. But now the source of nativist hostility had simply dried up. Immigrants were not the enemies—indeed, the Great Depression hit them just as hard, if not harder, than the native-born. Economists still have not settled the question of what happened in 1929, whether it was bad monetary policy, lowered spending, or something else entirely. One thing, however, seemed clear: Immigrants were not the cause and nativism was not an option. The New Deal contained no immigration provisions and nobody suggested that it should. Although President Franklin Delano Roosevelt won the votes of most recent immigrants when he ran for election in 1932 (and went on to appoint many Catholics and Jews to his administration), he appears to have accepted the 1924 National Origins Act and generally considered large-scale immigration a thing of the past.[6] Immigrants might have become scapegoats in the 1930s, but they did not. Immigration simply was not a political issue.[7]

Yet immigration was an academic issue that both reflected and helped shape a national psyche moving ever closer to the liberal idea of Americanization advanced by Frances Kellor and her contemporaries. The 1930s saw growing interest in intergroup relations—an interest marked by intellectual curiosity rather than worried hand-wringing or noisy chest-thumping. Out of the depths of economic despair came a rebirth of cultural confidence. When Madison Grant published a new book in 1933 that expanded on the race theories he had advanced almost 20 years earlier, he was met with a mixture of outrage and ridicule.[8] Much more in tune with the time was *Our Foreign-Born Citizens* by Annie E. S. Beard. It was a collection of inspirational profiles of famous immigrants like Alexander Graham Bell, Andrew Carnegie, Samuel Gompers, Knute Rockne, Nikola Tesla, and dozens of lesser lights. "The author was inspired to write this book by the Americanization movement of the day," wrote Beard in a 1929 preface.[9] Although she died in 1930, her edifying book would be printed in updated editions by the same publisher through 1968.

The public at large seemed ready to rethink its opinions of the newest immigrants. The United States really was filled with racial and ethnic diversity, thanks largely to the recent waves of large-scale immigration. It seemed like an ideal time to plumb the implications of this fact, since such research would not contain the layers of political meaning that it would have had during the frenzied years right after the First World

War. Moreover, the new immigrants from eastern and southern Europe by now had had enough time to adjust to life in the United States. If they were Americanizing, it would show. If they were not, that would show, too. The assimilation question might finally have an answer.

A loose collection of historians and social scientists devoted themselves to these matters. Their interests and views were varied and complex, but basically they had faith in both the ability of the United States to transform foreigners into Americans and the capacity of the immigrants themselves to adapt to their new home. They were not activists, but scholars. They did not urge Americanization as an ideal, but described it as a reality in the lives of ordinary immigrants and their families. They rejected both Horace Kallen's notion of cultural pluralism and Israel Zangwill's melting pot. Each was too far out of touch with the workings of actual immigrant communities. Kallen's anti-assimilationism did not mesh with how many of the foreign-born and even more of their children were abandoning Old World habits in favor of new American ones. Zangwill, on the other hand, did not have enough of an appreciation for the persistence of ethnic patterns. Intermarriage might eventually wipe away many ethnic distinctions, but in the 1930s ethnicity was still a salient feature of American life. At best, the melting pot simmered. It certainly did not boil.

In 1937, Francis J. Brown and Joseph S. Roucek published one of the first books that began to assess the recent experience with immigration along these lines. It was a lengthy collection of articles by a number of authors and called *Our Racial and National Minorities*.[10] The term *cultural pluralism* ironically enjoyed a sort of renaissance on its pages, but it had been stripped of its Kallen-like radicalism. "There certainly could be no harm in preserving intact the best of the various cultures, but, as a matter of fact, some degree of acculturation is inevitable, and a new and superior culture will emerge," wrote one of the book's contributors.[11] As historian Philip Gleason has pointed out, none of the authors cited Kallen as a reference source, even though an entire section of the book was titled "The Trend toward Cultural Pluralism." Kallen's name appeared nowhere in a 66-page bibliography.[12] He was mentioned only once, without description, in a list of Jewish American intellectuals. Roughly half the book was devoted to encyclopedic treatments of racial and ethnic groups, ranging from "The American

Negro" and "British Americans" to "Bulgarian Americans" and "Hawaiian Minority Groups." Despite such categorization, most of the entries measured how well each group had broken out of its pigeonhole. Finnish Americans: "The Finns are becoming Americanized with reasonable speed."[13] Latvian Americans: "Another interesting characteristic of the Lettish immigrants is the ease with which they tend to assimilate."[14] Armenian Americans: "They become conscientious and devoted citizens; learn the Americanization requirements with great rapidity; and become assimilated amazingly and exceedingly well."[15] Assimilation, in the editors' view, was both a description of social reality and a mark of success.

Despite this apparent enthusiasm, these new scholars were not Americanization apologists. William Carlson Smith said as much in 1939 in his "natural history" of assimilation, *Americans in the Making:* "The author's interest in this study has not been motivated by any desire to start a reform movement. It has been his desire to *understand*— to study immigrants as *persons,* as *human beings.*"[16] Smith offered a straitlaced, descriptive account of the immigration experience, ranging from reasons for migration to assimilation's ripple effects on the children of immigrants. Although he came down hard on the destructive final days of the Americanization movement—"The idea of rigid standardization is preposterous," he wrote[17]—Smith implicitly approved of assimilation, and even used the terms *assimilation* and *Americanization* interchangeably. He also considered their effects unavoidable. *"Assimilation is inevitable,"* he stressed. "No matter what the situation may be, a change takes place in the immigrant who spends some time in America."[18] Unlike Brown and Roucek, Smith did cite Kallen—but only to discard his ideas swiftly. If a regime of ethnic federations were ever to arise, he wrote, "assimilation would fuse [the groups] ultimately . . . the separate entities would tend to disappear."[19]

Other academics wrote in this new vein as well. Many were like Smith, critical of compulsory Americanization. Yet there remained a general consensus among them that voluntary assimilation—along the lines of what the original Americanizers had advocated—was both a reality and a positive force in the lives of immigrants and the nation. "Foreign-born to the number of almost fifteen million are still part of the American population, but they are no longer immigrants," remarked the historian Marcus Lee Hansen in an influential 1937 lecture. "By one adjustment after the other they have accommodated themselves and reconciled themselves to the surrounding world of society, and . . . they became what the natives called 'Americanized.'"[20] In *We Who Built America,* a 1939 book that made much ado about immigrant contributions to the United States, Carl Wittke noted with optimism that "The fusion of immigrant strains will of course continue for many years."[21] Other scholars showed how immigrants and their descendants melted ethnically, if not religiously. In a 1944 academic article, Ruby Jo Reeves Kennedy advanced the theory of the "triple melting pot," in which ethnicities blended but the traditions of Protestantism, Catholicism, and Judaism remained distinct. In 1955, Will Herberg fleshed out this thesis and popularized it in *Protestant–Catholic–Jew.*[22]

The Second World War also had a remarkable effect on national confidence by promoting a we're-all-in-this-together attitude that erased the lines of ethnicity. A 1945 edition of Brown and Roucek's book carried a new title that captured the upbeat spirit of the day: *One America: The History, Contributions, and Present Problems of Our Racial and National Minorities.* As the pair wrote in the preface to this revised and updated edition, "in the period between the two editions and in the crucible of war we are moving toward a cultural democracy. We have become and will remain One America."[23] After the war, ethnic divisions continued to erode as assimilation entered a rapid development phase. Educational opportunities and migrations out of cities and into suburbs opened new doors to Americanization. A bustling economy shattered class divisions. Measured against their parents' position, the children of immigrants actually made more socioeconomic progress during these years than did native-born whites.[24]

The war itself amplified the propositional basis of American nationhood and opened new avenues to Americanization. Knowledge, not ancestry, determined loyalty to the United States and the American cause. George Washington "does not represent the past to which one belongs by birth, but the past to which one tries to belong by effort," wrote anthropologist Margaret Mead in her wartime study of American culture *And Keep Your Powder Dry.*[25] In this formula, Americanization was not awarded from on high to the lucky few. It was achieved through effort, and open to people from all sorts of backgrounds. In 1944, President Roosevelt reminded Americans that among those fighting and dying in the war were "the Murphys and the Kellys, the Smiths and the Joneses, the Cohens, the Carusos, the Kowalskis, the Schultzes, the Olsens, the Swobodas, and—right in the middle of them—the Cabots and the Lowells."[26] Popular culture reflected this trend of inclusion, too. Think of the typical wartime movie, with its ragtag cast of GIs that included a few old-line Americans as well as an Italian, a Jew, a Pole, an Irishman, and often a Hispanic (played by Desi Arnaz, for example).[27] It did not matter where their parents had come from. They were all doing their patriotic duty. They were all Americans.

Even as they chronicled assimilation, the new intellectuals remained keenly aware of the country's immigrant presence. Almost 25 percent of the population in 1945 was either foreign-born or had at least one foreign-born parent. The first language of roughly one in seven Americans was not English.[28] Despite their essential optimism about Americanization, none of these scholars was blind to the racial and ethnic problems of the time. They understood that assimilation was a generational process that could fill immigrants with self-doubt about their identity. They acknowledged the conflicts it created between parents and children. They criticized people who tried to deny immigrants their heritage, or who suggested that ethnic loyalties were incompatible with devotion to the United States. They were also sympathetic to the plight of blacks and Asians who were forcibly kept apart from the American identity. Yet they reveled in the American freedoms that allowed immigrants to mingle as they pleased in the mainstream, in the ghetto, or in both, and they held out enormous amounts of hope that the same advantages would extend to Asians and blacks as well. There was a general sense among them that prejudice was beginning to vanish, even the most virulent strains of it. In *An American Dilemma,* a landmark study of race relations published in 1944, Swedish social scientist Gunnar Myrdal wrote that "*not since Reconstruction has there been more reason to anticipate fundamental changes in American race relations.*"[29] His nearly one thousand five hundred pages of detailed examination of the state of black America offered a troubling portrait, but Myrdal remained sanguine: "There is no doubt, in the writer's opinion, that a great majority of white people in America would be prepared to give the Negro a substantially better deal if they knew the facts."[30] Although this growing sentiment of sympathy toward blacks and optimism about their future did not directly affect immigrants, it illustrates an underlying point that does: Americans of all racial and ethnic backgrounds were seeing the lines of race and ethnicity begin to matter less. In many instances, they still mattered a great deal. But what seemed increasingly important was that they were all Americans joined in common citizenship. Positive change appeared almost inevitable. One of the main goals of Americanization—that people living in the United States be seen as individuals, not members of racial or ethnic groups—was taking concrete form.

IMMIGRANT ROOTS

The most important contribution of this new scholarship on immigrants came from Oscar Handlin. The son of Jewish immigrants from Russia, Handlin was a precocious boy who tested into Brooklyn College at the age of 15, started Harvard graduate studies at 19, and earned his Ph.D. in history at 25 in 1940.[31] Although his remarkable academic career would reach into the 1990s, it was front-loaded with brilliant achievements. His first book, *Boston's Immigrants,* grew out of his doctoral research on the Irish and was published in 1941 to an enthusiastic reception. It fit neatly into the new body of scholarship fermenting around the question of immigration—indeed, towered over much of it—and won the American Historical Association's prestigious John H. Dunning Prize. Another book followed: *Commonwealth,* a study of the colonial government and economy of Massachusetts. Next came *This Was America,* a selection of writings on American life and culture by foreign visitors, edited by Handlin. Accomplished though they were, these works provided only the slightest clue of what was to come: the most powerful written expression of the immigrant's central place in American life.

With the publication of *The Uprooted* in 1951, Handlin firmly established his reputation as one of the most important American historians—and *the* most important immigration historian—of the 20th century. The legendary opening lines of the book make clear its great ambitions: "Once I thought to write a history of the immigrants in America. Then I discovered that the immigrants *were* American history."[32] *The Uprooted* seemed unconventional for a student of history. There is hardly a proper noun on its pages and only a handful of references to specific figures or events. Instead, it is the epic of the 35 million nameless people who pulled themselves free from the soil of their familiar peasant lives and migrated to America and the unknown between 1820 and 1920. They had no idea of what to expect or what the future would bring, only the hope that it would turn out for the best. Usually the transition was painful. The shock of the New World left permanent scars and profound disillusionment. By the time immigrants understood what had happened to them—and very few ever would understand—it was too late to go back. They had become a new kind of person, beholden to two worlds at the same time, but neither fitting into nor being totally accepted by either of them.

Handlin tells a bitter story of alienation, especially when contrasted with the romanticized picture of immigrants passing through Ellis Island and easily finding a place for themselves in an America that welcomed them. "The old folk knew then they would not come to belong, not through their own experience nor through their offspring," wrote Handlin.[33] The author endowed his book with a literary grace rarely found in scholarship, an element that made his seemingly dim view all the more unsettling. His metaphor of uprootedness is well chosen. The word *culture*, after all, comes from the Latin *cultus*, which means cultivation. To be uprooted from the life-giving soil of one's culture is a transforming disruption of custom and habit, and almost an act of violence. Handlin "achieves some of the grave, moving eloquence of the Psalmist," wrote Milton Rugoff in his *New York Times* review of the book.[34] A better comparison, actually, might be Ecclesiastes.

Because of this, *The Uprooted* has been cited often as a sort of elegy, a tale of quiet desperation. And to be sure, sorrow saturates its grand story. And yet there was more—a deep undercurrent of optimism about what the immigrant experience meant for the American nation. To Handlin, the immigrant was a uniquely American archetype, and the metaphor of uprootedness resonates far beyond the boundaries of a single immigrant life. In the final pages, the metaphor embraces all Americans, who are an uprooted people. "A society already fluid, the immigrants made more fluid still; an economy already growing, they stimulated to yet more rapid growth; into a culture never uniform they introduced a multitude of diversities," wrote Handlin. "The newcomers were on the way toward being Americans almost before they stepped off the boat, because their own experience of displacement had already introduced them to what was essential in the situation of Americans."[35] In a sense, the immigrants made America more American.

This transcendent vision erases traditional distinctions of race, ethnicity, class, and place of birth and unites all Americans as the figurative children of immigrants. The subtitle of *The Uprooted* was *The Epic History of the Great Migration that Made the American People*. Migration *made* America. Immigration was a source of cohesion rather than division. It was the shared experience of immigration, rather than the mere extensions of categories forged in Europe or elsewhere, that defined us as uniquely American:

> We are come to rest and push away our roots more deeply by the year. But we cannot push away the heritage of having been once strangers in the land; we cannot forget the experience of having been all rootless, adrift. Building our own nests now in our tiredness of the transient, we will not deny our past as a people in motion and will find a place in our lives for the values of flight.
>
> That also must be so. In our flight, unattached, we discovered what it was to be an individual, a man apart from place and station. In our flight, through the newness, we discovered the unexpected, invigorating effects of recurrent demands upon the imagination, upon all our human capacities. We will not have our nest become again a moldy prison holding us in with its tangled web of comfortable habits. It may be for us rather a platform from which to launch new ascensions that will extend the discoveries of the immigrants whose painful break with their past is our past. We will justify their pitiable struggle for dignity and meaning by extending it in our lives toward an end they had not the opportunity to envision.[36]

The Uprooted put Americans of both native and foreign birth on the same plane and treated them as equals. It took traditional American traits like individualism, restlessness, creativity, entrepreneurship, disregard of status, and risk acceptance and projected them onto the immigrant. Or perhaps more accurately, it suggested that Americans have these characteristics because of immigrants. In either case, Americans became immigrants and immigrants became Americans in Handlin's equation. Americans' roots may have been uprooted, but they were still roots. Like an ivy, they found new crevices from which to hang.

The Uprooted won the Pulitzer Prize for history in 1952. Although Handlin's name already had been well-established among professional historians before the book's publication, this honor elevated him above the field. More important, it introduced his ideas to a wider audience. Although *The Uprooted* sat atop a mountain of research, it had been written for a general readership. It enlisted the help of primary sources, but integrated them into the text rather than cited them directly. It was a popular book written with scholarly authority, but without scholarly pretense. In 1966, a company that published study guides similar to Cliff's Notes devoted one of its Study Master volumes to the book. "The Uprooted has brought intellectual order to a field where formerly there were only bits and pieces of research and scattered monographs," it said.[37] According to the *Harvard Encyclopedia of American Ethnic Groups,* a massive reference work with more than one thousand pages of small type, *The Uprooted* is "doubtless the most widely read and influential book on immigration history."[38]

Handlin and his colleagues regularly described racial and ethnic diversity as cornerstones of American nationhood, but they also accepted the idea of immigrants voluntarily assimilating into American life. They were, in their way, Americanizers. They both leveled old nativist assumptions about who could become American and dispelled the Kallen model of cultural pluralism. They knew that ethnicity could serve as a source of stability and order in a strange milieu, but understood that out of *pluribus* could—and did—come *unum.* In a 1983 book on the history of immigration and ethnicity, Thomas J. Archdeacon called the postwar years a "repressive cultural environment."[39] In reality, major vistas of opportunity were opening up to the progeny of eastern and southern Europe. If some barriers to full participation in public life remained, they were on their last legs.

In 1956, the proto-multiculturalist Horace M. Kallen capped off the immediate postwar period with a substantial revision of his anti-assimilationist theory of cultural pluralism, first advanced during the heyday of the Americanization movement 40 years earlier. He did not call *Cul-*

tural Pluralism and the American Idea a revision, but that is what it was—and it located his views much closer to the pro-assimilation ideas of Handlin and the new scholars. Gone was the entrenched racialism of "Democracy versus the Melting Pot." Now Kallen wrote of an encompassing "humanity of man" that seemed to fill the cultural gaps he had previously placed between racial and ethnic groups.[40] He was much more sensitive to the need for national unity, and proposed the American Idea as a force that would bind disparate people together. This was similar to what the Americanizers advocated when they spoke of immigrant identification with the American way of life. He did not use the word *assimilation,* but he seemed to describe it when he wrote that "individuals may enter such a group [e.g. a culture or nationality] by birth, by immigration, by initiation, by compulsion."[41] Kallen still cast a slant eye toward Americanization, but he also acknowledged the potential benevolence of a liberalized version. And he thought he saw one developing. "Americanization seeking a cultural monism was challenged and is slowly and unevenly being displaced by Americanization, supporting, cultivating a cultural pluralism, grounded on and consummated in the American Idea," he wrote.[42] Whereas Kallen's aggressive support of *pluribus* previously had drowned out any place for *unum,* here the two reached a happy medium. His change of heart shows how far the idea of Americanization had come in four decades. The fact that few people at the time recognized that Kallen had abandoned some of his early radical thoughts and embraced some of the moderate ones already developed by Americanizers and their kin perhaps says even more. Full-blown Americanization was setting in. Over the next 10 years, it would reverse the legislative defeats of the 1920s.

A LEGISLATIVE TRIUMPH

At the base of a flagpole just 75 yards away from the Statue of Liberty, President Lyndon Baines Johnson signed into law a bill that instantly Americanized U.S. immigration policy. With the flick of Johnson's pen, the country abandoned its legacy of national-origin quotas in place for more than 40 years and founded on the assumption that some immigrants made better Americans than others because of their biological identity. "This measure that we will sign today will really make us truer to ourselves both as a country and as a people," said Johnson. The president made clear that the United States in 1965 was a nation dedicated to a political proposition, and not to some kind of mythic common ancestry. "Our history this year we see in Vietnam. Men are dying—men named Fernandez and Zajac and Zelinko and Mariano and McCormick," said Johnson. "Neither the enemy who killed them nor the people whose independence they have fought to save ever asked them where they or their parents came from. They were all Americans. It was for free men and for America that they gave their all, they gave their lives and selves."[43] This appeal to patriotism relied on the core idea of Americanization, the notion that people of all backgrounds can become faithful to the United States—faithful enough to die for it and to rest in patriot graves.

This accomplishment was an outgrowth of the new intellectual movement that favored assimilation. In the postwar years leading up to 1965, the government started to remove racial and ethnic barriers to full participation in American public life. The 1965 immigration law was a clear rejection of not just national-origins law but also racialist assumptions about American identity. Since 1924, the United States had experienced both economic catastrophe and a two-front, global war. It came out of this period with a vision of itself as a superpower destined to lead by setting its own moral example. As a consequence, it became increasingly difficult for the United States to ignore the second-class status of many of its citizens. If all men were created equal, then why were some more equal than others? Small measures began to widen opportunities for some groups that had been excluded from sharing in the American identity. Foreign policy considerations in 1943 had convinced Congress to repeal the Chinese Exclusion Act of 1882, making a handful of Chinese eligible for immigration each year and also allowing Chinese living in the United States to naturalize. The repeal of racist exclusion laws continued in 1946, when Asian Indians also received a small immigration quota and the ability to naturalize. That same year, Filipinos won the right to become citizens as well. These were small victories for Americanization—the national-origins quota system still severely limited Asian admissions for racial reasons. But nevertheless they began to undermine the current immigration law's racialist assumptions.

The cold war against international communism, lasting for roughly 45 years after the end of the Second World War, amplified the propositional origins of American nationhood and made more progress in the direction of racial and ethnic tolerance possible. Americans and Russians were not simply enemies pitted against each other over a territorial conflict, a succession dispute, or an ancient hatred. They were locked in a struggle over the meaning of freedom and equality. Being un-American in the 1940s and 1950s meant an ideological betrayal, not a questionable ancestry. McCarthyism may have had many faults, but nativism was not one of them. It pursued people not because of who they were, but because of what they believed. The Internal Security Act of 1950, for example, barred admission to aliens with communist affiliations and permitted some deportations. In some ways, this was a throwback to the Red Scare. Yet it had an entirely different tenor. It was not foreign birth that mattered so much as ideological conviction. Chinese allies from the Second World War were gaining acceptance. British communists were losing the ability to immigrate.

Liberal intellectuals have spent an enormous amount of time trying to draw links between the anti-Catholic Know-Nothing party of the 1850s, the anti-black and anti-immigrant Ku Klux Klan of the 1920s, and the anti-communist McCarthyites of the 1950s. Historian Richard Hofstadter, in a famous essay, called it the "paranoid style in American politics."[44] In a more recent book that also tries to pull in the antigovernment militia movements of the 1990s, historian David H. Bennett employs a blunter and more politicized description: "the American Far Right," or "the Party of Fear."[45] But there was an important difference between the pre-Second World War hatred and postwar counterparts. Americans could protect themselves from a McCarthyite witchhunt by ideological conversion. Yet immigrants, blacks, and, to a lesser extent, Catholics and Jews could not suppress the qualities their adversaries sought to locate and expunge. Immigrants would always be foreign-born, blacks would never be white, and Catholics and Jews often inherited their religion as if it were an ethnicity. This is not a defense of McCarthyism—but it provides an example of how ideological conviction and not place-of-birth, race, ethnicity, or religion increasingly defined American nationhood. If the enemy of my enemy is my friend, then in the 1950s anti-communist immigrants, blacks, Catholics, and Jews were seen as full Americans. This was a triumph for Americanization.

Many barriers to full Americanization remained, however. The Mc-Carran-Walter Act of 1952 reaffirmed the national-origin quota system and kept U.S. immigration policy weighted heavily in favor of northern and western Europeans. Leading intellectuals blasted the act as a failed opportunity to abandon race-conscious immigration. Senator Pat "Mc-Carran is not just a bitter old man resentful of the changing America within which he lives," wrote Oscar Handlin. "He is the symbol of a fossilized radicalism inadequate in its own day and mischievously incongruous in ours."[46] President Harry S. Truman had vetoed the new legislation because he wanted to move away from national-origin restrictions, but Congress overrode his wishes. Despite this apparent setback, the new law actually advanced the interests of Americanization, though not by as much as some would have liked. It removed all racial criteria for immigrant admissions. Asians from any country were now free to migrate to the United States so long as they fit below the low ceiling afforded them by the national-origins quota. Asian immigration remained a pittance, but lifting the near-total ban on immigrants from Asian countries represented a step forward. The McCarran-Walter Act also removed the racial and ethnic requirements for naturalization. For the first time, citizenship applicants would be judged as individuals, rather than mere extensions of potentially undesirable groups.[47] Immigration levels also rose during the 1950s to about 2.5 million immigrants—low by historical standards but roughly two-thirds more than had arrived during the entire 1930s and 1940s combined.[48]

In this environment of ideological patriotism and declining interest in racial and ethnic categorization, the United States could finally begin dealing with the condition of blacks in an honest fashion. Indeed, the civil rights movement for black Americans started its long march in 1945. Executive orders, federal laws, and judicial decisions chipped away at Jim Crow's authority. The intellectual foundations of legal segregation began to crack. Politicians who defended segregation increasingly had to assure their audiences that they were not advocating racism and that segregation was not discriminatory—it was not just separate, it was also equal. They were wrong, but as public opinion shifted toward tolerance, they had to improvise.

In his 1957 book *Race and Nationality in American Life,* Handlin expressed the optimism with which many liberals viewed their time: "The origins of racism lie in the comparatively recent past and we may, in our lifetime, see it run its full course."[49] They would see no such thing. But their cheerfulness about the future inspired them to try to correct the injustices of the day. This sentiment would eventually lead to the passage of the two most important pieces of legislation to come out of the civil rights movement: the Civil Rights Act of 1964, a broad antidiscrimination law, and the Voting Rights Act of 1965, which involved the federal government in securing the right to vote for southern blacks. Indeed, the struggle to win legal remedies for discrimination against blacks dominated domestic politics. Immigration took a backseat, but at least it had hitched a ride. In fact, it is unlikely that the Immigration Act of 1965 would have come about were it not for the growing revulsion against anti-black racial categorization.

The national-origins quota system did not fall down overnight. The congressional override of Truman's veto of the McCarran-Walter Act revealed the strength of a racialist immigration policy as recently as 1952. In spite of this defeat, the momentum was on the side of Truman and Americanization. President Dwight D. Eisenhower had suggested loosening the quota system and admitting more immigrants, a policy that Vice-President Richard Nixon supported during his 1960 presidential campaign. The victor of that race, John F. Kennedy, also had been a strong advocate of immigration reform. His *A Nation of Immigrants* cited immigration as a source of national strength.[50] Two years into his term, President Kennedy proposed a five-year phase-out of national-origins quotas. He did not, however, make a strong push for this legislation before his assassination in 1963, and Congress had taken no action. In his 1964 State of the Union address, President Lyndon B. Johnson called for an end to the quota system.

Immigration was only a minor issue in that fall's presidential race, but when Congress reconvened in 1965 it began to draw up plans for major reforms. The status quo had a handful of defenders. North Carolina Senator Sam Ervin praised the "national and uniform mathematical formula recognizing the obvious and natural fact that those immigrants can best be assimilated into our society who have relatives, friends, or others of similar background here." He called the current policy "a mirror reflecting [the racial and ethnic makeup of] the United States."[51] As historian Roger Daniels points out, however, Ervin's mirror was as bent out of shape as those found in fun houses at carnivals and amusement parks.[52] It did not reflect the contemporary United States, but our nation in 1890. More important, a growing number of Americans found offensive the notion that race and ethnicity were important factors in explaining any given individual's potential to assimilate. This was especially true under the current law that assumed so many Greeks, Italians, Poles, and other new immigrants who had Americanized were posing problems due to the very nature of who they were. The real debate in 1965 was not about whether to keep national-origins quotas, but how to replace them. Congress ultimately opted for a system that emphasized family ties, skilled labor, and refugees from communist countries.

Nobody expected that the legislation would radically alter immigration patterns. Critics of the bill worried that lifting national-origins provisions would encourage Asian immigration, but the Johnson administration and congressional supporters countered by saying that the bulk of the post-1965 immigrants would be European. Indeed, Johnson conspicuously did not refer to Asians in his speech at the bill's signing ceremony. If Congress had known in 1965 that its reforms would open the door to more than 18 million immigrants over the next three decades—about one-third of them from Asia—they may not have passed the new law. There was no intent to deceive by the bill's backers. They were just plain wrong about what the bill would bring. What ultimately carried the bill to passage was the powerful symbolism of an immigration policy that did not discriminate on the basis of national origin. Ideals were what motivated reform in the first place, and in the end they were enough to trump popular fears about an Asian invasion. From then on, immigrants gained admission to the United States because of individual characteristics, not racial or ethnic attachments. The new law became another example of a political document that was better than the environment out of which it came, of universalism rising above origins still bound by particularism and triumphing over them. As President Johnson put it shortly before he signed the Immigration Act of 1965 into law: "Those who do come will come because of what they are, and not because of the land from which they sprung."[53] It was about time.

THE WHITE MAN'S MULTICULTURALISM

At the moment when race and ethnicity seemed to matter less than ever before, they suddenly began to matter more. The story of how the civil rights movement reversed course after achieving its political goal of colorblind law is an oft-told tale.[54] For years the movement had devoted itself exclusively to securing equal rights for all individuals, regardless of their race, color, religion, or national origin. After passage of the 1964 Civil Rights Act, 1965 Voting Rights Act, and a few companion pieces of legislation, however, it abandoned the philosophy that had made its pleas so compelling. Terry Eastland notes that "Black leaders historically had sought equal laws as well as an improvement in the condition of blacks generally."[55] Once colorblindess was written into the law of the land, they focused on ameliorating the social and economic condition of blacks through more active use of government power. Instead of equal opportunity for individuals, they embraced the concept of equal outcomes for groups. In other words, attempting to guarantee that blacks would have an even shot at employment or fair access to the voting booth was not enough. The state now had to make sure that blacks had equal representation in different professions and in public office. The subsequent deconstruction of colorblind justice—set in motion by President Johnson with a series of executive orders and bureaucratic decrees, then advanced further by President Richard Nixon's Philadelphia Plan and other measures—amplified racial consciousness in controversial new ways. The consequences of this development are still being contested in the 1990s in the debates over racial preferences and multiculturalism. Today these conflicts usually are defined in terms of race, but in the 1960s and 1970s they had crucial ethnic parallels. Indeed, before there was a legal regime of racial preferences for blacks, Hispanics, and Asians, there was multiculturalism for the descendants of eastern and southern Europeans.

Just as the civil rights movement aided in the repeal of racist immigration laws, the civil rights transformation spurred on an intellectual movement that boldly rejected the assimilationist viewpoint that had dominated mainstream academic thinking for nearly three decades. In their 1963 study of race and ethnicity in New York City, the most distinguished sociologist of his generation and a future U.S. senator bluntly declared that "The point about the melting pot is that it did not happen."[56] Nathan Glazer and Daniel P. Moynihan went on to assert in *Beyond the Melting Pot* that ethnicity is a permanent feature in American life. A "final smelting" of the population into "a single American nationality" has always "seemed to lie just ahead—a generation, perhaps, in the future," they wrote.[57] And it might never arrive. The pair pointed to "some central tendency in the national ethos which structures people . . . into groups of different status and character."[58] Italian Americans living in New York City may not be the same thing as Italians living in Rome, but they were certainly something unto themselves—they were, in short, *"a new social form."*[59] Glazer and Moynihan did not partake in the racialism of Kallen's early work, but they advocated a form of cultural pluralism that placed a heavier emphasis on group solidarity than individual Americanization. They were right to argue against Israel Zangwill's vision of hasty amalgamation—it did not happen. But this did not mean that the melting pot would never happen. Yet Glazer and Moynihan took their idea a few steps further. In addition to being unrealized, they wrote, the melting pot ethic was not desirable. It had "outlived its usefulness."[60]

Handlin came under withering scrutiny the next year in an important academic publication, the *Journal of American History.*[61] Rudolph J. Vecoli challenged the assumption in *The Uprooted* that the immigrant experience had defining similarities for all of its participants. "This interpretation is open to criticism on the grounds that it fails to respect the unique cultural attributes of the many and varied ethnic groups which sent immigrants to the United States," wrote Vecoli. He went on to argue that immigrants from southern Italy in the late 19th century had experiences that were markedly different from those supposedly lived by Handlin's immigrant-everyman.[62] "The historian of immigration must study the distinctive cultural character of each ethnic group and the manner in which this influenced its adjustment in the New World," Vecoli concluded.[63] This was a victory for ethnic particularism. Vecoli saw trees, not the forest. *Of course* Handlin painted his canvas in broad strokes, and *of course* not every single immigrant went through the exact same process of adjustment and assimilation. Yet *The Uprooted* made an enormous—and worthwhile—contribution to Americans' understanding of what the immigrant experience was like, what it meant for the country, and how it forged national unity. Vecoli, however, doused Handlin's universalism in an atomistic critique.

Over the next few years, this intellectual discontent with assimilation only grew louder. "America is going through a period of re-ethnization," wrote Murray Friedman in 1970.[64] He was not talking about the newest immigrants arriving after 1965, but the descendants of the "new immigrants" from eastern and southern Europe. In *Overcoming Middle Class Rage*, a collection of essays edited by Friedman, a wide variety of writers refuted the melting-pot thesis of merging identities and argued that ethnic attachments among white people were strengthening, not weakening. "Re-ethnization" seemed to mean de-Americanization, since it gladly allowed group identity to trump American individualism. Assimilation was on the outs. Vecoli made an appearance, again blasting the historiography of Handlin and his colleagues: "Ethnic studies thus have long suffered from the blight of the assimilationist ideology," he complained.[65]

The book heralded the coming of a new pluralism that mirrored the old cultural pluralism of Horace Kallen in important ways. The authors made many sensible and intelligent observations about the persistence of ethnicity, but they also often slid into the role of cheerleaders bubbling over the wonders of ethnic diversity. To call them naive is needlessly harsh. They were keenly aware of the challenges posed by ethnic heterogeneity. Yet this did not prevent a rash of wishful thinking. "And while the demons of suspicion and distrust prove very hard to exorcise from interethnic relationships, such suspicion and distrust are not, I am convinced, inevitable. If they can be eliminated, ethnicity enriches the culture and reinforces the social structure," wrote priest and sociologist Andrew Greeley. The prospects for reaching this goal, however, were bleak. As Greeley himself noted: "It may be possible to isolate ethnicity from suspicion and distrust, but no one has yet figured out the formula for doing so."[66]

The chief problem with the new pluralists was that they did not offer a convincing formula of their own for overcoming ethnic conflict. Americanization and its emphasis on individualism offered such a strategy, but they would have none of it. "The idea that we are a nation of individuals is largely a fiction . . . [it was] Fashioned, in part, by older-stock groups as a means of maintaining their power and primacy," Friedman wrote cynically.[67] Ethnicity was intractable, according to the new pluralists. Greeley went so far as to suggest that there was no such thing as an Irish American. Instead, there were American Irish. There were also Irish Irish.[68] In other words, nationality might change, but ethnicity remained the same. It persisted as the denominator in any kind of cross-cultural equation. And as any fourth-grade math student knows, different denominators cannot join themselves together.

The new pluralists felt more comfortable retreating into the realm of formalized group rights. Irving M. Levine and Judith M. Herman did not endorse but gave serious consideration to an idea advanced by the American Indian activist Vine Deloria: "It is imperative that the basic sovereignty of the minority group be recognized. . . . Recognition of new interpretations of the Constitution based on the concept of the group could be a vital step in this process." With words that have added shock-value in light of what happened in South Africa, Deloria also noted that in his brave new world of ethnicity, "everyone would have a homeland."[69] This kind of thinking soon began to seep into the political mainstream. In 1969, Senator George McGovern presided over a special rules committee of the Democratic National Committee. After hearing months of testimony on party procedure, he declared that "We have heard from every conceivable ideological point of view . . . from the young, the old, the black, and the white in every region of our country."[70] Astonishingly, McGovern made no distinction between race and ideology. To him they were apparently one and the same.

Since ethnic diversity was so desirable in the minds of the new pluralists—dubbed "ethnic-niks" by Harold R. Isaacs in an insightful review for *Commentary*[71]—they thought that the federal government should serve as a sort of cultural curator intent on preserving white ethnic identities. In 1970, Congressman Roman C. Pucinski, a Chicago Democrat, introduced a bill to have the federal government create and finance a series of Ethnic Heritage Studies Centers that would teach white ethnic children about their white ethnic heritage and also promote the idea of cultural pluralism. Friedman took this occasion to remark on the "hopeful signs that, perhaps for the first time in our history, we are beginning to come to grips with our tribal past and present."[72] During congressional hearings, Pucinski declared, "I find the whole doctrine of the melting pot frankly very repugnant. I don't want to be melted down to a monolith."[73] Ironically, the new pluralists were the most monolithic of thinkers. They championed diversity of ethnicity, but ignored diversity within ethnicity. For them, each ethnic group was its own monolith. The hearings from 1970 contain 363 pages of witnesses wallowing in an orgy of group narcissism. According to the historian Arthur Mann, "the supporters of the Pucinski bill seldom expressed interest in others. They wanted government funds to underwrite the study of their own ethnic group . . . they had in mind a curriculum that would celebrate their own kind and make their own young feel proud. Their separatist approach was identical to, because it was influenced by, the black-studies movement."[74]

Although the proposed legislation failed on its first go-round, right before the 1972 election President Nixon signed a scaled-back version. Well before then, however, members of the elite culture had abandoned the idea of the great American melting pot. Several months before Nixon embraced government-sanctioned white multiculturalism, poet W. H. Auden wrote in the *New York Times:* "Whoever invented the myth that America is a melting pot? It is nothing of the kind and, as a lover of diversity, I say thank God."[75]

White ethnic tribalism encouraged a victim mindset. The worse off you were, the better your position to generate sympathy and seek redress from society. And it was every group for itself. In 1969, Baltimore social worker Barbara Mikulski (elected to the U.S. Senate as a Democrat in 1986) put the conflict in stark terms: "Ethnic Americans do not feel that black people are inferior but regard them as territorial aggressors on their residential and employment turfs." Black claims on society were not unique, according to Mikulski. The plight of white ethnics was just as bad: "Those who remain blue-collar workers are the field hands and we who moved up into the white-collar positions are the house niggers with all of the brainwashing that it implies."[76] Being a Polish American in the late 1960s was apparently a lot like slaving away on the cotton plantation. If blacks could demand compensatory justice in the form of federal largesse such as antipoverty programs and hiring quotas, then so could the white ethnics. The National Confed-

eration of American Ethnic Groups, a Washington-based special interest claiming 67 affiliate organizations and 18.6 million individual
members, demanded a larger piece of the public pie.[77] Before long,
white ethnic groups created a paradigm of oppression that mimicked
the one used by blacks. Instead of the white establishment exploiting
nonwhite minorities, however, they spoke of a WASP establishment exploiting white ethnics.

The most sophisticated statement of the new pluralists and white
ethnic political aims came in 1972 with the publication of Michael
Novak's *Rise of the Unmeltable Ethnics*. Novak was a man of the left, a
radical Catholic theologian of Slovak descent. (He has since drifted
rightward, a classic example of a neoconservative.) Novak criticized liberal intellectuals for assuming that the great masses of working- and
middle-class whites were a bunch of racist louts standing in the way of
black progress. The politics of protest ignored white ethnics' legitimate
aspirations and feelings of group pride, he said, and now it was time to
find a place for them in public policy. Like all of the new pluralists,
Novak identified ethnicity as an important part of selfhood. The
essence of his book might be captured in a single phrase: "People un-
certain of their own identity are not wholly free."[78] In other words,
membership in a collectivity is the path to genuine freedom. Yet as
Robert Alter countered in a thoughtful essay devoted to Novak's book,
"People preoccupied with their own identity are not wholly free."[79] Indeed, Novak's ethnic mystique contained impermeable boundaries:
"Upper-class Quakers *think* and *feel* in a way I cannot think and feel;
Jewish intellectuals tend to live and breathe out of writers, concerns,
and experiences I can emulate as second nature, but not as first; certain
Irish Catholics exhibit emotional patterns I can follow but not find native to me," he wrote.[80] There may have been some kernel of truth in
this statement, but if this was freedom, it seemed awfully confining. It
did not leave much room for individuality—and even less for the cross-
ethnic experience of Americanization. White ethnics, in Novak's mem-
orable title, were unmeltable.

Ethnic attachments and Americanization, of course, are not necessarily incompatible, and Novak did not suggest they were. His book at-
tempted to find a respectable place for ethnicity within an American
creed, not to deconstruct American democracy. Yet the extremely

polemical nature of Novak's book in 1972 did cause some confusion and it prompted several critics to question its commitment to the universal values that make ethnic life possible within the United States. These disputes were generally resolved in public exchanges, but they never went away entirely. Multiculturalists in the 1990s occasionally would cite *Rise of the Unmeltable Ethnics* as one of their movement's founding texts. Novak responded harshly to these claims in a 1996 preface to the second edition. "I abhor the new thing and disavow the allegation of paternity," he wrote, singling out the anti-American sentiments found in so much multiculturalism. Despite this, Novak also went out of his way to knock Arthur M. Schlesinger's important 1992 book, *The Disuniting of America,* for its "coercive monoculturalism."[81] The multiculturalists of today may not be right when they call the Novak of 1972 an ally, but their confusion is certainly understandable. The Novak of 1972, after all, once wrote that "The dangers of divisiveness on the one side and of homogenization on the other are equally depressing. It is my view that in America, at least, it is homogenization that is now more ominous."[82] Twenty-five years later, these words seem almost laughably off target. And yet this sentiment animated the new pluralism. It is easy to see why multiculturalists would be so eager to appropriate it.

To some extent, white ethnics were revolting against the inversion of Americanization, triggered by the prevailing anti-authority attitude of contemporary radicalism. Basic American* institutions and traditions came under reckless and relentless attack. White ethnics—indeed, Americans generally—did not like what they saw happening to their country during the late 1960s and early 1970s. The rules of the game had started to change. They had been told to obey the law, but now they saw criminals go unpunished and police officers derided as pigs. They had been told to work hard, but they saw welfare becoming a lifestyle choice. They had been told to commit themselves to American political principles, but now they saw open talk of revolution become stylish. A series of events and trends served to undermine confidence in a strong national identity: the uncertainty of Vietnam, the rise of black militancy, the emergence of feminism, the betrayal of public trust at Watergate, and the growing drug culture. When *Newsweek* asked a group of distinguished historians in 1970 to reflect on what ails the

American spirit, they drummed up divergent views. Richard Hofstadter said that "If I get around to writing a general history of the recent past, I'm going to call the chapter on [the] '60s 'The Age of Rubbish.'" Arthur M. Schlesinger had a rather different opinion: "the turmoil, the confusion, even the violence may well be the birth pangs of a new epoch in the history of man."[83] Many other intellectuals shared Schlesinger's view and openly questioned the very nature of American society. Some went further, even hoping for the destruction of its norms. Fascism was right around the corner if America continued along its present course, they predicted. Herbert Marcuse said that "as far as I'm concerned, one can speak with complete justification of an incipient fascism" in America. The president of Howard University even declared that "we conquered Hitler, but we have come to embrace Hitlerism."[84] There was something foul in the heart of America, and the very idea of turning people into Americans was thus a corrupting project to be avoided by enlightened minds.

To a certain extent, the rise of white ethnic consciousness was a reaction against such self-evidently wrong nonsense as this. Theirs was a search for an America they could believe in. Yet the vast majority of white ethnics did not abandon faith in the concept of Americanization. The new pluralism never really caught fire among the masses. It was not a popular movement that swelled up from the grass roots, but an intellectual style that trickled down from the top. Ethnic identity was a real force in American life, but its power much diminished. Much of it was nostalgia. In 1937, Marcus Lee Hansen described what has come to be known as Hansen's law.[85] In short, it says that the third generation wants to remember what the second generation tried to forget. This means: First-generation Americans—the immigrants—came to the United States and adjusted to life here with some difficulty but essentially with success. The paradox of their lives is that their foreignness never allowed them to fit in completely, but they also consciously departed from their Old World ways. Their children—the second generation—socialized into American norms but remained haunted throughout their lives by the fact that they were only a single generation removed from peasantry in Europe. They constantly strived to prove themselves as red-blooded Americans. The third generation—grandchildren of the immigrants—were thoroughly American, lacking most of the foreign cultural patterns that had marked their parents. Often they could not speak the language of their grandparents. They felt no need to prove themselves, as their parents did. They were completely comfortable with their Americanness. Nobody could call them into question. But they wanted to know more about their past and toiled to disinter what their parents had buried. Hansen's law appears to have been borne out by the white ethnic revival. By the 1960s, of course, the third generation of eastern and southern European immigrants was rapidly reaching adulthood.

If the 1950s were the Uprooted decade, in which Oscar Handlin set forth an inspiring and unifying vision for a nation of immigrants, then the 1970s were the Roots decade, in which Americans kindled an interest in their diverse heritages. Yet the 1970s also demonstrated that the boundaries of ethnicity were much more permeable than the theorists of the new pluralism had assumed. Movies like *Fiddler on the Roof* and *The Godfather* were smash hits, but moviegoers did not have to be Jewish or Italian to appreciate them. Indeed, they were popular precisely because they appealed to a broad market. Alex Haley's *Roots* became a best-seller and one of the most-watched television specials of all time. Haley wrote about his own family history, telling the inspiring story of how his African ancestors were transported to the United States, where they participated in the tragic black American experience of slavery and suffered from a legacy of discrimination. One of the great ironies of *Roots*, however, is that even though it seemed to fit neatly into the new pluralists' notion of a particularist revival, it climbed only part of the family tree. "If Alex Haley had traced his father's bloodline, he would have traveled twelve generations back to, not Gambia, but *Ireland*," noted Ishmael Reed in 1989.[86] Haley told a compelling story, but to suggest that *Roots*—as well as the many books and movies like it—served as proof that Americanization had failed and that the melting pot did not work is incorrect. Separatism may have informed the intellectual *zeitgeist*, but it did not reflect what was really going on.

RETURN TO THE MELTING POT

The point about the melting pot is that it did happen, at least in reference to the descendants of eastern and southern European immigrants.

By the 1970s and 1980s, ethnicity among whites was headed toward meaninglessness. Sociologist Richard D. Alba noted in 1990 that "Insofar as ethnicity has a role, then, it is increasingly voluntary, dependent on deliberate actions of individuals to maintain activities and relationships that have ethnic character."[87] Ethnic identity was becoming symbolic. That is, white people were more likely to *feel* ethnic than *be* ethnic. Intermarriage rates between the conglomeration of ethnic groups that composed the category of white people had been so high throughout the course of the 20th century that relatively few of them could meet the requirement of common ancestry that binds single ethnic groups together. By the 1980s, in fact, a majority of U.S.-born non-Hispanic whites were of ethnically mixed ancestry.[88] Measured by almost any indicator—educational attainment, occupational mobility, English-language usage, residential patterns, and, of course, intermarriage—the assimilation of white ethnic groups was essentially complete.[89] Americanization had worked well. The immigrants from eastern and southern Europe—the people who had inspired the Americanization movement—as well as their descendants had found a place for themselves in an American society still dedicated to the principles outlined two centuries earlier.

The so-called white-ethnic revival was a charade led by intellectuals more interested in prescribing personal behavior than in describing generational assimilation. It represents the monumental failure of the new pluralism to come to grips with the reality of Americanization—a reality that Oscar Handlin and his colleagues had revealed years earlier. The new pluralists wrongly assumed the most important thing about Americans is that few of them had much of anything in common. To see the spectacle of white ethnics advancing this agenda did great harm to the ideal of assimilation to which Americans traditionally had clung. Back in 1971, during this movement's heyday, an Italian-American organization called the melting pot "a myth which has been perpetuated by the elite-dominated American educational system to commit cultural genocide on our people."[90]

Such outlandish rhetoric would be amusing if it did not have poisonous side effects. The descendants of eastern and southern Europe had become Americanized in substantial ways. For intellectuals to suggest something to the contrary, when the United States was beginning to re-open the doors to millions of immigrants from Asia, the Caribbean, and Latin America—immigrants who also would need to be met by Americanizing institutions—was profoundly irresponsible. It undermined faith in assimilation and encouraged a search for untested alternatives to an ideal that had functioned quite well. If Americanization did not work for white ethnics, after all, then how could it possibly succeed for the newest immigrants, most of whom were not even white? This apparent rejection of an American tradition by the self-proclaimed leaders of people who had benefited in critical ways from that tradition paved the way to our present assimilation crisis.

PART TWO

THE PRACTICE OF
AMERICANIZATION

Chapter 6

THE PROBLEM OF
GROUP RIGHTS

In 1991, the Democrat-controlled California legislature passed a bill that would have imposed a massive racial and ethnic quota scheme on the state's public universities. The most onerous section of the proposed law would have required schools to make their graduation classes reflect the state's racial and ethnic composition. In the weeks and months before Republican Governor Pete Wilson vetoed the bill, a vigorous debate concerning individual and group rights raged throughout the state. The most stirring moment came when a tall, slender Pakistani immigrant named Ali Raza appeared before a committee of politicians to testify against the bill. He read most of his remarks from a prepared statement. As he concluded, however, he looked up from his notes and gazed at Assemblyman Tom Hayden, one of the bill's chief sponsors. In his heavily accented, high-pitched voice, Raza said: "When I was young, my father would tell us stories at the dinner table. He would open the story by identifying the family from which the character of the story came. One day I asked him, 'Dad, what's the difference whether or not a person comes from or belongs to a particular family?' My father replied: 'Son, it matters in Pakistan what family one comes from.' And then he added: 'If you want to be judged on the basis of your individual performance, you should go to America.'"¹ Raza had come to America and was outraged that a group of politicians would try to alter what he took to be its fundamental meaning.

Raza understood what the Founders meant when they declared that "all men are created equal." Today, many public figures, most of them born and raised in the United States, seem to have forgotten. Racial and ethnic identities should be a private concern of no particular interest to the government. When the state gets into the business of treating them differently, however, it creates a collection of interest groups engaged in an adversarial relationship with each other and with their perceived oppressors in mainstream America. If a racial or ethnic group can claim that it has a past history of discrimination, then it immediately becomes eligible for a series of special entitlements from the government. This has an enormous impact on today's immigrants, because about 85 percent of them during the 1990s are racial and ethnic minorities that, according to the federal government, automatically qualify as disadvantaged. This defies common sense—foreign-born newcomers almost by definition cannot have experienced a past history of discrimination in the United States. Immigrants traditionally have been enterprising achievers and they remain so. Now they have a powerful political motivation to boast of their downward mobility, since victim status confers its own rewards. They have not asked for this supposed privilege. Indeed, many of them, like Ali Raza, actively resent it. But it is given to them anyway.

When the government places a premium on differences and a penalty on commonality, it retards the natural process of assimilation by offering a motive for groups to remain distant from Americanization. It gives them a reason to say that they are so unlike everybody else that they cannot possibly be expected to compete on the same playing field, live by the same rules, or conform to the same standards. The result is a poisonous atmosphere of constant suspicion, hostility, and recrimination. It resembles the bitter rivalries of Bosnia, Chechnya, and Rwanda more than the American ideal of *E pluribus unum.* Today, this problem is almost entirely the creation of government policy and its system of racial and ethnic classification. It does not occur naturally. The actual voting patterns and intermarriage rates of these so-called groups suggest that they are anything but monolithic entities. And yet the cult of group rights remains one of the most significant threats to the Americanization of immigrants.

IDENTITY POLITICS, THEN AND NOW

Identity politics have a long history in the United States. Just as union members, senior citizens, and gun owners may think that they have a set of common political interests, so may racial and ethnic groups. These perceived interests can vary widely, from Chinese Americans in Los Angeles wanting economic policies that are friendly toward family-owned restaurants to Nicaraguan immigrants in Houston following election returns in their home country. These interests grow naturally from the nexus of identity and circumstance. Other groups may oppose them, but the fact that interest springs partly from identity is not in and of itself troubling—and it is certainly of no special concern to the government. Having a home-grown concern for one's heritage is healthy. Americanization, properly understood, has no quarrel with this type of sentiment.

In the past, identity politics often have been generated organically at the grassroots level. They were local and diverse, varying from place to place and time to time. The late-19th and early-20th-century Tammany Hall Irish of New York City, for instance, voted overwhelmingly for Democrats. In Philadelphia, however, Irish Americans were mostly Republicans. Even when the first Catholic presidential candidate Al Smith ran as a Democrat in 1928 against the Republican Herbert Hoover, the Irish helped deliver all seven of Philadelphia's congressional districts into GOP hands. Immigrant voters in Chicago demonstrated their unique interests as well. They turned the mayor's office over to another party six times between 1911 and 1931.[2] Immigrant political views in New Haven, Connecticut, also displayed chameleon qualities. According to Robert Dahl, each wave of newcomers in that community seemed to change color, supporting the party opposed by the wave before it. The Yankees were Republicans. The Irish were Democrats. The Italians were Republicans. The Jews were Democrats. Despite exceptions to these rules, this back-and-forth pattern essentially held in New Haven.[3]

Immigrants were not sorted into political interest groups by some

far-off entity. They gathered together on their own in a process that relied entirely on the freedom of association, not federal assignment. The
government often resisted ethnic categorization. In 1818, Irish groups
in New York and Philadelphia petitioned Congress for a western land
grant on which to settle. But Congress refused, noting that it did not
want officially sanctioned ethnic communities filling up the land.[4] At
other times, natives would try to sort by group. In the early 20th century, restrictionists blasted the new immigration from southern and
eastern Europe. They were clearly more concerned with group designa-
tions than with individuals. For the most part, however, the restrictionists did not have the force of the state behind them. They had to
wait until 1924 and the National Origin Quota Act, which cut immigration levels and tried to control its ethnic makeup, before they had
their day. Yet even then, group distinction affected the people whom
the government kept outside more than those it let in. Once admitted,
immigrants were expected to become Americans no matter what their
background. Although the remnant of Asian immigrants from the late
19th century were still denied naturalization, the government by and
large treated foreign-born American citizens not as members of groups,
but as individuals deserving equal treatment under the law.

For all of their cohesive strength, however, grassroots identity politics have severe limits: They only work on the local level. Their devotees rarely can present themselves as leaders of broad-based coalitions.
The country's largest Polish American communities in Buffalo,
Chicago, and Detroit traditionally have supported the Democratic
party, especially in the first half of the century. Between 1888 and
1912, for instance, the Polish vote in Chicago averaged 61 percent for
the Democratic presidential candidate. (The only aberration occurred
in 1904, when the popular Theodore Roosevelt headed the Republican
ticket and the Democrat Alton B. Parker attracted a mere 41 percent of
Polish votes.[5]) Polish Americans had a great deal of influence in these
cities and politically controlled portions of each. Yet none of the politicians who thrived in any of these areas achieved national stature. The
first Polish-American politician to do that was Edmund Muskie, who
came from the Yankee hinterlands of Maine. He rose to prominence in
the 1950s as a governor and then a senator. In 1968, he ran for the Democratic presidential nomination and wound up as the party's vice-pres-

idential candidate. He also served briefly as Secretary of State in the Carter administration. The son of an immigrant, Muskie could not rely on a substantial Polish-American presence in Maine to propel his career. Instead, he had to make nonethnic appeals to a wide spectrum of voters. Voters did not see Muskie as a Polish-American politician, but rather as a politician who happened to have Polish ancestors. Many of them probably did not even know that much and did not care. Put simply, Americanization underwrote Muskie's success.

A similar story comes out of the Irish-American political experience. The Irish, of course, are closely identified with the urban machine. More than any other immigrant group, they have relied on public employment and patronage for economic and social advancement. The best-known Irish American politician, however, is not Boss Tweed (whose parents were actually Scottish immigrants), James Michael Curley (twice elected to public office from a Boston prison), or even Plunkitt of Tammany Hall (perhaps the country's most famous ward boss). He is John F. Kennedy, the first American of Irish ancestry and the first Catholic to become president. Although many Irish Americans hung Kennedy's portrait in their homes for distinctly ethnic reasons, to the rest of the country Kennedy was more Harvard cool than Irish machine. Americans did not see him as an ethnic character. His background may have won him Irish and Catholic votes and lost him Protestant ones, but his appeal ultimately eclipsed any kind of ethnic or religious bloc-voting that went on in his favor. His success and the *Camelot* mystique that followed it were distinctly American phenomena. Today Kennedy is remembered more as a genuinely American icon than as an Irish boy who did good. His triumph, like Muskie's, is a model of political Americanization.

Today, however, political Americanization has a powerful adversary. This new challenger tries to take the weakness of grassroots identity politics—the fact that its particularism falters beyond the local level—and make it an asset. To do so, it attempts to forge nationalized political identities that owe their very definitions to government action. They rely on what the historian David A. Hollinger calls the "ethnoracial pentagon."[6] In this scheme, every American falls into one of five color-coded categories: black, brown, red, white, or yellow. These colors correspond to the five racial and ethnic groups recognized by the

Census Bureau and most civil rights legislation: black, Hispanic, Native American, white, and Asian American. Individual Americans certainly retain a host of individual rights, but they also may gain special benefits accorded to certain sides of the ethno-racial pentagon. When that happens, it means that not all individuals are equal in the eyes of the law. All men may be created equal, but some groups are more equal than others, and membership has its privileges.

Throughout American history, the state has used nationalized identities as a tool to favor the rights of one group over those of another. The institution of slavery—America's original sin—is perhaps the most clear-cut example of this. After slave emancipation, Jim Crow and the law of segregation did much the same thing, if in a less malignant way. Immigration also has played a role in this history of group rights and nationalized identity politics. In 1812, the Federalists unsuccessfully fought against universal white suffrage because they feared it would increase the immigrant Irish vote in New York City.[7] They wanted to keep a group of people locked out of full citizenship because they thought it would help their current political standing. The Chinese Exclusion Act of 1882 tried to ease nativist concerns by barring Chinese immigrants from entering the United States. The only way to accomplish this, of course, was to treat all Chinese as members of a disfavored group, rather than as individuals who may or may not have warranted admission on a case by case basis.

Old-fashioned, nationalized identity politics are different from today's identity politics in that their chief purpose was mass disenfranchisement. Today's identity politics, on the other hand, are supposedly benign methods of expanding the political franchise to include everybody. Looked at this way, the old identity politics were bad and the new identity politics are good. But the truth is more complex. Both the old and the new identity politics share something in common: They are manufactured by elites and thrust on the people. Instead of rigging public institutions to profit white Americans, today's identity politics assign certain benefits to nonwhites—preferential treatment in college admissions, employment, congressional redistricting, and other areas. Yet even if segregation (old-time identity politics) and preference programs (new-fangled identity politics) are separate species, they come from the same genus. Because each allows the government to assign value to skin color (or the notion that a group has a past history of discrimination), each is wrong for the same reason. Today's quota of inclusion could easily become tomorrow's rationale for exclusion. Civil rights advocates who endorse the current system of racial and ethnic spoils are flirting with danger, because they refuse to defend the principle of colorblind government—a principle that, if maintained, would guarantee minorities equal protection during times of trouble.

Americanization says that membership in any particular racial or ethnic group is a private matter. The only important public concern is that we are all individual Americans. Journalist Clarence Page likes to say that Americans get along a lot better as individuals than as groups—and he is right. If for no other reason, it is very important that the government treat its citizens as individuals rather than as groups. Indeed, this was a main goal of Congress in 1952, when it finally banned the practice of denying naturalization to people on the basis of their race or ethnicity. How ironic for immigrants to find that, after going through a colorblind naturalization, American government at every level makes color-conscious policy.

Certain immigrants, of course, may receive a short-term political payoff in accepting the new racialized regime of group rights. The benefits of affirmative action can mean an Ivy League education for someone who might otherwise miss it or a business contract for a firm that might otherwise be poorer. But group rights are ultimately a bad deal for the supposed beneficiaries. They sponsor a perverse competition between upward mobility and disadvantage. Immigrants are strivers by nature—it takes a special kind of person to uproot and migrate to a new and unknown land. But group rights are underwritten by failure, or at least the perceived inability to enter the social and economic mainstream. Immigrants' self-appointed political and civil rights leaders—themselves rarely immigrants—constantly say that hate will keep them down, that success is too elusive. These leaders are practically forced into making this argument, of course. If they did not, there would be no rationale for special privileges passed out on the basis of disadvantage. For immigrants, the effect of this rhetoric is dispiriting. They can become disenchanted with their new home, thinking that any setback, no matter what its source, can be traced to a hostile system of institutionalized prejudice. Since Americanization relies on the immigrant's voluntary adoption of American life, these words clearly have a delaying effect on assimilation. What sane immigrants would want to become Americans in an America that does not welcome them? Because the political culture of group rights encourages the foreign-born to think along these lines, the tiny, short-term benefits that it delivers are little more than hollow victories won at the expense of Americanization.

This nationalization of identity politics has another harmful effect on the assimilation process. It saps the native-born of the Americanizing spirit. Immigrant advocates constantly say that racial and ethnic minorities are forever mired in poverty, unable to escape it on their own, and in need of special help from the government to get out. This kind of rhetoric fails to inspire ordinary Americans to advance the assimilation process. They may understandably begin to form negative opinions of immigrants, thinking that since newcomers in the past did not have a battery of special government protections, today's arrivals must be fundamentally different and forever incapable of joining the American nation. These attitudes dilute the critical contribution the native-born make to Americanization.

Taken to its logical extreme, the theory of group rights allows some immigrants to defy the most basic American legal principles. In 1987, Dong Lu Chen, a Chinese immigrant living in Brooklyn, murdered his wife with a claw hammer after she admitted to having an affair. During his trial two years later, the defense put an anthropologist on the witness stand who testified that in Chinese culture, the terrible shame of having an unfaithful wife made such drastic action understandable. Chen never went to prison. Instead he was sentenced to five years probation on a manslaughter charge. In legal circles this has become known as the "cultural defense": if an action is acceptable in another culture, then it should be acceptable in the United States. Margaret Fung of the Asian American Legal Defense and Education Fund hailed the Chen decision because she opposes "the idea that when people come to America they have to give up their way of doing things." The cultural defense does not always work, but it has cropped up—usually to have charges reduced—in several recent cases involving child abuse, kidnapping, and rape. As Duke University law professor Doriane Lambelet Coleman has written, however, "the use of cultural evidence risks a dangerous balkanization of the criminal law, where non-immigrant Americans are subject to one set of laws and immigrant Americans to another."[8]

Yet the main threat of racialism is that it subverts the goal of immigrant assimilation by encouraging the foreign-born to focus their political thinking on old attachments instead of on the new ones that they may acquire in America. There are many examples of this in American political life, but perhaps none better than the current regime of voting rights. According to political scientist Peter Skerry, the Voting Rights Act "is the single strongest incentive for Mexican Americans and their leaders to define themselves as racial minority claimants."[9] It essentially guarantees racial and ethnic groups—in current practice, this means blacks and Hispanics—the right to live in congressional districts in which members of their group will make up a majority of eligible voters. This strategy of empowerment relies explicitly and totally on group rights, rather than the more traditional path of political Americanization and its theme of transcending the suffocating particularism of identity politics. It implicitly accepts the principle that in politics, only blacks can represent blacks, only Hispanics can represent Hispanics, and only Asians can represent Asians. The sinister corollary of this logic, of course, is that only whites can represent whites. Going further, the current regime of voting rights entitles some American citizens to receiving election ballots and materials in non-English languages—even though naturalized citizens are supposed to have passed an English test. Finally, it insists that noncitizens—even illegal aliens—be counted in congressional reapportionment. In other words, when Congress parcels out its 435 seats in the House of Representatives to the states on the basis of their population, illegal aliens and American citizens carry equal weight in the distribution process. This creates a United Nations nation—a country made up of bickering factions divided by their race, ethnicity, and language. The United States strives to be something else, a place where race and ethnicity do not have an iron-fisted influence on political life, a place where common citizenship and the principles to which that citizenship is dedicated pull together Americans of all races, ethnicities, and religions. Before that can happen, the United States must remove this high obstacle to political Americanization.

THE VOTING RIGHTS REGIME

In the fables of the civil rights movement, the Voting Rights Act of 1965 does not occupy as prominent a place as the 1954 *Brown* v. *Board of Education* ruling, the 1963 "I Have a Dream" speech, or the 1964 Civil Rights Act. Yet it undeniably has had as dramatic an effect on public policy as anything to come out of that era. Throughout the Deep South, blacks deliberately had been denied access to the voting booth by hostile state and local governments, even though the 15th Amendment to the U.S. Constitution had secured their right to vote almost a century earlier. They were forcibly kept away from political participation in many areas as late as the 1960s. One of the primary tools for keeping black voter registration low was the literacy test. Ostensibly intended to prevent illiterates from going to the polls on election day, the tests often were applied only to blacks, and the questions were obscure. According to Abigail Thernstrom, "southern registrars were observed testing black applicants on such matters as the numbers of bubbles in a soap bar, the news contained in a copy of the *Peking Daily*, and the definition of terms such as *habeas corpus*. By contrast, even illiterate whites were being registered."[10] As a result, few blacks voted and even fewer ran for public office. Congress did not ban literacy tests in 1965, but rather insisted that they be applied to all potential voters without regard to race or ethnicity. This made democracy a reality for many southern blacks for the first time. In Mississippi, the consequences were stunning. In just two years, black voter registration rose from 6 percent to 60 percent.[11] In 1964, only 103 blacks held public office in the United States. By 1994, this number had increased to 8,406.[12]

One of the reasons for the triumph of the original Voting Rights Act was its specificity. It searched for discrimination where it existed—in the Deep South—and stamped it out. The federal government monitored balloting in the states with spotty records and allowed other states, which did not deny voting rights to blacks, to go about their business. Like so much civil rights legislation, however, the original intentions of the authors of the Voting Rights Act were soon subverted. As the emphasis of the civil rights movement shifted away from opportunities and toward outcomes, so did the interpretation of voting rights. No longer were racial and ethnic minorities to be granted equal access to the ballot box, now they were to be guaranteed that the ballot box would produce equal results. And the provisions would no longer apply merely to blacks in the South, but to minorities everywhere. By the early 1970s, Hispanics were on their way to becoming a crucial voting rights constituency. How they got there is an instructive tale.

The Hispanic expansion started in the early 1970s with a voting rights lawsuit filed by the Mexican American Legal Defense and Education Fund (MALDEF) on behalf of Puerto Ricans in New York. Puerto Rico is not a state, but its residents are U.S. citizens by birth. When they move to the mainland, they are entitled to vote in the same elections as other Americans. Yet many of them cannot communicate well in English, and MALDEF argued that English-language literacy tests discriminated against Puerto Ricans as a class. The courts agreed, and said that people who had been educated in Spanish-language Puerto Rican schools would be allowed to take their New York State literacy tests in Spanish. It seemed like a minor and limited exemption at the time, but civil rights groups would soon take full advantage of this decision. MALDEF had established the legal principle that holding elections in English wrongly blocked Hispanics from the ballot box.[13]

The immediate challenge for activists on the federal level was to expand the Voting Rights Act beyond the narrow provisions that left most Hispanics outside of its jurisdiction. They wanted to be covered just as the southern blacks had been, and set out to demonstrate that Hispanics had been subject to the same kind of discriminatory treatment as blacks in the Deep South. Their reasoning was not persuasive. There were isolated examples of discrimination, but nothing comparable to the widespread and systematic abuses against blacks in the South. The Civil Rights Commission said that the numbers on Hispanic voting behavior "do not paint the shocking picture that, for example, the 1965 statistics on Mississippi did."[14] Moreover, Hispanics were not shut out of public office. They recently had served as governors, senators, and members of Congress in Arizona, New Mexico, and Texas. Hundreds of Mexican Americans held local offices. In short, there was little evidence to warrant the federal government's massive intervention, and quite a bit that suggested everything was more or less okay.

Yet the civil rights groups ultimately prevailed during congressional reauthorization of the Voting Rights Act in 1975 when they built on their courtroom success in New York. They equated printing English-language ballots and election materials with administering literacy tests, which had since been made illegal everywhere. People whose first language was Spanish needed special protections to vote, they argued. This was an absurd claim. Literacy tests in the South were used almost exclusively to keep blacks away from elections. Low Hispanic voter turnout in other places was mainly due to the fact that so many of them were not citizens. Either they had not naturalized (Mexicans have among the lowest naturalization rates of any national-origin group) or were in the country illegally. In short, they were not entitled to vote. Despite this evidence, Congress agreed with the advocates. In the future, federal voting rights regulations would kick in whenever language minorities made up at least 5 percent of the population of a political district and less than half of the district's citizens were either registered to vote or had voted in the 1972 presidential election.

What's more, the 1975 law required that bilingual election materials be made available to voters in every county in which the language-minority population had an illiteracy rate—defined as failure to complete the fifth grade—above the national average. This included many jurisdictions with Hispanics because immigrants from Mexico and other Latin American countries often were poorly educated. In many cases they were not even citizens, and so could not vote. Yet the noncitizens counted toward the bilingual trigger anyway. Interestingly, language minorities were not defined by language (a cultural characteristic), but by ancestry (a genetic one). The category included only "persons who are American Indian, Asian Americans, Alaskan Natives, or of Spanish heritage."[15] French Canadians living in Maine, the Poles of Chicago, and the Pennsylvania Dutch received no special assistance.

The Voting Rights Act came up for renewal in 1982, and again Congress broadened its purview. The act now would apply to every political jurisdiction in the United States, whether or not it had a history of denying the vote to any group. More important, however, racial and ethnic groups were given a greater opportunity to demonstrate that they were the victims of bias. If a district were accused of discriminatory voting practices, the only way it could defend itself would be to show "the extent to which members of a protected class have been elected to office in the state or political subdivision." In other words, they would have to demonstrate that members of racial and ethnic groups did not simply have equal access to the voting booth, but that they also occupied public offices in sufficient numbers. At-large and multimember districts were especially vulnerable. To comply with the new rules, hundreds of cities and counties—including large jurisdictions such as Chicago, Dallas, and Los Angeles—had to create single-member districts with safe seats for minority politicians.

On the congressional level, most of the action took place after the 1990 Census spurred state legislatures into redrawing the district maps, as they have occasion to do after every census. The 1990 Census, however, was the first held under the new voting rights provisions. It also counted a record number of Hispanics, whose population rose from 14.6 million in 1980 to 22.4 million in 1990. The biggest change, however, was in the number of congressional districts that contained Hispanic majorities. Because the federal government was telling the states that they had to increase their minority officeholders, the cartographers assigned the task of redrawing district maps made sure to bunch Hispanics together like never before. The number of Hispanics in Congress jumped from 10 in 1992 (before the Census took full effect) to 17 in 1994 (after redistricting was complete).

Voting districts can assume all kinds of shapes and sizes, but compactness is generally considered a virtue. Of course, politicians always have fiddled with their district lines to protect incumbency. The word *gerrymander*—"to manipulate district boundaries unfairly"—has its origins in an 1812 dispute in Massachusetts. But never before was race-driven districting so rampant. New census technologies allowed reapportionment committees literally to look block-by-block at the racial and ethnic makeup of neighborhoods. The result was a series of oddly formed congressional districts that had no rationale other than to make sure that they elected either a black or an Hispanic to Congress. They meander this way and that, connecting entirely different communities of voters simply due to their similar racial and ethnic makeup. Because of their strange shapes, Abigail Thernstrom has called them "bug-splat districts."[16]

The fact that the districts look awful is not the most important concern here. Aesthetics matter in redistricting, but only to a point.

The real offense goes back to the nature of the voting rights legislation advancing the idea that only blacks can represent blacks and only Hispanics can represent Hispanics. (It would probably like to assume that only Asians can represent Asians, but integration and residential patterns make it virtually impossible to create a majority-Asian congressional district anywhere in the United States.) If immigrants are to join a broad American political community, then they should understand that in the United States, anybody can represent anybody. Race and ethnicity may be salient features of our political life, but they certainly should not be hardwired into our political institutions through a homeland policy that recalls South African apartheid. With colorblind congressional districting, there will still be places in which blacks represent blacks and Hispanics represent Hispanics. But there will also be places where whites represent blacks, Hispanics represent whites, and Jews represent non-Jews. The United States is a place where Colin Powell would be president, if only he would announce his candidacy. Must we actually tinker with Virginia's congressional map so that Powell, living in the Washington suburb of McLean, can have enough blacks in his home district to win a seat in the House of Representatives? The answer is no. Virginia itself elected a black man, Douglas Wilder, to the governor's mansion in Richmond, just a few blocks away from the old Confederate White House of Jefferson Davis. To assume that Americans like Powell and Wilder need race-based help is to elevate group identity over the common bond of American citizenship. Immigrants should not hear this message. Unfortunately, our political culture often hollers it at them.

In recent years, the voting rights regime has taken other approaches harmful to immigrant assimilation by focusing on language. In 1992, Congress said that counties with more than 10,000 residents who speak the same language and are not proficient in English must have access to bilingual voting assistance, which can include foreign-language sample ballots, registration cards, election notifications, nomination papers, polling place signs, and voter instructions. The National Asian American Pacific Legal Consortium (NAAPLC) estimated that 31 percent of Chinese-American voters in New York City and 14 percent in San Francisco used some form of bilingual assistance in the November

1994 elections. Although these figures are probably overstated—NAAPLC is an advocacy organization that supports bilingual ballots—proportions anywhere near this magnitude are worrisome.[17] As Boston University president John Silber noted in congressional testimony in 1996, bilingual ballots "impose an unacceptable cost by degrading the very concept of the citizen to that of someone lost in a country whose public discourse is incomprehensible to him."[18] Not everyone need speak English all of the time in America, but it must be the lingua franca of civic life. Because the voting booth is one of the vital places in which citizens directly participate in democracy, it ought to be the official language of the election process.

Bilingual ballots also have raised practical concerns. Los Angeles County, for example, has struggled to produce sample ballots in English, Chinese, Tagalog, Japanese, Vietnamese, and Spanish. "I don't think there's any machine out there that could accommodate all those languages," said Rosa Garcia-Viteri, head of the county's multilingual voting.[19] New York City has had to purchase entirely new voting machinery because its old equipment does not have enough room to include all of the Chinese characters that the law says it must provide. No word on what the city will do when the new machines that can display up to five languages at one time must add a sixth. Even if they address this issue, there is always the possibility of human error. On a 1993 New York ballot question, faulty translators printed the Chinese character for *no* instead of *yes.*[20] The problem can become even stickier. Ballot initiatives often are worded very carefully. But will ballot translations always convey the precise meaning of every initiative? In a deliberative democracy, they must. Otherwise the halls of government will echo with miscommunication.

In addition to these concerns, immigrants who become citizens should not need bilingual ballots. To naturalize—and thus gain the vote—the foreign-born must demonstrate the ability to speak, read, and write simple English. A handful of them are granted exemptions in what is known as the 50/20 rule—naturalization applicants who are over the age of 50 and have lived in the United States for 20 years do not have to meet the English requirement. But they only make up an estimated 7 percent of all citizenship applicants.[21] The other 93 percent have to pass the test. So why must we assume that they lose their English skills on election day? In fact, most do not. California's Yuba County, which lies about 50 miles north of Sacramento, is required by federal law to provide voting materials in Spanish. In 1996, it spent nearly $30,000 on them for the primary and general elections. "In my 16 years on this job," says Frances Fairey, Yuba County's registrar of voters, "I have received only one request for Spanish literature from any of my constituents."[22] If English were not an important part of American citizenship and the right to vote, the United States would never have asked naturalization applicants for almost the entire 20th century to take exams. In the meantime, foreign-language voting sends one more message to immigrants that assimilation is not an important part of participatory democracy.

The voting rights regime sends another, and perhaps more troubling, message as well: Citizenship is not an important part of participatory democracy, either. The rules of congressional apportionment are strangely hostile to the notion that citizenship is a cornerstone of the American political system. In ordering a decennial census, the Constitution makes no reference to the citizenship status of U.S. residents.[23] The courts have interpreted this to mean that everybody, no matter what their citizenship, must be counted. That much makes sense. But what does not make sense is the claim that all people counted, no matter what their citizenship, must affect apportionment decisions equally. So Congress gives the same measure to citizens, legal permanent residents, and illegal aliens when it counts heads for districting purposes. In other words, people who cannot vote carry as much weight as those who can. People who are in the country illegally matter as much as citizens. Instead of sticking to the principle of "one person, one vote," they have permitted the concept of "one person, no vote" to take hold.

The House of Representatives has 435 seats, which are spread among the states on the basis of population, determined by the decennial census. During the 1990s, the average congressional district contained more than five-hundred-fifty thousand residents. The three largest states, California, New York, and Texas received 52, 31, and 30 seats in the House, respectively. Seven states received only one seat.[24] California, New York, and Texas also attract a disproportionate number of this country's noncitizens and illegal immigrants. They are correspondingly rewarded with more congressional districts—and thus a greater influence over national affairs through the size of their congressional delegations and electoral-college clout.

Illegal immigrants and other noncitizens are not dispersed uniformly within each state. They tend to concentrate in certain areas. Lots of noncitizens find themselves in just a handful of districts. The result is a number of congressional districts that have very few eligible voters. Turnout is dismal, and politicians are elected to Congress with just a handful of votes. In the 1996 elections, for example, many congressional districts saw more than two-hundred thousand voters go to the polls. Yet in California's 33rd District, Representative Roybal-Allard won with less than forty-eight thousand votes. No congressional district in the country cast fewer votes that year. The 33rd District is in Los Angeles and includes sections of that city with large numbers of illegal aliens and noncitizens. Roybal-Allard allegedly provides them with representation in Congress, but does she really? How is she held accountable to these constituents?[25] She is not, and her district would qualify as a modern-day rotten borough. According to the political scientist Peter Skerry, elected officials from these areas "respond more to the politicians or advocacy groups responsible for the creation of their districts than to those whom they formally represent."[26] This is representation without representation, and it is a problem in Hispanic districts generally (although often not as severely as in the case of Roybal-Allard). In 1994, only 56 percent of Hispanics in the United States were citizens. Although roughly 1 in 10 adults was Hispanic, only 1 in 16 adult citizens was Hispanic.[27] The congressional districts with the lowest voter participation are consistently majority-Hispanic districts, since so many nonvoters live in them.

The problem comes full circle when congressional districts are ethnically gerrymandered to create safe seats for Hispanics. Their boundaries often are drawn to include thousands of people who cannot vote. Take New York's 12th District. Created after the 1990 Census to ensure that Hispanics in New York City would elect one of their own, it runs through parts of Brooklyn, Manhattan, and Queens. Its appearance is bizarre, described by the *Almanac of American Politics* as "a serpentine-shaped entity. . . . Stitched together, often by the thinnest of threads."[28] Its boundary lines change direction a remarkable 813 times. Representrative Nydia M. Velazquez won reelection in 1996 with less than sixty-two thousand votes. Velazquez says that each of her five-hundred-seventy-seven thousand constituents receives proper attention, and perhaps they do. But what a weird introduction to American political life for the immigrants who live there. In February 1997, a federal court struck down the 12th District because of its clearly race-driven boundaries.[29] This is a positive step, and possible only because several recent Supreme Court rulings look askance at the deliberate creation of majority-minority districts. Yet the political impulse to create them has not died, and what rises out of the ashes of this particular 12th District remains to be seen.

The wicked assumption of racial and ethnic gerrymandering is that only Hispanics should represent Hispanics because only Hispanics can understand Hispanic concerns. But remember the flip side of the same argument—only non-Hispanic whites can represent non-Hispanic whites. Following this logic to its conclusion would doom Hispanics to the barrio. Their political success would peak with election to the occasional congressional district. Because Hispanics do not represent a majority of voters in any state, they would never be able to elect one of their own to a statewide office. That means no governors or senators, and certainly no Mexican-American Kennedy. For political Americanization to work, immigrants must be allowed to break free from the stifling conformity of identity politics and be counted as individuals.

To a certain extent, that is already happening. Despite the best efforts of activists who claim to speak for the silent masses, Hispanic and Asian American political behavior cannot be easily categorized. One widely held belief is that there is an Hispanic vote or an Asian vote. It is true that both Hispanics and Asians occasionally display political tendencies, but each group also contains remarkable diversity. The reality of Hispanic and Asian American political behavior shatters the false notion on which the empire of identity politics is built—that all the members of a racial or ethnic group are carbon copies of each other, that they represent a monolithic entity of like-minded clones. They do not, and perhaps the real-life political choices of the huddled masses make that case better than any theory.

HOW THE RAINBOW COALITION REALLY VOTES

A yellowed newspaper clipping inside a black frame hangs on the office wall of Alfredo Cardenas. The article is from the October 29, 1904, edition of *La Libertad*, a Spanish-language newspaper. It describes two local officeholders, the county sheriff and treasurer. "Those are the last two guys in Duval County to win election as Republicans," says Cardenas, the mayor of the small south Texas town of San Diego, about an hour's drive west of Corpus Christi. "Until me, that is," he adds with a smile, pointing to the two pictures of George Bush that hang behind his desk.[30] As a Republican in south Texas, Cardenas is an oddity. For most of the 20th century, the Democratic Party has dominated his section of the state in something that approximates one-party rule. Democrats are everywhere, like the scrubby mesquite trees that clutter the landscape. Republicans, on the other hand, are about as rare as a snowfall: Your uncle can probably tell you a story about the last time he saw one. "Down here, you're born three things," says Laredo school board member Bebe Zuniga, "A Hispanic, a Catholic, and a Democrat."[31]

In Miami, you are also born three things, at least if you are Cuban: Hispanic, Catholic, and Republican. When the Cuban-born Ileana Ros-Lehtinen was elected to Congress as a Republican in a 1989 special election to fill the seat left vacant by the death of Democrat Claude Pepper, she carried an estimated 90 percent of the Hispanic (mostly Cuban) vote. Since then, her 67-percent-Hispanic district has returned her to Congress with big margins of victory. Three years later, Florida's growing population compelled it to add another district in Dade County—the 21st congressional district. It contained a Hispanic population of 70 percent. No Democrat has even tried to run there. It would be political suicide, since Cubans so overwhelmingly favor the GOP.[32]

When taken as a national group, Hispanics fall somewhere between the two extremes of Mexican Americans in south Texas and Cuban Americans in Miami. They tend to support Democrats, but not overwhelmingly. One study estimates that 41 percent of all Hispanics are Democrats, 24 percent are Republicans, and 27 percent are independents.[33] Party preference in presidential elections appears to have fluctuated a good deal. Hispanics prefer Democrats, but a sizable minority appear to vote Republican. In 1980, President Carter won 59 percent of the Hispanic vote to Ronald Reagan's 33 percent. When Reagan ran for reelection in 1984, he had made some inroads into the Hispanic vote, boosting his support to 37 percent. His challenger Walter Mondale, however, managed to pull in 62 percent. In 1988, Michael Dukakis more than doubled George Bush's Hispanic vote, 69 percent to 30 percent. Bill Clinton won 55 percent of the Hispanic vote in 1992, compared to Bush's 29 percent and Ross Perot's 16 percent.[34] Hispanic distribution on the electoral map ironically appears to increase Republican odds of winning the White House. If no Hispanics had voted in the 1992 presidential election, three states would have switched how they voted: Florida (25 electoral votes) would have gone for Clinton, Colorado (8) and New Mexico (5) for Bush. In other words, Bush pocketed 12 electoral votes because of Hispanic support.[35]

Hispanics flocked to the Democratic party in 1996, when they gave more than 70 percent of their support to Clinton. Only 21 percent voted for GOP candidate Bob Dole—a smaller proportion of the Hispanic vote than any Republican presidential candidate had earned in at least 25 years. Data also suggest that Democrats made substantial gains among Cuban voters and may have carried 85 percent of Hispanic voters who had just become citizens. A number of factors probably contributed to these results, but most important almost certainly was the perception among Hispanics that Republicans, because of their welfare reform efforts and threats to reduce family-based legal immigration, are hostile to immigrants.[36] GOP-sponsored public policies were not nearly as harsh as some of their detracting demagogues made them sound, but appearances always matter in politics.

Hispanics are widely considered an important part of the Democrats' rainbow coalition of minority groups. Of the 19 Hispanics in Congress, for example, 16 are Democrats. That might indicate that 84 percent of all Hispanics are also Democrats, but, as the presidential election results indicate, the math really does not work that way. In some races, high levels of Hispanic support provide Republican candidates with the winning edge. The Los Angeles media widely attribute Republican mayor Richard Riordan's victories in 1993 and 1997 to Hispanic voters.[37] In Texas, Republicans say that Governor George W. Bush received between 35 and 40 percent of the Hispanic vote in his successful 1994 bid for office.[38] "Many Hispanics are Republican but they just don't know it," says Frank Guerra, a San Antonio political consultant who has managed the campaigns of Representative Henry Bonilla, the only Republican of Mexican descent to serve in Congress. "Marketing research tells us that Hispanics are more brand-loyal than any other racial or ethnic group in the country. That's why they're voting for Democrats. But they have become more Republican in recent years. It's only a matter of time."[39]

Despite the success and optimism of some, Republicans appear to be in a no-win political situation, especially if Hispanic immigrants continue to enter the United States and vote for Democrats at the rate they currently do. For every candidate who does well by attracting 40 percent of the Hispanic vote, 6 of 10 Hispanic voters are still casting their ballots for Democrats. Yet to some academics, "the dynamics of social trends among Hispanics seem to favor the Republican Party."[40] Hispanics may not be moving toward the GOP as fast as Republicans might like, but they are clearly doing it. Upward mobility plays a big part in this equation. As Hispanics become better educated and more prosperous as a group—something that is happening with a certain amount of inevitability—they will move toward the GOP, which traditionally represents high-education, high-income parts of the population. According to Barry A. Kosmin and Ariela Keysar, "as time and social mobility affect the Hispanic population, support for the Republican Party should increase. Moreover, as the older generation dies out, college graduation rates increase and Hispanic household income rises, we should expect that support for the Democratic Party will be reduced."[41]

Asian-American political behavior is even more varied. In one sense, it is very difficult to determine Asian-American voting behavior because there is really no such thing as an Asian American. Chinese, Filipinos, Indians, Japanese, Koreans, Vietnamese, and others share no common tongue, faith, or history. They are lumped together by the federal government's bean counters and Americans generally. Yet they are remarkably diverse groups with very different interests. Japanese Americans, for instance, are a well-established group that has reached rough parity with non-Hispanic whites on a variety of socioeconomic indicators. Southeast Asians, however, are overwhelmingly first-generation Americans who arrived as poor, displaced refugees.

Many Asian Americans are becoming candidates for public office. Every election cycle seems to bring its share of Asian-American firsts. In November 1994, Ben Cayetano of Hawaii (D) became the first Filipino to win election as governor. Two years earlier, Jay Kim (R-Calif.) became the first Korean-American member of Congress and Nao Takasugi (R) became the first Asian American since 1976 to enter California's legislature.[42] This emergence also is visible on the grassroots level. By winning a seat on the Westminster, California, city council, Tony Lam recently became the first Vietnamese refugee elected to office in the United States.[43] In 1996, Gary Locke (D) became the highest-ranking Chinese American officeholder in the country with his election as governor of the state of Washington.

Some data on the political preferences of Asian ethnic groups do exist. A *Los Angeles Times* poll, for example, found that about two-thirds of Vietnamese Americans registered to vote in Southern California consider themselves Republicans. This comes as no surprise, since so many of them fled a communist regime and quickly identified with the GOP's cold war philosophy. Koreans are considered a fairly Republican group. Chinese and Taiwanese also appear to lean in the GOP's direction. As with the Vietnamese, much of this springs from anticommunist sentiments. Japanese Americans, however, are overwhelmingly Democratic and most Filipinos probably are as well. Indian political preferences are less clear, but when they run for office they are much more likely to do so as Democrats. In 1994, six ran for Congress in the Democratic primaries. (Only one won, and then he lost in the general election.)

Exit polls have shown a clear tendency among Asian Americans as a group to favor Republican candidates. In the 1996 presidential race, Asian Americans voted 49 percent for Bob Dole compared to 42 percent for Bill Clinton. Asian Americans also supported the GOP candidate in congressional elections 53 percent to 42 percent. They were more likely than whites to vote Republican in both cases. In 1992, Asian Americans supported George Bush by 55 percent to 29 percent for Bill Clinton and 16 percent for Ross Perot. Among the general population, Clinton prevailed with 43 percent of the vote, compared to 38 percent for Bush and 19 percent for Perot. Only white evangelical Christians and self-identified Republicans had a higher rate of support for Bush. In California, Asian Americans gave Clinton 45 percent of their support, compared to 40 percent for Bush and 15 percent for Perot, according to the *Los Angeles Times*. Asian GOP support in California still outpaced levels in the state's general population, which gave Bush less than one-third of its vote. Back in 1988, George Bush took 54 percent of the Asian vote nationwide to Michael Dukakis's 44 percent. In 1984, Ronald Reagan may have beaten Walter Mondale by a 70 percent to 30 percent margin among Asians. Perhaps the Republican National Committee knew what it was doing when it opened a special Asian American Affairs Office in 1989—beating the Democrats, who claim to speak for ethnic minorities, by a year.[44]

Internal Republican polling data show that most GOP support among Asians comes from the immigrant generation, with U.S.-born Asians remaining politically independent. A similar finding appears in a 1984 study by University of California researchers Bruce E. Cain, D. Roderick Kiewiet, and Carole J. Uhlaner. Their survey showed that 42 percent of foreign-born Asian Americans identified with the GOP, compared to 32 percent with the Democrats. Yet among Asians born in the United States, 43 percent considered themselves Democrats and 37 percent Republicans. The survey also asked for opinions on specific political issues, and the foreign-born Asians were much more supportive of increased defense spending and gun control than other racial or ethnic groups. Asians born in the United States had political opinions very similar to those of non-Hispanic whites.[45]

The generation gap is critical. Nearly two-thirds of all Asian Americans are foreign-born, according to the 1990 Census. The children of these immigrants will not necessarily mimic their parents' political behavior. "There's no telling where the younger Asians will go, and they will be a big part of the population before too long," says Paul Shie, a political scientist at Southeastern University and a Republican consultant. "The older generation lived through the civil rights movement during the 1960s, so they were pulled toward the civil rights advocates in the Democratic Party," he says. Younger U.S.-born Asians will not share that experience.

The next generation of Asian Americans may not share any kind of ethnic political experience at all. Although immigrant enclaves like Manhattan's Chinatown, Los Angeles's Koreatown, and Orange County's Little Saigon still exist, most of the Asian population is highly dispersed. Ten percent of Californians are Asian, but the state has no Asian-majority voting district—even on the state assembly level. The most successful Asian-American politicians—Rep. Jay Kim, Rep. Robert Matsui, and former Rep. Norman Mineta—do not come out of ethnic political backgrounds. Kim got his start on the Diamond Bar City Council and then became mayor. Matsui served for seven years on the Sacramento City Council. Mineta was the mayor of San Jose. None has represented a district with more than 15 percent Asian residents, so their careers are built on the support of non-Asians.

These numbers on Hispanic and Asian American political behavior say many things, but chief among them is the fact that neither is a monolithic group. Of course, that could change if group rights were to become a permanent fixture in American political life. Group rights are a fairly new phenomenon, and there is no telling how they will affect the political attitudes of Hispanics and Asians in the years to come. If these new populations begin to believe what their self-proclaimed leaders constantly tell them—that they cannot fit into the mainstream because of who they are—then they imperil the goals of Americanization. There is, however, one final enemy of group rights whose role in this debate is not yet properly understood: intermarriage and miscegenation.

THE NEXT MELTING POT

The Census Bureau currently predicts that sometime in the next century, probably soon after the year 2050, the United States will become a "majority minority" country. That is, minorities will outnumber non-Hispanic whites. In its latest population projection, the Census Bureau says that by 2050 the non-Hispanic white population will have dwindled to 52.7 percent of the population, down from 75.7 percent in 1990. Halfway through the next century, it proclaims, 21.1 percent of all Americans will be Hispanic, 15.0 percent will be black, 10.1 percent will be Asian, and 1.1 percent will be American Indian.[46]

There is only one problem with this prediction: It is completely wrong. For starters, nobody knows what the racial and ethnic makeup of the United States will look like in the future. Demographers can make guesses, but these guesses are based on highly tenuous assumptions regarding fertility, immigration, and other factors. Demographic predictions are like meteorological forecasts, except that instead of merely looking to next weekend, they squint decades into the next century. Anybody who has spent a few rainy days at the beach knows the unreliability of even these fairly modest attempts at seeing into the future. The truth is, nobody knows how many children the average American woman will have in 2020, or how many Cambodian immigrants will arrive in 2030, or what war, epidemics, or economic pressures will do to family size in 2040. History says as much. So-called population experts in the 1930s, for instance, were unanimous in guessing that the U.S. population would decline sharply. None of them predicted the postwar baby boom or increased immigration at century's end.[47] The size of America's population has gone from 123 million in 1930 to almost 270 million in 1998.

Demographic forecasters face an even trickier problem, however, when they talk about race and ethnicity. The ethno-racial pentagon erected by the Census Bureau—and relied on by demographers who speak of the minority majority—will soon implode. It will collapse under the weight of its own artificiality. The questions of who belongs to what race or ethnicity will become increasingly confused as more and more Americans marry people of different racial and ethnic backgrounds and have children. This is how it worked in the past. The Ellis Island generation of immigrants came from all over Europe. Although the ethno-racial pentagon today teaches Americans to think of all these people as white, in reality they were a diverse group of folks who spoke a variety of languages, followed different faiths, and often did not even like each other. The racial theorists who divided European whites into three categories—Nordic, Alpine, and Mediterranean—might well have offered their own predictions about when the United States would find itself host to a majority non-Nordic population. In fact, some of them did. They called it race suicide.

It was all nonsense. The progeny of Europe were soon marrying each other. Today, a majority of U.S.-born non-Hispanic whites are of mixed ancestry. That is, they are more likely to be part-English, part-German, or part-Polish than wholly English, wholly German, or wholly Polish. Whiteness, in fact, is a racial category almost unique to the United States. It exists largely because of high levels of cross-ethnic intermarriage among European immigrants and their descendants. There are, of course, white people in Europe. But more than that, there are Dutch, Finns, Italians, Russians, and Spaniards. To speak of them all as the same does an enormous disservice to their diversity and to how they think of themselves. Intermarriage essentially has wiped out this diversity among white Americans, who can trace their ancestry in many different directions. In the last census, 13 million Americans found their tangled family tree too confusing to label. When asked their ethnicity, they replied "American" or "United States."[48] This kind of generational Americanization among European immigrants and their children has worked so well that many people forget it ever happened.

It looks like it may happen again with the new immigrants and their children, even though so many of them are not white. In 1990, 30 percent of all marriages including an Asian American also included a non-Asian, usually a white. These marriages produced more than 314,000 children. Nearly one out of every five Asian-American births was to a mixed-race couple.[49] This miscegenation can have fairly dramatic effects. Half of all Japanese Americans now marry someone who is not Japanese, for example. In 1989, there were 39 percent more births to exogamous couples consisting of one Japanese parent and one white parent than to endogamous couples of two Japanese-American parents. This was not a one-time statistical fluke, but the start of the long-term trend. Before long, there will be more Americans of partial Japanese ancestry than total Japanese ancestry.[50]

Hispanic intermarriage rates are similarly high. More than 28 percent of the marriages involving Mexican Americans included a non-Hispanic in 1990. For Puerto Ricans the rate was 35 percent, and for Cubans it was 26 percent. Marriages involving other Hispanic groups included a non-Hispanic almost 44 percent of the time. Over 1.3 million children were born to these mixed marriages.[51]

These intermarriage rates inch upward when controlled for nativity. Many immigrants arrive in the United States already married, so the prospect of first-generation Americans marrying someone of a different background is much lower than it is for their children. Second-generation Americans—people who have at least one foreign-born parent—provide a better glimpse at how well the melting pot percolates. In a study of New York City marriage records issued in 1991, second-generation Hispanics showed a high rate of intermarriage with non-Hispanics. Among second-generation brides, 66 percent of those of Cuban ancestry married non-Hispanics, as did 53 percent of Mexican Americans, 56 percent of Central Americans, and 41 percent of South Americans. Similar rates prevailed among second-generation grooms. Dominicans were a good deal less likely to marry non-Hispanics: 24 percent of second-generation Dominican brides married non-Hispanics. This may be due to the fact that many Dominicans are racially black, and blacks have a much lower intermarriage rate with whites than various white ethnic groups (including Hispanics) have with each other.[52]

The problem with the ethno-racial pentagon is that it cannot accommodate children born to interracial marriages. They do not fit snugly into this racialist scheme like the missing piece of a puzzle. They are more like the extra pair of brackets left over from a build-it-yourself project. You know they belong somewhere, but cannot find a convenient place to put them—and ultimately wonder if you have done the job correctly.

Intermarriage becomes more common over time and down the generations. Just as second-generation Americans are more likely to intermarry than their immigrant parents, third-generation Americans are more likely still. At some point, intermarriage ceases becoming intermarriage. It becomes simply marriage. When an Irish American married an Italian American 75 years ago, it was probably a big deal in the neighborhood. But no more. In the future, everyone will have a Korean grandmother.

The Census Bureau has given some thought to this matter, and it may include a new multiracial category in the 2000 Census or allow people to check off more than one racial box. Either of these options is only a temporary measure. The mestizo population of Mexico became so intertwined that the Mexican government has not asked a race question on its census since 1921.[53] The United States may expect to see something similar happen, as the ethno-racial pentagon becomes less and less reflective of the American population. There may come a time when a majority of Americans can trace their ancestry to Asia or Latin America. They will trace it to Europe, too. What really matters is that

Americans stay dedicated to the principles of American nationhood. If they do, the complexion of the United States may change, but its character will remain the same. Perhaps the best way to undermine the ideology of group rights is to permit this natural process of assimilation to work its way down the generations as people of mixed background marry and have children. Just imagine the poetic justice of a new melting pot of immigrants from all over the world eradicating the regime of group rights—something that the native-born white politicians of the 1990s have refused to do.

Change may not come easily, so Americanizers should not place all of their hopes on this scenario. The concern is that if immigrants learn that group rights matter most, assimilation may not affect today's immigrants as powerfully as it did their predecessors. The United States right now is closer to the ideal that all men are created equal, no matter what their race or ethnicity, than ever before—and probably closer than any polity has come. Ending the government's preoccupation with racial and ethnic distinctions would help Americanize immigrants immediately, because it would teach them by example that what matters most in the United States is not the color of your skin, the genetic makeup of your parents, or even where you were born. What matters is that Americans are all individuals dedicated to a proposition—and deserving equal protection under the rule of law.

Chapter 7

THE NATURALIZERS

Linda Wai frowns. She reads the words on the test, but not all of them register. English is, after all, her third language. Her first language is Chinese, as she was born on the mainland before the Second World War. She picked up her second language, Spanish, in Costa Rica, where her family moved during the 1950s. Only after 1977, when she immigrated to the United States, did she begin to learn English. But older people do not learn languages as easily as children, and Linda Wai is an old woman. Even now, almost twenty years since coming to America, she struggles with the English on her citizenship exam.

Across the desk, Dan Childs finishes reviewing the thick collection of forms, fingerprints, and photos in Wai's citizenship application folder. "Let's take a look at this," he says, reaching for Wai's test. Childs, an INS airport officer on a three-month detail to conduct citizenship interviews in Arlington, Virginia, scans her exam. Wai must answer 7 of 12 questions correctly to pass. Childs can tell right away that she is a borderline case. His own subjective analysis of her responses will make the difference between approving Wai's application for citizenship or denying it. She clearly has answered 5 questions correctly. Number six, however, is a problem. "Who was the first president?" it asks. Her answer: "George Washing." Childs smiles and decides to test her orally: "Who was the first president, George Washing?" "Yes, George Washington," she says. "All right," mumbles Childs to himself, giving her credit.

That makes six. Wai needs one more to pass. But the rest of her exam is filled with blanks and half-answers. Childs tries to prompt her again orally. Can she name one of her two Senators in Congress? No. What is the Bill of Rights? Silence. Wai squirms in her seat. She does not know that the only thing standing between her and citizenship is one correct answer, but she senses that the interview suddenly has soured. Childs moves to a question on the exam that Wai did not answer completely, thinking that maybe she can fill in the gaps if he pushes her. "Who was Abraham Lincoln? What did he do?" he asks. Wai lowers her eyebrows, tightens her lip, and leans her small body forward. "He make everybody the same." "Yes, but what did he do?" "He make everybody the same," she says again, nodding her head. "Who did he make the same?" "Everybody." "Right. Who in particular?" Wai stutters, but fumbles her way forward. "You know. The colored people." "But what were they, why did he have to make them the same?" continues Childs. "Oh, I don't know. I know the word in Chinese." "I want to hear it in English. Why did he make them the same?" "He had a very good heart." "Yes, but what were they? What did he have to do to them?" "I don't know," Wai says with increasing despair. Childs pauses, and starts again: "What were they doing?" "They working hard, so hard. All the time very hard," she says rapidly. Childs stops and thinks. He still has not heard the word *slave* or *slavery*. What to do?

Wai wrings her hands, then blurts out: "When I first come to Washington, D.C., I go to Lincoln"—a reference, apparently, to the Lincoln Memorial. "He freed them from slavery," says Childs, stressing the last word. "Oh, yes," says Wai with a worried look. Childs decides to give her credit. "I'm not going to make her come back in 10 weeks for a re-exam over this," he says later. When Childs tells her that she has passed and can now become a citizen, Wai starts to cry. "Long time I wanted America. I hope America when I little girl," she stutters as she weeps. She thanks Childs half-a-dozen times and shakes his hand twice. As she walks out of the cubicle, she points to her red purse and her blue-and-white-striped sweater. "Today I wear America colors," she says, thanks Childs one more time, and steps away.[1]

DUMBING DOWN NATURALIZATION

In the mid-1990s, the United States saw massive numbers of immigrants seek citizenship. In 1995, more than 1 million of them applied for naturalization, up from an annual average of only two hundred thirty thousand in the 1980s. This rush to citizenship offers both an opportunity and a danger for Americanization. The opportunity is to help more immigrants become Americans than ever before and to protect the country from multicultural conflict. The danger is that to cope with a crushing volume of applicants, the INS will lower its naturalization standards and devalue citizenship like a peso.

The naturalization of Linda Wai reveals both the best and the worst aspects of how immigrants earn citizenship. At its best, it exposes deep attachments and a sense of belonging. It allows the built-up human capital of cultural assimilation to pay off by extending the political franchise to people who have found a place within American society after years of living in it and becoming familiar with it. Preparation for the tests and ceremony of citizenship has long been a powerful instrument of unity, an engine of assimilation that turns newcomers into U.S. citizens who understand our political traditions and are proud to be Americans. A citizenship ceremony is among the most moving events in American public life. Patriotic songs and colorful speeches fill the program. The event concludes with a duty-bound oath in which immigrants forsake foreign allegiances and pledge themselves wholly to their new country. As new citizens pick up their official citizenship papers, they also receive small American flags and voting information. Friends and family greet them outside. That day will be remembered the way most Americans remember graduations, weddings, and the birth of children.

All of the difficult moments leading up to citizenship reinforce its meaning for participants. To naturalize, immigrants must live in the United States for five years as legal residents. They must pass an FBI criminal background check. They must demonstrate the ability to speak, read, and write in simple English and discuss basic information about U.S. history and government. Imagine an American moving to Japan, learning to speak the language as well as read and write kanji script, and reciting facts about the shogunate, the Meiji restoration, and Admiral Togo. It's a tough assignment, but it's also roughly on par with what the United States has demanded of its citizenship applicants since 1907, when uniform rules for naturalization took effect. Only those immigrants who really want citizenship will get it. And when they do, they swell with a satisfaction that most other Americans can never experience. Ultimately, naturalization does more than merely grant a set of political entitlements. It infuses new citizens with a sense of duty, responsibility, and loyalty. Who can doubt that Linda Wai will make a great American?

Despite this, the INS is currently threatening to lower its standards to the point where naturalization is no longer a meaningful experience. Our notion of citizenship has cheapened since the turn of the century. The INS's Nats section, as the employees call it, has been swamped in recent years with more citizenship applications than it can handle. More than a million citizenship applications are backlogged. It can take more than a year for an immigrant to schedule an interview. The agency never has functioned very well, and with 1996 setting a new record for naturalization petitions, it has assumed a bunker mentality. Like a school that promotes problem students into the next grade because to hold them back would risk controversy, the INS now pressures its examiners to push potential citizens through the system quickly, even if they are not ready. Agents hint that their superiors are more concerned about meeting a numbers-driven agenda than making sure everybody does a good, thorough job. "We have about 15 minutes for each interview," says Childs. "If I want to take a little extra time to question something, it really backs things up. We're always behind schedule, even if things go smoothly. I usually skip my lunch hour just to catch up. You can guess what you want about the INS giving us so many appointments and so little time." What's more, scoring 7 out of 12—and allowing considerable lenience in how applicants arrive at the 7—does not exactly set a high performance standard for the test on U.S. history and government.

The immediate danger, however, is not that the INS already sets the citizenship bar too low, but that it will drop the bar altogether. In 1996, the agency mistakenly granted citizenship to hundreds if not thousands of criminal aliens whose convictions should have blocked naturalization. One internal audit discovered that one hundred eighty thousand immigrants awarded citizenship did not undergo a mandatory FBI criminal background check.[2] In California, an INS district office looked the other way as an activist organization actually helped noncitizens register to vote—over the protests of INS agents who warned their superiors about these violations.[3] Critics accused the Clinton administration of running a voter mill. The *Washington Post* proceeded to uncover documents that appeared to verify these charges.[4]

Worse still, INS Commissioner Doris Meissner has suggested eliminating the mandatory personal interviews to save time.[5] In an article solicited by the INS, Arnold Rochvarg, a professor at the University of Baltimore School of Law, recommended that interview exemptions be granted to large classes of applicants.[6] As many as 20 percent of successful citizenship applicants now take their tests on U.S. history and government away from the INS and under the auspices of private testing agencies. Under honest vendors, this exemplary program resembles student SAT testing. But the INS's total lack of oversight and quality control has allowed hucksters into the business. Bribery and corruption are disturbingly common, and the fact that the INS has looked the other way despite warning signs speaks to how low it might let the naturalization process sink.[7] The interviews that Meissner and Rochvarg do not value and which the INS already has started to skirt form the crux of the entire naturalization process. To eliminate them suggests, quite strongly, that meaningful naturalization is not a concern of the INS and its top managers. A battery of civil rights organizations egg them on. Hispanic activist Harry Pachon says that the National Association of Latino Elected and Appointed Officials promotes naturalization because citizenship "is the missing ingredient to Latino empowerment strategies."[8] In other words, naturalization is not an important aspect of the complicated assimilation process, but a political power grab. The easier, the better. Leticia Quezada of the Los Angeles School Board wants to break down the distinction between citizens and noncitizens entirely by giving the vote to people who have not naturalized. She even equates her views with the historic efforts of removing sex and race as barriers to the ballot box. "At one time only white males could vote," she says. "My position is that it's time we cross the line in terms of citizenship."[9] Susan B. Anthony, Martin Luther King, Jr., and the other champions of equal opportunity must be rolling in their graves.

Despite these attacks, naturalization remains a vital force in the assimilation of immigrants. Since 1907, more than 13 million foreign-born people have become citizens—full members of American society and ready to take part in democratic decision making. No decade in the 20th century has seen less than 1 million people seek naturalization.[10] The word *naturalization* means, literally, to make natural, or to put on a level with what is native. And in a political sense, that's exactly what it does. Naturalized immigrants immediately experience near-total political assimilation. They may not lose their accents when they receive their papers, but they do shed the political distinctions that divide noncitizens from citizens. Citizenship grants immigrants the right to vote, hold certain government jobs, and carry a U.S. passport. It provides better opportunities to sponsor the immigration of relatives. It also mandates jury duty, when called. There is only one legal difference between a native-born citizen and a citizen who has been naturalized: Under Article 2, Section 1, of the U.S. Constitution, the president must be born in the United States.[11]

Yet naturalization does much more than turn newcomers into voting members of the republic. It provides them with a gateway to American civil society and the ability—no, the right—to say, "I am an American." Immigrants who naturalize have by virtue of their status demonstrated an understanding of American life and a willingness to commit themselves to the principles that support it. They may even know more about these matters than the native-born, thanks to the educational aspects of the naturalization process. In a day when many people are starting to question immigrants' commitment to the melting pot ethic, a renewed faith in naturalization might ease anxieties. Despite this, naturalization has received scant attention from scholars and the media, except when a voter registration scandal erupts in highly partisan circumstances. A public debate over immigration continues to rage, but few people have critically examined the process by which the United States turns immigrants into citizens.

It was not always this way. Americans once expected immigrants to become citizens, and they took a great interest in whether or not naturalization occurred. They knew that citizenship did more than award political entitlements. The value of naturalization lay in its ability to transform foreign nationals into patriotic Americans. This was a growing concern at the time, since the millions of newcomers from eastern and southern Europe, in the minds of many natives, were of questionable loyalty to the United States. The fact that some of them participated in strikes and advocated radical ideas did not enhance their popularity. Virtually all native-born Americans—even those who outright opposed the new immigration—agreed that naturalization was fundamental to the newcomers' successful integration into American life. Their confidence in the assimilative capacities of naturalization was so strong that when President William McKinley fell to the bullet of the anarchist Leon Czolgosz—an American by birth but of obvious foreign parentage—in 1903, the Americanizers looked to naturalization, not restriction, as the solution to domestic turmoil.[12] After McKinley's death, the Sons of the American Revolution (SAR) rushed to press with a small leaflet entitled *A Welcome to Immigrants and Some Good Advice* and urged immigrants to become citizens as quickly as possible. SAR and other groups would repeat this bit of counseling in the years ahead. "The immigrants of today may be the good Americans of tomorrow, if they are made to know their privileges and their duties in their adopted country," argued a group of activists in 1911.[13] Thousands of other contemporary documents give voice to this same belief. Naturalization sat at the very core of Americanization.

WHO NATURALIZES—AND WHY?

Few immigrants come to the United States because they want to be naturalized. Nothing could be further from their minds. They are not even eligible for it until they have completed five years of permanent legal residency. Assimilation, however, does not wait. It is impatient. It starts to work on newcomers immediately—at first, almost by osmosis—as they pick up a few words of English and become familiar with American habits, customs, and mores. The decision to naturalize comes gradually, if at all. The choice is very difficult for immigrants, since it gets snagged in thorny questions about loyalty, identity, and family.

Even though naturalization leads to full membership in American society, it also can seem like a betrayal of a person's past. The experience can become downright gloomy if immigrants equate becoming American with snuffing out their heritage. Perhaps it recalls nothing so much as that bittersweet moment in family life when a child moves out of the family home for good. The son lingers at the door, wanting to stay just a little bit longer but knowing that he must leave. It is not hard to put off citizenship. Immigrants can always naturalize. But once done, they can't go home again.

The Americanizers believed that making a home in the United States came with a few obligations. Obeying the law and leading productive lives were two of the responsibilities shared by natives and immigrants alike. Americanizers also wanted the foreign-born to naturalize. If you want to live here, the thinking went, then become an American. It's part of the deal. Refusing to naturalize was like objecting to an employer's drug test—what do you have to hide? There is a certain logic to this attitude, even as it sparks resentment among the foreign-born. The best Americanizers considered citizenship a privilege that they wanted to share. They did not want to coerce people into naturalization, but they considered an immigrant's acquisition of citizenship of vital importance. This belief translated into policy recommendations. When the Committee for Immigrants in America outlined a seven-point program in 1915 to help the foreign-born assimilate, it advocated an "increase of facilities for naturalization and for coordination of educational requirements with educational facilities" as an important piece of the plan.[14] Significantly, this faith in naturalization went beyond the advocates of immigration. In its 1911 report endorsing restrictions on immigration levels, for example, the Federal Immigration Commission said that "as far as possible those excluded should be those who come to this country with no intention of becoming American citizens."[15] For them, the desire to naturalize was a prerequisite to walking through the golden door. This sentiment has faded in recent years, even though the U.S. Commission on Immigration Reform has promoted the idea of naturalization.[16] In 1996, the Center for Immigration Studies suggested that immigration policy (the question of who gets in) should look more favorably on the types of immigrants who are likely to naturalize than on those who are not.[17]

More than one-third of the roughly 40 million people who have immigrated during the 20th century have become citizens.[18] Of course, many of these millions never even qualified for citizenship due to death or repatriation. Others opted out because they feared that they would fail the English-language requirement or the civics test. Becoming an American citizen requires an engagement with American society that goes beyond political allegiance. Whatever the case, the choice is not random. Naturalization requires a fair amount of paperwork and a lot of personal endurance. Those who go through the entire process, almost without exception, will have given the matter a good deal of thought. Today, about half of all eligible immigrants become citizens. Slightly more than 50 percent of all adult immigrants who had arrived before 1985 were citizens in 1989, according to the 1990 Census.[19]

As with any characteristic of assimilation, naturalization takes time, and the rate of naturalization increases over the years. The average immigrant who naturalizes does so after living in the United States for about eight years. Asians and Africans tend to naturalize more quickly than other groups, taking about seven years. Europeans hold off for 13 years and immigrants from Canada and Mexico wait even longer. By the end of 1995, about 42 percent of immigrants who arrived in 1982 had naturalized, as had about 46 percent of those who came in 1977.[20]

Naturalization levels typically have followed immigration levels, but with a delay of several years—and a few notable exceptions. As with the general flow of immigration, the number of naturalizations rose fitfully in the first part of the century, bottomed out in the middle, and began to inch upward again in the 1960s. Times of trouble can upset this pattern. German immigrants, in particular, have rushed to citizenship during conflict. The First World War inspired a record number of naturalizations, which actually peaked in 1919, the first full year of peace, at more than two hundred thousand. The Second World War also put a spike in the naturalization chart. In 1944, close to four hundred forty-two thousand immigrants became citizens—more than any other year in U.S. history until the 1990s, when four separate circumstances conspired to push the number of naturalizations to an all-time high of more than 1 million.[21] First, more immigrants are eligible for citizenship today than ever before, thanks to high levels of legal immigration in recent years and the illegal alien population that received amnesty under the 1986 Immigration Reform and Control Act. It is only natural that citizenship applications would rise on the heels of this increase.[22] Second, the Mexican government has proposed lifting the property restrictions it currently imposes on Mexican citizens who pledged allegiance to another flag, which is usually the United States.[23] Third, the INS ruled in 1994 that all legal immigrants holding green cards issued before 1979 had to have them renewed—for a $75 fee. Many decided that they would rather pay an extra $20 and shoot for full citizenship instead.[24] Finally, some immigrants perceive the current political climate—embodied by measures like California's Proposition 187 and new limits on noncitizen welfare eligibility—as opposed to their interests. This belief has inspired thousands of newcomers to seek the legal status that will prevent the unpredictable world of politics from abridging their rights or denying them benefits.[25] The surge in naturalization probably will continue to the end of the century, as more than 1 million naturalization applicants now find themselves stuck in a massive INS backlog that will take years to reduce.

The demographics of naturalization also track the broader pattern of immigration. Just as the 1965 immigration reforms altered the racial and ethnic makeup of the immigrant population, so too the population of those who naturalize. During the 1960s, more than 60 percent of all new citizens were European.[26] By 1969, European domination had slipped to 52 percent, but still outpaced the Asian and Hispanic share of all naturalizations (16 percent and 11 percent, respectively).[27] Two decades later, however, Asians made up about half of all naturalizations and Hispanics—mainly Colombians, Cubans, Dominicans, and Mexicans—contributed another 25 percent. Only 11 percent of new citizens were European, with Polish and Portuguese newcomers leading the way.[28]

The rate of naturalization varies on a country-by-country basis. As a general rule, immigrants from African, Asian, and European countries tend to have higher naturalization rates than newcomers from Caribbean and Latin American countries.[29] In a sophisticated study of immigrants who arrived in 1973 from six countries, sociologist Zai Liang found that Asians were more likely than other groups to have become citizens by 1989. Nearly two-thirds of Chinese and Korean men had naturalized, compared to 46 percent of Cuban men and 50 percent of Colombian men. Canadians and Mexicans had the lowest rates of all: only 17 percent of Mexican men, 20 percent of Mexican women, 20 percent of Canadian men, and 15 percent of Canadian women had naturalized.[30] The quality of life in an immigrant's country of origin plays an important role in these variations. A high per capita GNP in the home country decreases the odds of naturalization, for example. Countries with communist or socialist regimes tend to produce immigrants with a greater desire to become citizens, as do countries that churn out refugees. The distance traveled to reach the United States also has a positive effect: Every mile makes citizenship more likely. This helps explain why Canadians and Mexicans—whose homelands seem to share little in common except for the fact that they both border the United States—have among the lowest rates of naturalization among immigrant groups. Sociologist Philip Yang considers all of this good support for his "reversibility hypothesis," or the idea that immigrants who can reverse course and head back home without much economic or political difficulty will be more likely to do just that—and thus turn down American citizenship.[31]

As the Americanization movement predicted, strong attachments to American institutions increase the likelihood of naturalization.[32] Younger immigrants, for instance, become acclimated to life in the United States during their formative years. They are more likely to become citizens than older immigrants. A study in southern California of newcomers who arrived during the 1970s found that only about 40 percent of Asian immigrants were citizens in 1990, but that more than two-thirds of those who were young adults in 1980 had naturalized. Latino immigrants as a whole were far less likely than Asians to naturalize—only about one out of five 1970s arrivals had become citizens by 1990. But the youngest Latinos also saw their naturalization rates double during the 1980s.[33] For immigrants generally, the odds of naturalizing appear to peak at age 39. This suggests that the perceived benefits of citizenship increase with age and then, during an immigrant's fifth decade of life, begin to drop off.[34]

Families also appear to play a strong role in the decision to naturalize. Married immigrants are 18 percent more likely to become citizens than those who are single. Immigrants with children gain a 14 percent edge over those who are not parents. These results make intuitive sense.

Marriage and children promote stability rather than mobility and increase a family's connections with some of the basic institutions of American life, such as churches and schools. Also, the U.S.-born children of immigrants are automatically U.S. citizens, which may increase the incentive of their parents to stay in America and become full members of its political community.[35] One of the biggest reasons immigrants say they want to naturalize, especially among those hitting middle age, is because they have children born in the United States. Higher levels of education, higher-skill occupations, and higher household income all correspond to higher rates of naturalization as well. In addition, immigrants receiving public assistance are less likely to become citizens than those who do not.[36]

Finally, immigrant communities play an important role in the decision to naturalize. Urban concentration and a large number of compatriots encourage citizenship, apparently because immigrants moving into these environments can draw on the experiences of their more assimilated brethren. Becoming a citizen is much easier when neighbors know the rules of naturalization and can explain them in a familiar language. Members of an immigrant group with 70 percent of their compatriots living in a central city are 77 percent more likely to become citizens than those with a 30 percent urban concentration. The size of the immigrant population living in the United States is also influential. Immigrants from countries that send lots of other newcomers are more likely to naturalize.[37]

HOW NATURALIZATION WORKS

When it comes to U.S. history and government, Americans expect foreigners to know more than high school students. Or so it would seem. To gain American citizenship, after all, immigrants must pass a civics test. The questions are not difficult—What is the Constitution? or How many terms can the president serve?—but they are fundamental to a basic understanding of how the United States functions as a political body. About 90 percent of the immigrants who actually sit for this exam at their local branch of the INS pass it and go on to naturalize successfully. When taking the same test, American high school students don't do nearly as well.

That's what Greg Gourley learned when he visited high school class-rooms in the Seattle area during the winter and spring of 1995. Gour-ley, a part-time community college instructor, administered the same exam used in the Seattle INS office to nearly 300 students. "I was nosy and curious," he says. "I wanted to see how many of our kids could do what we require of immigrants." The result? "A little over 50 percent of them passed," says Gourley. "I told the rest of them to be glad that they're native-born. Otherwise they would have to wait for months be-fore they could take another crack at becoming citizens. And even then they might fail it again."[38]

The fact that American high school students don't know much about history or government should come as no surprise to people fa-miliar with education statistics. Low standards are the rule, not the ex-ception. According to the U.S. Department of Education, nearly 6 in 10 high school students lack a basic understanding of American his-tory.[39] So it may seem ironic that the newest Americans are made to learn material fit for a Civics 101 course. You can graduate from high school without knowing anything about George Washington, appar-ently, but it's hard to become an American citizen if you can't name the first president.[40]

The challenge is to help immigrants reach the point where they can pass the naturalization exam, since passing the test represents a certain understanding of American life. The more that make it here, the closer we come to the Americanizing ideal of allowing the foreign-born to participate fully in civil society. Some of the requirements for citizen-ship are quite simple, but the farther immigrants travel down the road to naturalizing, the more complicated the demands on them become. An effort to improve civics education among the foreign-born would help more of them make it all the way.

Potential citizens must meet a few basic requirements. Others fol-low, but these three provide a starting point: (1) Applicants must be at least 18 years of age. Children automatically gain citizenship as soon as both of their parents become citizens. If one of their parents natural-izes, but not the other, the citizen-parent can make a special petition. (2) Applicants must have immigrated legally. In other words, they must be legal permanent residents. (3) Applicants must have lived in the United States for at least five years. If the applicant is married to a U.S.

citizen or has served in the U.S. armed forces, the period is three years. For all applicants, one-half of this residency must be spent physically within the United States.

Once immigrants satisfy these categories, they can make their formal application for citizenship and enter the INS bureaucracy, which has a terrible reputation for preventing people from naturalizing due to anything but actual merits. One study estimates that one-third of all applicants are neither formally approved nor denied citizenship. Instead, they remain in limbo, a bizarre category called nonapproval. Frustration with the INS and its inefficiencies leads many applicants to abandon the whole project. It becomes too much of a hassle.[41] In a study of recently naturalized Hispanics, Robert R. Alvarez reports that the "slow and often poor service" of the INS creates a "mystery of citizenship" that confuses the entire naturalization process.[42] The INS is simply plagued with problems. A division of the Department of Justice, it is "broadly dysfunctional" and "perhaps the most troubled major agency in the Federal Government," according to the *New York Times*.[43] A report issued by the Center for Equal Opportunity concluded that the INS suffers from "chronic ineffectiveness" that only "comprehensive structural reform" can begin to address.[44] For an outfit that provides so much of what immigrants want—the ability to come to America, reunite with family members, and become U.S. citizens—the INS has an unbelievably low standing among the people it purports to serve. It usually takes more than a year to complete naturalization.[45] In the view of many immigrants, the INS is not a helping hand, but an obstacle to overcome. One of the best reasons to naturalize, some say, is to make sure that they never will have to confront the INS again.

Despite these aggravations, millions succeed in naturalizing. Step one in the actual application involves paying a $95 fee and filling out the convoluted N-400 form. The N-400 can be very intimidating, especially for those who do not speak excellent English. Men, for example, must prove that they have registered for the draft. That's not a tall order for people who have saved their selective service cards or know where to call. The INS itself offers little assistance to those with questions, unless they can wait in line for several hours on a weekday. Uncertainty about what to do can cause delays, and delays can stretch for months, and months can turn into years. Naturalization is easy to put off, especially for people working more than one job and living paycheck to paycheck. Some immigrants turn to lawyers for help, although it usually costs hundreds of dollars to have an attorney shepherd a citizenship candidate through an entire naturalization. To combat these problems, many community organizations provide free or inexpensive assistance in filling out the N–400.

Naturalization applicants eventually have to demonstrate good moral character. In practical terms, this means that they must prove that they are not criminals—or at least that the federal government does not know them to be criminals. Part of the citizenship application includes submitting a complete set of fingerprints for an FBI criminal background check. While not infallible, this prevents many people from naturalizing. Major crimes—what the INS calls "crimes involving moral turpitude"—rule out naturalization. A felony conviction often blocks citizenship, but a single case of shoplifting does not. The N–400 application form also asks several questions about moral character whose answers are not verifiable: Have you ever been a habitual drunkard? or Have you ever received income from illegal gambling? They depend totally on the honesty of the applicant and stop almost nobody from becoming a citizen.

Another consideration involves political ideology. Immigrants who belong to an organization that advocates the overthrow of the U.S. government cannot become citizens. Recent affiliation with the Communist Party can halt naturalization, although frequent exceptions are made for people whose membership was involuntary. Those who were affiliated with the Nazi government of Germany also are barred, although this rule becomes more archaic every year. Finally, applicants must answer in the affirmative to this question: Do you believe in the Constitution and form of government in the U.S.? Once again, the N–400 application form covers this territory—and winds up denying naturalization to only a handful each year. Historian John Palmer Gavit illustrated the question's ineffectiveness with a classic anecdote in *Americans by Choice,* first published in 1922. In the court of a judge who insists that every naturalization applicant be familiar with the Constitution, an Irish man is ordered in the morning to come back that afternoon after reading the Constitution or having it read to him.

"Well, did you read the Constitution to him?" demanded the judge of the citizen who was acting as mentor of the petitioner.

"I did, your Honor; I read it to him—all of it."

"Is he ready to swear that he is attached to the principles of it?"

"He is, your Honor; when I got through readin' it to him he said he thought it was a blame fine Constitution."[46]

THE INTERVIEW

Once the N–400 is complete and the INS decides that the applicant has met the basic requirements of citizenship, an interview is scheduled. This is the hardest part of any citizenship application, at least in the minds of most immigrants. It is the key moment of the entire naturalization process, the place where immigrants must demonstrate a level of Americanization that not all of them can meet. One of the biggest concerns revolves around its unpredictability. Citizenship candidates do not know what to expect. Friends and family members probably have related their own experiences—and also spread a few urban myths, like the story of the guy who was deported for admitting that he once received a parking ticket or the rumor that immigrants must spit on the Mexican flag to become citizens.[47] After all of the complicated forms are filled out and filed, after a waiting period that can last more than a year, and after studying the basics of American history and government, the line between mere residency and full citizenship often comes down to the personal judgment of an INS examiner who may be in a bad mood. Almost without exception, applicants walk into the interview with their hearts racing. Some handle their nerves better than others, but all of them desperately want to succeed.

In truth, virtually every person who makes it this far will become a citizen. The interview itself is a one-on-one encounter that lasts about 15 minutes. Nobody is allowed to accompany the naturalization applicant except for a lawyer, though few actually employ one. The INS examiners' first priority is to make sure that every form in the citizenship application is complete and that the FBI criminal background check has not turned up anything unsavory. The examiner's second task is to determine their citizenship candidates' English-speaking ability. Examiners have almost complete discretion over this matter, although a skeletal set of standards exists. Naturalization applicants do not have to be fluent, but they must be able to speak, read, and write simple English. Immigrants can claim an exemption from this requirement if they meet what is known as the 50/20 rule—if they are at least 50 years old and have lived in the United States as a legal permanent resident for at least 20 years. There is a corresponding 55/15 rule as well. Exempted candidates still must pass the history and government examination, however, though they may take it in their native language.

Determining the ability to speak English is the least formal part of the English-language requirement and can be done through normal conversation. A common trick among INS examiners turns on the swear-in (to tell the truth, the whole truth, and nothing but the truth) conducted before each interview. It measures an immigrant's ability to understand spoken English. When an applicant first walks into the interviewer's office, the interviewer asks him to raise his right hand. But instead of raising his own right hand, which the interviewer must do to administer the oath, he waits for the applicant to move first. One of three things can happen. If the right hand goes up, so does the examiner's and the interview moves ahead. If the left hand shoots up—a surprisingly common reaction—it is usually due to nerves. A simple remark, "Your other right hand," typically fixes the mistake. If no hands spring up and the applicant stares blankly, there is a problem.

Assuming that this first encounter moves along without any hitches, a short conversation on just about any topic can then follow as the examiner begins to flip through the candidate's application folder. Some examiners discuss particular aspects of the N–400 with the applicant. Common questions drawn from this form include: Have you ever been a communist? Do you pay your income taxes? Have you ever claimed to be a citizen when you were not? An interviewer who wants to probe language ability more deeply might ask applicants where they work, whether their spouse is a citizen, or why they left the country at a certain time. Interviewers can determine the ability to read and write English in several different ways. Some ask the applicant to read the first few lines of the Oath of Allegiance, although the word "potentate" is a common trouble spot. Writing a simple sentence dictated by the examiner—"This is a good day." or "The cat plays with the ball."—completes the language part of the interview.

The test on U.S. history and government is next. The exams are all of a type, their content drawn from a series of short books published by the INS. Their actual administration can vary considerably among different INS districts, which are allowed to develop their own testing procedures. They may be conducted orally or in written form, for instance. Applicants who pass a fill-in-the-blank test generally are assumed to have met the English-language reading and writing requirements. The questions are simple enough: Who was the first president of the United Sates? Why do we have a holiday on the 4th of July? Who makes the laws in the United States? They also may ask applicants to name their governor or one of their senators. Some questions have several possible answers. If a test asks Who was Abraham Lincoln? an INS examiner will accept any of these responses: the 16th president, author of the Emancipation Proclamation, author of the Gettysburg Address, president during the Civil War, or the president who freed the slaves. Some of the questions are a little tricky. If asked Who elects the president? most Americans will say, "the people." The correct answer, however, is the electoral college. If asked, Which countries were our enemies during the Second World War? the response must include Italy, as well as Germany and Japan. Naming each of the 13 original colonies and identifying the Chief Justice of the Supreme Court are two more examples of questions beyond the reach of many native-born Americans. A thoroughly prepared citizenship applicant will know, among other things, the origin of the flag and its meaning, the reasons why we celebrate certain national holidays, the responsibilities of each of the three branches of government, the terms of office for the president and members of Congress, and a series of important names and dates.

Passing the exam does not require anything like a perfect score. The INS district office in Arlington, Virginia, offers a test with 12 questions. Citizenship applicants are told to answer 10 of them. Of the 10, they must have 7 correct responses. Seven out of 12 is 58 percent—not a great mark on a chemistry exam, but good enough for government work, apparently. The INS office in Seattle, which oversees the entire state of Washington, uses an oral test with 16 questions—8 in history and 8 in government. Four correct in each category earns a passing grade. The most common form of test is oral and includes 10 questions, of which 7 must be answered correctly.[48] (If these standards seem surprisingly low, keep in mind the pass rate among American high school students.) In truth, the majority of test takers do not squeak by, they do quite well. Most score in the 80 to 90 percent range. Scores of 100 percent are common.

Self-proclaimed immigrant-rights advocates often complain that the exams are excruciatingly difficult. During a symposium at Georgetown Law School, for instance, Karen Narasaki of the National Asian Pacific American Legal Consortium told the story of "an elderly Chinese woman [who] killed herself because she was so stressed out" about passing the naturalization exam. "She committed suicide rather than becoming a burden on her family. It's not as unintimidating as you might be led to believe," she said.[49] Perhaps this actually happened, but it hardly seems like an indictment of the whole naturalization system. Another panelist at the same event suggested that esoteric questions about obscure constitutional amendments are common.[50] This is simply not true. Arguments like these are made for the single purpose of watering down naturalization requirements.

Good test takers study and naturalization applicants are no different. Dozens of immigrant aid organizations distribute study guides, sometimes in a language other than English, and help applicants prepare for the exams. It is possible to acquire booklets from the INS that cover American history and government and even to practice the answers to 100 Typical Questions listed on a free INS handout.[51] Most successful applicants, however, have done more than engage in rote memorization. By and large, they have developed a basic understanding of how American political institutions function. The history questions lend themselves more easily to memorization, because the INS makes little attempt to connect facts and themes. The history questions also seem to have a few offbeat selections. They include figures like Patrick Henry and Francis Scott Key, but not Franklin Delano Roosevelt or Mark Twain. Henry and Key are clearly worth knowing, but should they take the place of Roosevelt and Twain?

The larger problem is that the exams essentially test trivia. One common question asks the length of a U.S. senator's term in office. The answer, of course, is six years. The important point, however, is not that senators serve for six years—or five years, or seven years—but that they have to face the public every so often in an election. Instead of asking about length of term, a better question might ask why elected officials have terms in the first place.

This much can be said of the exams: They cover material that every American ought to know. They also have remained remarkably consistent over time. *Naturalization Made Easy: What to Do and What to Know,* an inexpensive booklet first published in 1908, makes this clear.[52] Written by a pair of San Jose lawyers and available in updated editions through the 1920s, the pamphlet purports to be "A Book of Instruction for Aliens Wishing to Become Citizens." The authors note, "There does not seem to be any regular set of questions asked at these hearings [i.e., the interviews], the aim being to ascertain just what your standard of intelligence is, and just what you know about this country, its institutions, and its laws, and the examination may take a wide or narrow scope, depending very much upon the examining officer."[53] They go on to encourage a well-rounded education in American history and government. To that end, they provide the full text of both the Declaration of Independence and the U.S. Constitution and encourage naturalization applicants to read them.[54] They also offer seven pages of questions that applicants should be prepared to answer.[55] Virtually all of them could appear on an INS civics test tomorrow, with a few exceptions like How do Territories become States? and Who invented the cotton gin? The only questions that might get asked today, but could not have been asked at this book's time of publication, involve presidential term limits (adopted in 1951 in the 22nd Amendment), the Second World War, and Martin Luther King, Jr.

Another book, *Americanization Questionnaire,* first came out in 1924 and was available in reprints through the 1940s.[56] It offers a rather long subtitle: "Containing the Questions usually asked of Aliens applying for Citizenship Papers,—together with their Answers, and other valuable information for those interested in Americanization work." Like *Naturalization Made Easy,* it includes the Declaration of Independence and the U.S. Constitution. It also provides 55 pages of questions and answers for interview preparation. The books go into much greater detail and have the purpose of not only preparing immigrants for naturalization but also helping them adjust to life in America. A question like Why should every man carry life insurance?

probably never appeared on any naturalization exam, but this book asks it anyway.[57] Either of these books, with a small amount of revision, could prepare today's immigrants for citizenship.

The Americanization movement of the early 20th century was responsible for many of the books and pamphlets that helped immigrants become citizens. Its members also viewed the classroom as an important tool, both to teach newcomers how to speak English and to impart them with the value of citizenship. The Sons of the American Revolution described their work and the work of other Americanizers this way in 1911: "The millions of aliens in the United States are being taught what the nation stands for, what it means for them to become a part of the body politic, participating in the duties and responsibilities of active citizens in an intelligent manner."[58] Immigrant aid organizations, community colleges, and adult education programs continue to offer citizenship training courses today, but their impact on the foreign-born population is not as great as it was 80 years ago. Part of the problem is that public agencies like the INS do not encourage immigrants to enroll in citizenship education. Lack of funding is not the reason, since civics instruction is fairly low-cost—its participants can pick up the tab. Rather, they have not engaged in the types of innovative partnerships with local groups that can boost interest in naturalization, make the INS operate more efficiently, and ultimately Americanize people who might otherwise be left out of the system. An exception to this rule, however, could recently be found in Seattle, Washington. With a bit of creative thinking, it may have lessons for the entire country about how best to naturalize immigrants.

HOW NATURALIZATION CAN WORK BETTER

Justice Barbara Madsen, Acting Chief Justice of Washington State's Supreme Court, stands in the middle of a second-story room at Highline Community College. "Can you think of one more reason why Referendum 48 was not such a good idea?" she asks a group of students sitting to her left. It's a Wednesday night in November and yesterday was election day in Washington. The state voted on a number of ballot initiatives, including one that would restrict the state's ability to regulate landowners' property rights. The measure lost by a 3-to-2 margin, but Madsen has chosen to resurrect the debate in Greg Gourley's citizenship class. She has split the students into three groups. One argues in favor of the proposal, one argues against, and one—nine students meant to represent the state's nine Supreme Court justices—will issue a verdict.[59]

It's just another night for Gourley. He has become used to watching public figures perform in his citizenship classes around the Seattle area. He invites them to visit his students—each of them an immigrant applying for naturalization—and talk about what they do. "The politicians love this," laughs Gourley. "They smell votes."[60]

For three hours a night, four nights a week Gourley teaches his students what they need to know to pass the INS naturalization exam—plus a lot more. Like test takers everywhere, many naturalization applicants simply want to earn a passing grade. Gourley teaches to the test, but includes a lot of information that probably will not be on it. "Being a citizen is about more than just passing an exam," he says. One of the first lessons his students receive, for example, is about the Pledge of Allegiance. After the third or fourth week of class, everybody has memorized it. They recite it at the start of each class, even though none will be asked anything about the pledge during their naturalization interview. Gourley likes teaching the pledge for two reasons: First, at least one answer to a question on the INS test lies buried in its words. "What kind of government does the United States have?" The answer is not a representative democracy, or a constitutional democracy, or even a plain old democracy. The answer is a republic, as in "I pledge allegiance to the flag of the United States of America and to the republic for which it stands." Second, learning the pledge immediately gives these immigrants something in common with most native-born Americans. "Just about every kid in the United States knows that pledge," says Gourley. "It's important for these people who are going to be citizens to know it, too."[61]

Gourley has an objective at the start of each class. He usually wants to read through a few of the questions that might appear on the INS exam and engage his class in a call and response. He also zeroes in on a particular topic. In one class about halfway through the term, for instance, he reads the Preamble to the Constitution and distributes a copy to each student. This leads into an impromptu discussion of

American symbols. A student in the back of the room pulls out a $1 bill and asks about the eye and the pyramid. "I've heard it has something to do with secret societies," he says. Gourley, however, challenges the claim, offering a short lecture on how that symbol made its way onto American currency. He also discusses two Latin phrases that appear on the bill: *E pluribus unum* and *Novus ordo seclorum*. This information probably has never appeared on an INS exam anywhere. Gourley teaches it anyway. "I don't know if any of this will make them better Americans," says Gourley. "But I hope it does."[62]

Gourley is one of a handful of educators in the Seattle area to participate in a pilot program with the local INS office. Students who enroll in one of the 21 citizenship classes offered by community colleges, churches, and immigrant aid organizations in the region receive special consideration from the INS. They are screened for English fluency and pay a tuition of $60–$120, depending on where they learn, in addition to standard INS application fees. Instead of waiting half a year between submitting their applications and having their INS interviews, as is common in Seattle, students have the wait cut to 10 weeks. On the first two nights of class, they complete their N–400 forms. Instructors such as Gourley are experts in filling out these applications and can handle all of the tricky questions that might arise. After the second class, the forms are submitted to the INS, which immediately begins processing them. Weeks three through nine are spent in the classroom learning about citizenship and preparing for the INS exam. On the 10th week, students take the exam either by traveling as a group to the INS office next to the Kingdome in downtown Seattle or by allowing a pair of INS examiners into their classroom to proctor the test and conduct the interviews. Students who pass are sworn in as citizens immediately. In 10 weeks, they go from prospective naturalization applicants to full-fledged citizens. The initiative is enormously popular. Hundreds of immigrants have signed up on waiting lists to participate.[63]

In fiscal year 1995, Seattle's INS office processed more than twelve thousand naturalizations. About 15 percent of the applicants gained citizenship by going through the classes—an option they did not have just a few years earlier. INS District Director Richard Smith created the program—the only one like it in the country—to improve the INS's public image. "The only publicity we used to get was when a TV crew would show up outside our building and film the long lines of people huddled in the cold waiting to get in," says Cheryl Zeh, INS's senior examiner in Seattle. "But they love what we're doing with this outreach program. It's very popular."[64]

Its popularity partly comes from the fact that participants get to avoid most of the unpleasantness of dealing with INS bureaucracy. The Seattle INS office locks its doors every day at 2:30 P.M. because it cannot assist people who arrive any later. It also goes into a virtual shutdown every other Friday because lenient civil service guidelines allow federal employees to construct work schedules that make every other Friday a holiday. If the INS wants to learn why it has an unsavory reputation in the community, it need look no further than the sorts of barriers it puts between itself and the people it supposedly serves. Most of the citizenship students are simply glad to avoid spending hours trying to ask a quick question about completing their N–400s.

Students also take the classes because they have some learning to do. "The Soviets didn't teach us anything about America—nothing true, anyway," says Viktor Bozhko, a Ukrainian refugee taking a citizenship course at Lake Hills Baptist Church in Bellevue. "This is the best way for me to learn about my new home," he adds.[65] Says the Cuban-born Ramon Negrin, one of Gourley's students at Bellevue Community College: "This is a good refresher course. It's making me proud to be an American."[66] Citizenship classes have been popular in the area for years among immigrants planning to naturalize. Only the link with INS and the expedited service are new.

One of the chief virtues of the program is that its students rarely fail their interviews—the pass rate is 98 or 99 percent. That helps the INS, which does not have to devote time to correcting mistakes on application forms or scheduling reexams. Students are not calling or going to the INS office with questions, because their instructors can handle most of the problems that they face. It's as if the INS were contracting out the work and improving its efficiency. The students, after all, pay for these additional services through their tuitions. Despite this, the program is not cost-effective, says Zeh, when the INS has to send examiners out to remote locations or pay them overtime to conduct interviews at night. But once this problem is resolved—perhaps by making all students take their exams at the INS office during business hours, or charging a special fee for those who must test at night—the Seattle office may have the model for a program with national appeal. Not only does it make the INS more efficient but it also gives immigrants an education that will make them better Americans. "Some people have said that this is just a shortcut to citizenship, but these people really are getting intensive instruction in what it means to be a citizen," says Scott Winslow, Director of Continuing Education at Highline Community College.[67]

Cal Uomoto agrees. "Our goal is not to get them citizenship, but to make them citizens," he says. Uomoto is the local head of World Relief, a refugee services provider that offers classes through churches. "Our motto is 'Register once, vote twice, write thrice.' We make them registered voters right after they naturalize. Then we encourage them to vote in two elections, so they can get the hang of it. Finally, we tell them to write three letters to elected officials to become used to political communication," he says.[68] World Relief teacher Bob Salisbury, for example, has his students write letters to the president. "When they get a response—and they always do—it's very exciting for them, especially those who are just starting to learn about democracy," he says.[69]

These citizenship courses deepen immigrants' understanding of U.S. history and government. They turn borderline naturalization applicants like Linda Wai—who barely became a citizen—into testers who ace their exams. They also can bring new people into the system by instilling those who otherwise would hesitate to apply with the knowledge and confidence they need to pass. Even immigrants who probably would have tested successfully without the course learn something new. Receiving 20 to 30 hours of citizenship instruction over 10 weeks would teach something to just about anybody, from a thoroughly assimilated immigrant to a well-educated native. The INS has neither the resources nor the capability to offer a full-blown citizenship education program to all the immigrants who might profit from one. Fortunately, as the Seattle experiment shows, private groups and local agencies can pick up the slack in a way that actually makes the INS more efficient, by providing the immigration service with candidates whose credentials are in perfect order.

According to the Center for Civic Education, "Education has a civic mission: to prepare informed, rational, humane, and participating citizens committed to the values and principles of American constitutional democracy."[70] This mission is doubly important for immigrants, most of whom cannot fall back on childhood stories about patriot Nathan Hale's regret that he had "but one life to give" for his country, or Abraham Lincoln's determination that government "of the people, by the people, and for the people shall not perish from the earth." Yet they must learn such stories, for this is the stuff of which citizens—citizens of a nation dedicated to a proposition—are made. Benjamin Franklin once remarked that our Constitution offers Americans "a republic—if you can keep it." Turning immigrants into citizens, into Americans who cherish both their freedoms and their responsibilities, may be the surest way to keep this republic safe through the ages.

CEREMONY

Rex Tung taps the heel of his foot and chews his thumbnail. "I want to make clear to people that I'm an American citizen. I want to prove myself to them," he says in a flash of confidence as he fidgets in his seat and waits to take his oath of citizenship. Tung came to the United States from Taiwan as a 17-year-old in 1984. He will soon graduate from George Mason University with a master's degree in international business.[71]

About a dozen feet to Tung's left sits Raul Vallejos, motionless. A tall man from Peru, his knees knock into the row of seats before him. "I've lived here so long—since 1980," says Vallejos, an accountant who married an American. "My children are here. It's about time I became a citizen."[72]

Tung and Vallejos both live in Fairfax County, Virginia. They never have met before and probably never will meet again. But on this October morning, they sit beside each other waiting for their citizenship ceremony to begin. More than 500 other citizenship candidates from 82 countries join them in a dimly lit high school auditorium just a few miles south of the Capital Beltway. Friends and family sit and stand in the back of the big room, pointing, waving, and taking pictures. One walks up and down an aisle with a video camera, sweeping its gaze over a crowd of men in suits and women in dresses.

Everybody stands quietly as a color guard from the county police department marches to the front of the auditorium. When the Holms Middle School Choir starts the national anthem, most of the audience either sings or hums along. Next comes a series of three short speeches, all heavy on civic boosterism and loaded with references to freedom and opportunity. Two of the speakers call America a nation of immigrants and cite the Statue of Liberty. One refers to Ellis Island. "Because of people like you, we'll continue to be the greatest nation in the history of mankind," says INS District Director William J. Carroll in his thick Brooklyn accent, right before launching into a story about his Italian grandfather. "Love your country and it will love you back," says the head of the local chapter of the Daughters of the American Revolution, which will give a small American flag to every new citizen at the end of the ceremony.

After the speeches, Carroll returns to the podium and reads the name of every country of origin represented in the auditorium, starting with Afghanistan and ending with Vietnam. Citizenship candidates stand when they hear their homeland called. The patriotic sentiment that has marked the ceremony so far comes to a close. The mood turns official and solemn. "Raise your right hand and repeat after me," says Carroll. Everyone obeys and recites the Oath of Allegiance, which includes no words about freedom or opportunity, only duty:

> I hereby declare, on oath, that I absolutely and entirely renounce and abjure all allegiance and fidelity to any foreign prince, potentate, state or sovereignty, of whom or which I have heretofore been a subject or a citizen; that I will support and defend the Constitution and the laws of the United States of America against all enemies, foreign and domestic; that I will bear true faith and allegiance to the same; that I will bear arms on behalf of the United States when required by law; that I will perform noncombatant service in the Armed Forces of the United States when required by the law; that I will perform work of national importance under civilian direction when required by law; and that I take this obligation freely without any mental reservation or purpose of evasion; so help me God.[73]

Carroll pauses for a moment, peering into the silent audience. A baby cries out in the back of the room. "Congratulations, you're Americans."

Chapter 8

THE FAILURE OF
BILINGUAL EDUCATION

Students march into Nora Kato's second-grade class after morning recess and take their seats. Reading is next on the agenda in room A4—a 35-minute lesson on pronouncing words with a double *e*, such as *feed*, *kneel*, and *meet*. Every day, language is one of the most important subjects taught at Willmore Elementary School in Westminster, California. More than 90 percent of its students are Hispanic or Vietnamese, and most do not speak English as their first language. The fact that so many of Kato's second-graders speak it well is testimony to the school's heavy emphasis on English acquisition.

But it's not always a smooth road. Right before Kato begins her lesson, she pulls a pair of Vietnamese girls away from their desks and asks them to sit at a table in the back of the room. As she leads the rest of the class in phonics, teaching assistant Cuong Truong works with the two girls. He quietly reads from a picture book called *Farmer Duck*. That's not the only difference. Kato speaks to her class entirely in English. She is a good teacher with 28 years of experience. Truong, however, reads in Vietnamese. He never uses a word of English, even though the story includes text in both English and Vietnamese. The two girls are new to the United States, so it's understandable that they would have trouble in a room full of fluent English-speakers. Yet they do not develop their English skills this morning. Teaching English is not in Truong's job description. Like several other aides on campus, he spends a few hours each morning talking to students in their native language. The girls do not even learn to say the word *duck* in English. They never even hear it spoken to them.

They will probably do all right in the long run. Willmore's principal and most of its teachers are committed to helping their kids learn English. But it's a struggle, as state bureaucrats hassle the school district over its lack of a full-fledged bilingual education program that stresses native-language maintenance. At the start of the 1995–96 school year, in fact, Willmore was forced to set up two Spanish-language classrooms against its will. The state government also compelled teachers to take rudimentary foreign-language classes to keep their certification. There's a sense of creeping regulation at Willmore, a sense that a school on the front lines of Americanization is seeing the state slowly pressure it to move where it does not want to go. The teachers persevere and most of the kids hear plenty of English, but it is not at all clear that things will stay this way. "A lot of people want us to go in a different direction," said Harvey Morris, Willmore's principal.

Willmore Elementary and its staff appreciate the importance of teaching English to immigrant children.[1] Yet Willmore and many schools like it are slowly falling under the influence of bureaucrats, who have abandoned pedagogy for ideology because they are far removed from the daily concerns of educating kids. Thousands of children in the United States do not hear more than a few words of English during the entire school day. Thousands more hear some English, but not enough—certainly not enough to approach anything like fluency. Much of this crisis comes directly out of federal policy, which has coerced hundreds of school districts around the country to adopt teaching programs that value students' native-language maintenance over their English acquisition. This crisis chiefly derives from the fact that schools have lost faith in a core tenet of Americanization: non-English-speaking children must learn English. This is a major failing, since so much of the success that immigrant children will have in life depends on how well they learn English in the schools. Education is important for everybody, but for immigrant kids it takes on special meaning because they have so much more to learn. They need to develop English language skills as quickly as possible. This is partly because elementary students are at a perfect age for gaining another language with relative ease.[2] It is also because they are expected to perform academically as well as their English-speaking peers. Nobody will give them any breaks for being immigrants.

During the first part of this century, the public schools considered teaching English to immigrant children one of their most important functions. Education historian Diane Ravitch rightly warns against buying into the "popular myth that the public schools had single-handedly transformed immigrant children into achieving citizens."[3] Many other assimilating pressures were at work on this earlier genera-tion of immigrants, and it took more than the schools to get the job done. But schools are critical, and far too many educators do not think that the public schools should even try to help turn immigrants into Americans through language training. Josué M. González of Colum-bia University's Teachers College, for instance, writes in *Reinventing Urban Education* that "Spanish should no longer be regarded as a 'for-eign' language."[4] Some reinvention. Because of this attitude, thou-sands of children do not learn to communicate well in English. A revived Americanization movement would refuse to disable immi-grant children through poor language training or see them trapped in linguistic ghettos. We know that these kids are capable of learning English, and we know how to teach it to them. Now we only have to do it.

ENGLISH IN AMERICA

If the American identity is based on a proposition, then where does a cultural characteristic like the English language fit in? For starters, it oc-cupies a somewhat uneasy place within the American identity because it does not contribute to national self-definition in as meaningful a way as the Declaration of Independence or the U.S. Constitution do. Eng-lish does not reinforce American exceptionalism; it is either the most popular or the official language of many countries, among them Aus-tralia, Belize, Canada, India, Ireland, Jamaica, Namibia, Pakistan, South Africa, and Zimbabwe. As the language of global commerce, it is undeniably the most popular second language in the world. There is nothing intrinsically special about the fact that Americans speak it.

None of this is to say that English does not matter. Quite the contrary, it matters a great deal. It matters because it is our common language. Roughly 97 percent of American households include English speakers, according to the 1990 Census. (And the vast majority of the 3 percent that do not speak English are made up of recent immigrants who are busy learning it and whose U.S.-born children will grow up understanding it.) No nation is complete without a culture, not even a nation that dedicates itself to a proposition. The English language is without question a vital part of American national culture. Once again, there is nothing intrinsically special about it—except that it is ours.

The American founders understood the tremendous need for a common language. In 1751, Benjamin Franklin asked "Why should Pennsylvania, founded by the English, become a Colony of *Aliens,* who will shortly be so numerous as to Germanize us instead of our Anglifying them, and will never adopt our Language or Customs?"[5] John Marshall, who became Chief Justice of the Supreme Court in 1801, spoke to similar concerns:"The tendency . . . to preserve a sameness of language throughout our own wide spreading country, that alone would be an object worthy of public attention."[6] The Founders did not follow a strict English-only policy from the beginning. In the 1770s, the Continental Congress printed German translations of some of its proceedings, including the Articles of Confederation, to win German-speaking Americans' commitment to the cause of independence. French translations also were printed in a futile attempt to draw Quebec into the Union. After the adoption of the Constitution, however, the United States began to look much less favorably on state-sponsored bilingualism. In early 1795, Congress refused a motion to print all federal laws in German as well as in English. A popular myth, promulgated by German-friendly historians, says that the proposal lost by only a single vote. Yet as Dennis Baron has shown, the yeas and neas of the vote were not actually recorded. Nevertheless, the legend of German almost becoming a quasi-official language of the United States persists to this day.[7]

Several times during the 19th century, Congress rejected proposals to print laws and other government documents in German. In 1810, it voted down a petition from Michigan for French translations. Congress understood that a common language was a vital part of American nationhood. "Great inconvenience and confusion might result from having two separate texts for the same law, susceptible, as they necessarily would be from the imperfection of all languages, of different and perhaps opposite interpretations," it noted.[8] The federal government also delayed statehood for both Michigan and New Mexico out of concern that too many residents did not speak English. Michigan, after all, was originally settled by the French. (*Detroit* is a French word.) Most of present-day New Mexico was acquired in 1848 after the war with Mexico (and a sliver of it came with the Gadsden Purchase in 1853), and so the majority of its people spoke Spanish for some time after that.

If the principles of American nationhood were to be fully understood, Congress seemed to say on several occasions, then citizens must understand them in the same language—English. Of course, the United States clearly could live with some level of linguistic diversity. The Founders did not make any reference to language in the Constitution. Over the years, federal laws have mandated English in only a handful of circumstances, and then for narrow purposes: naturalization, air-traffic control, and product labels, for instance. Local governments have a great deal of freedom when it comes to language policy. Although 23 states have made English their official language, many services remain available to people who do not know a word of it. Non-English speakers in California (where English has been the official language since 1986) can dial 911 and talk to an operator in their native tongue. This service is available in literally scores of different languages.

Despite this liberalism on the local level, the United States has a need for a common language—a need amply fulfilled by English. Some people argue that the federal government should go ahead and ensure English its rightful place by formally proclaiming it the official language of the United States.[9] Yet it probably makes no difference whether or not the federal government makes English its official language. If Congress passed a law that declared Icelandic the official language, just about every American would continue speaking English anyway. What Congress says matters much less than what Congress does. One of the most significant dangers to Americanization is the fact that government has gotten into the business of promoting the retention of immigrants' native languages, often at the expense of their learning English. This actively blocks immigrants from participation in the country's common language and threatens to create non-English-speaking enclaves of people who cannot communicate with their fellow citizens. It is certainly possible for the United States to sustain some level of linguistic variation. The challenge of Americanization is not to stamp out foreign languages, but to guarantee that all Americans—native-born and foreign-born—can involve themselves in the common language of their democracy. That means English.

LINGUISTIC AMERICANIZATION

About 2.3 million school-age children in the United States were labeled as Limited English Proficient (LEP) in 1990.[10] They make up just over 5 percent of all children between the ages of 5 and 18. Although less than half are immigrants, the vast majority come from immigrant-headed households. And like immigrants generally, LEP students are highly concentrated in just a few places: California, Florida, Illinois, New Jersey, New York, and Texas are home to 72 percent of them.[11] Spanish is the mother tongue of 73 percent of them, followed by Vietnamese at 3.9 percent. No other language group makes up more than 2 percent of the LEP population.[12] Because of this, bilingual education is almost completely a Spanish-language phenomenon. With a few exceptions—the Chinese of San Francisco and the Haitians of New York City, for example—non-English-speaking students are not placed in bilingual education programs. Generally they are dropped into mainstream classes, where they might receive some special help but must learn English quickly, as a matter of necessity. For Spanish-speakers, however, the situation is different. They are much more likely to become eligible for a bilingual program that values native language preservation as much as English acquisition.

A study of immigrants in southern California shows how rapidly Americanization can occur for the youngest immigrants. Only about 22 percent of foreign-born Latinos spoke English very well in 1990. Among Latino immigrants between the ages of 5 and 14 when they arrived in the United States during the 1970s, however, about 70 percent spoke English very well in 1990. Asians showed a similar trend—39 percent of all Asian immigrants could speak English very well. Among those who had arrived between 5 and 14, however, the rate was more than 80 percent. Older cohorts for Latinos and Asians showed progress, but not nearly as much. Among immigrants aged 15–24 on arrival, about 30 percent of Latinos and 60 percent of Asians spoke English very well. For both groups, English-speaking ability declined with age. The youngest immigrants consistently made the largest gains in English language acquisition.[13] A survey of nearly 3,000 second-generation children in Miami and Ft. Lauderdale found that overwhelming majorities of Cuban-, Haitian-, and Nicaraguan-American youngsters preferred English to another language. According to the researchers, "what is at risk is the preservation of the languages spoken by immigrant parents"—not English.[14]

Given these numbers and figures, perhaps no institution has so much opportunity to do so much Americanizing as the schools. Children are young and impressionable when they enter kindergarten. For the next 13 years, schools have a unique chance to make their mark. Everything they teach—from the Pledge of Allegiance to proficiency in English—will have an enormous bearing on how their students fare in the United States. If the schools miss their opportunity, un-Americanized children grow up to become un-Americanized adults—at which point their Americanization becomes much more difficult and unlikely. The key is to reach people when they are young, when it is possible to make a big difference in their lives. Children have not fully socialized into any particular way of life, not even the culture of their parents. So introducing them to American customs, mores, and traditions—especially the English language—can have an enormous influence. Adults may forever struggle with the transition into American life, but children adapt easily. For immigrant kids, Americanization is no harder than growing up. After a few years they can seem no less American than someone with a family tree that stretches back to the *Mayflower.* They are technically members of the foreign-born first-generation, but they come closer to the assimilated habits of second-generation Americans. Korean immigrants like to split the difference. They have coined an interesting, computer-age term for such children: the "1.5 generation."

Immigrant families always have had to balance the competing aims of assimilation and tradition. This gives rise to an uncomfortable tension. On the one hand, immigrant parents want their children to learn what they need to know to succeed in the United States. They especially want them to become fluent in English. Parents often also want their children to learn about their heritage, including the ability to speak a language other than English. Too much Americanization can create family problems, especially if grandparent and grandchild cannot hold a simple conversation for want of a common tongue. The over-Americanized child also may gain the ability as well as some incentive to stray from home. A common complaint among immigrant parents is that for all of the wonderful freedoms and opportunities America offers, their children grow into people with whom they are at least somewhat unfamiliar. It is not that parent and child fail to love and respect each other, but that Americanization can create cultural clashes that would not have existed absent migration to the United States. These can involve everything from a failure to keep traditional religious observations to differences in opinion about the economic role of women in society. Language has the potential to make delicate situations even more fragile, especially if—as is often the case—children come to prefer English to the language they first heard their parents speak to them.

Policymakers do not have much business telling parents how to raise their children, and this rule applies as much to immigrant as native families. The question of children and language training becomes a public issue, however, when it arises in the public schools. Unlike today, schools during the first part of the 20th century had no problem stressing the importance of English acquisition. They, too, faced a large population of students who spoke little or no English. In 1911, the U.S. Immigration Commission reported that of all children enrolled in school, 58 percent had at least one immigrant parent. This was the national average. In some places, the rate was even higher. In Chicago, 67 percent had foreign-born fathers. In New York City, it was 72 percent.[15] Educators viewed English-language training as their most important duty to immigrant children. In his 1920 book *Schooling the Immigrant*, the superintendent of public schools in Boston, Frank V. Thompson, cited the "need of a common language" and noted that "the school can be the most important force in reducing materially the large degree of ignorance of our language among the foreign-born."[16]

The Americanizers made ample use of this powerful institution. Indeed, compulsory attendance laws partly grew out of the Americanization movement, which saw them as a good way of getting school-age children who could not speak English into the classroom.[17] The Americanizers did not pay as much attention to K–12 education as they did to adult education, mainly because they considered the importance of English instruction for children so obvious it was hardly worth mentioning. But when they did talk about it, they made it clear that English acquisition was a priority. "We furnish special classes sometimes for non-English-speaking children, but we do so merely for the purpose of enabling these children to enter the regular classes without delay," wrote Thompson.[18] Americanizers also linked language to citizenship. Children had to learn English if they hoped to become full participants in American democratic life. The "degree of [immigrants'] Americanization and their comprehension of American ideals and customs is often directly related to their command of the English language," wrote Thompson.[19]

Since Americanization was ultimately a strategy of inclusion rather than exclusion, Thompson was careful not to denigrate the native culture or language of immigrant children. "The assumption of a virtue inherent in the native by reason of his being an American, and of lack of it in the immigrant, may turn out to be an error in both respects," he wrote in his book.[20] But none of this took away from the immigrant's need to learn English, and the Americanizers used the public schools to promote English fluency among foreign-born children. They did not consider it the public's responsibility to preserve any immigrant's native culture. Indeed, the very idea of public schools assigning themselves such a task would have seemed ridiculous. For one thing, dozens of cultures were coming together in the classroom, each of them richly different. But more important, public schools could not possibly convey anything other than a cursory and artificial understanding of life in other countries. Culture has to begin at home, and that is where Americanizers wisely choose to leave it. Immigrant families took it on themselves to pass down their heritage to later generations. This often involved setting up after-school language lessons and Saturday classes, attending a certain kind of church or synagogue, and celebrating particular holidays. But it did not involve using public education as a tool for cultural preservation. It was privately inspired, and therefore authentic. The function of public schools was to equip children with what they would need to know to succeed in the United States. And that meant English-language fluency.

Today, this once unshakable faith in the importance of English acquisition has nearly collapsed among professional educators, although not among a public that still supports the goal of helping non-English-speaking children learn to communicate in the language of their new home. In a 1993 poll, 62 percent of Americans called for "teaching the children English at a more intense level." Only 22 percent said that "bilingual education is needed to maintain the native language of these children and enhance their self-esteem."[21] It has not collapsed among immigrants or Hispanics, either. They understand why their children need to learn English better than anybody. In a survey of Hispanic parents, 81 percent said that their children's academic courses should be taught in English rather than Spanish.[22] Yet single-minded dedication to English-language acquisition has fallen apart among many elites. Educators and politicians pay lip service to the virtue of learning English, but a disturbing number of them do not hold it as a conviction. In many places, native-language maintenance is now considered as vital as English acquisition. Bizarre ideologies have also worked their way into the picture. Bilingual education theorist Jim Cummins considers native-language training an important part of overcoming "institutionalized racism" and "Anglo-conformity."[23] The ramifications can be shocking. When Richard Bernstein of the *New York Times* visited San Fernando Elementary School in California, he heard so much Spanish that he compared his experience to traveling in a foreign country. "This could just as well be Mexico City or San Salvador, Grenada or Seville," he wrote.[24] Immigrant children sometimes succeed in spite of bilingual education, but far too often they fail because of it. There may be no better example of an American institution mis-serving its immigrant population than a bilingual education program that refuses to teach English.

PATHWAYS TO ENGLISH

There are dozens of different approaches to teaching English to children who do not speak it, each with its own name: Transitional Bilingual Education, Developmental Bilingual Education, English as a Second Language (ESL), Sheltered English, Structured Immersion, and Submersion. Each provides a different answer to the same question: How much of their native language must students hear to learn English? The question is peculiar, since common sense would dictate that English learners should hear as much English as possible, perhaps with a modest amount of special assistance when they first set out. If English constantly surrounds them, then they begin to absorb it almost automatically. ESL instruction, for instance, integrates LEP children with native-English speakers. Teachers may use special learning strategies to cope with the English learners, or these students may be pulled out of the classroom for up to an hour each day to receive assistance. Individual ESL programs vary in their particulars from place to place, but all subscribe to the idea that immersing students in the English language helps them learn it quickly and well.

Over the last two or three decades, however, common sense has not guided English-language instruction in the schools. In fact, federal policy has encouraged—and sometimes forced—school districts around the country to adopt bilingual education programs in which non-English-speaking students can receive as little as 45 minutes of English instruction per day. Education consultant Robert E. Rossier describes the logic this way: "In order for children to learn English, it is better for them to hear less English than to hear more English."[25] Supporters of bilingual education commonly say that the purpose of the program is to help children learn English. That was the original intent of federal laws supporting bilingual education, as well as of the many state laws that were passed in the 1970s and 1980s. Whenever Congress holds hearings on bilingual education, politicians of all stripes usually fall over each other proclaiming the importance of English. But learning English is not the only goal. In fact, bilingual education also supports a second outcome: native-language preservation. James J. Lyons, head of the National Association of Bilingual Education—a teacher union and lobbying organization with headquarters in Washington, D.C.—says that without native-language maintenance, children face "the risk of grave psychological harm." Worse still, he said, "they are being taught to disrespect their parents."[26] Given such dire scenarios, the goal of native-language preservation has come to eclipse the goal of English acquisition in many schools.

The theory of bilingual education—considered as a transitional approach to English acquisition, rather than an agenda of native-language maintenance—rests on three principles: Developing a first language well can help children learn a second language more effectively; students who are taught academic subjects in their native language will not fall behind in their studies while they learn a second language; and delaying the start of a second language until the age of eight or nine will avoid confusion and the threat of failing to become literate in any language, let alone two.[27] On this last point, some linguists argue that although children can pick up conversational skills in a second language fairly early, it takes five to seven years to develop a full understanding of it. The corollary is that young limited-English students will not be able to grasp abstract concepts in anything but their mother tongue.[28] Learning in a foreign language becomes imperative, and it crowds out time for English acquisition. The proponents of bilingual education say that English abilities will develop over time. "If kids aren't literate in their own language, how can they become literate in English?" asked Celina Quirindongo, a bilingual/special education teacher at King Middle School in Boston. Others, however, are not so sure.

Rosalie Pedalino Porter was a kindergarten teacher in bilingual education for five years in Springfield, Massachusetts. In 1980, she became director of bilingual education in Newton, Massachusetts—a position she held for 10 years. When she first started her career, Porter was completely dedicated to the principle of native-language maintenance. Over time, however, she began to question her own classroom practices: "Often I found that as I spoke in Spanish, they [her students] answered in English. *'Juan, que color es este?'* I would ask, as I pointed to a green box. 'Green' (pronounced 'grin') would be Juan's reply. So, I would correct him, *'Verde,'* and he would say again, 'Green.' In the early years I followed the curriculum and taught all subjects in Spanish, but I came to feel that I was going about things the wrong way around, as if I were deliberately holding back the learning of English."[29]

That is, in fact, what happens: Bilingual education teachers deliberately hold back the learning of English. In Boston's Russell Elementary School, Consuelo Ryan teaches her class of first graders almost entirely in Spanish. She occasionally orders a direction in English—"Freeze! Let me see your eyes" or "Put all of your papers away for me"—but she delivers nearly all of her academic lessons in Spanish. Storytime is in Spanish, too. Her students know some English. But they pick it up mainly from television and their peers, not educators. According to just about anybody who spends much time around limited-English children, oral skills develop rapidly. But reading and writing are much more difficult. Ryan does not even attempt it. "They get no formal reading or writing in English until the second grade," she says. "I have to make sure that they read well in their native language."[30] Elena Rivas, a fourth-grade bilingual teacher at Russell, says that she switches back and forth between the two languages about evenly.[31] Students in bilingual education at Russell are kept on a curriculum appropriate to their grade level, except for reading and writing English. Josefina Rodriguez, a third-grade bilingual teacher, says that her best students finish the third-grade reading subject matter (in English) suited for kids just starting the third grade.[32] In other words, her best students are exactly one year behind schedule.

When Rodriguez produces a print-out of students in Russell's bilingual program, it is not hard to find a child who has spent four years in bilingual education and reads English at the 8th percentile or a fifth-year student who is at the 13th percentile—another way of saying 92 percent and 87 percent of all Boston students read English better, respectively. That may not be the best measure of what these children really know, but it does suggest that kids in bilingual programs are clumped near the bottom of the heap when it comes to their English-reading ability. Perhaps this is to be expected, since they are struggling to learn a new language. Perhaps this is also the wrong expectation, since it does not expect much of them. Children often perform very well when they are challenged, and sometimes the youngest of them provide the biggest surprises. Yet at Russell, bilingual education can last a long time. The city suggests that children move into regular classes after three years, but never enforces this rule. "I try not to mainstream my kids because the bilingual program here is so strong," says Rodriguez.[33]

Archie Walsh, Russell's principal and a 43-year veteran of Boston schools, supports the theory of bilingual education but worries about how it functions in practice. "There's no question they learn English in their bilingual classes," he says. "But it's definitely possible to go from kindergarten through the 12th grade in the bilingual program." Parents are to blame some of the time, according to Walsh. Many of them want their children to stay in bilingual education for as long as possible, even after teachers have recommended that they move out. Walsh also complains that he is overregulated. The school board caps regular elementary school classes at 28. If Walsh hears of a student in bilingual education who is ready to move into a regular classroom, the caps can prevent him from making the switch. "If I had a kid who was ready to go right now, I might not be able to accommodate him," he says. "That's a shame."[34]

The gap in English ability between bilingual education students and others can linger for years. Teachers at Boston's King Middle School say that students in the bilingual program read and write in English at two or three years behind their grade level. Part of the problem is that the middle school must accept older students who are new to the country and did not have a chance to pick up any English when they were younger. That is only part of the problem. Students in bilingual education also can sink into a sort of complacency. "The main goal is to make them feel at home," says Celina Quirindongo, a bilingual teacher at King.[35] But according to another teacher at King (who asked not to be named), they can feel too much at home: "Those kids in bilingual education get addicted to the native-language support. Some of them have been in the program for six or seven years. They should get in and get out. And it makes no sense to me that any native-born kid should be in bilingual education at all."[36] Sonyan Wong, an ESL teacher at King, agrees. "I really believe in the bilingual program, but many Hispanic parents have become too comfortable with it. They think it is meant to continue their cultural heritage. That's wrong, that's not the purpose," she said. Wong is an immigrant from China who learned English in American schools. Although she can still speak her native tongue, she prefers English. Her children speak English as their first language, but she has enrolled them in after-school classes for proper instruction in Chinese.[37]

To criticize bilingual education is not to criticize bilingualism. Knowing two languages is of course better than knowing one. But knowing one well is better than knowing two poorly. And if students in the United States are going to master one language but not another, the schools would be wise to teach them English. Professional linguists like to point out that no one language is inherently superior to another language. Perhaps this is so, but the point exists in a vacuum, outside any kind of social context. Schools must believe without reservation that fluency in English will dramatically improve their students' ability to succeed in the United States. English might not be a better language than Spanish, but in America it's much more useful—as just about any immigrant will admit.

Bilingual speakers often refer to their ability to think in their second language. In other words, they become so comfortable with it that they do not require any kind of translation, either from another person or in their own minds. "To cross over this linguistic frontier should be the goal of all second language learners just as it should be one of the primary objectives of our schools to help all LEP students to achieve this level of linguistic competence," writes Rossier.[38] In *Forked Tongue: The Politics of Bilingual Education*, Porter recommends five steps for helping children learn English:

1. Provide as much time as possible to use and practice English.
2. Provide appropriate English subject matter for classroom work to enhance both language learning and academic achievement. Math is a good starting point because of the controlled vocabulary.
3. Promote rapid language learning and early integration with English-speaking classmates.
4. Discard the practice of instruction by translation and encourage students to think in English.
5. Make students feel both challenged and self-confident.[39]

Porter draws upon her experience as a classroom teacher in coming up with these five steps that almost seem like truisms. Yet scores of academics continue to argue against her commonsense prescriptions. When they discover poor results—bilingual education students who do not learn English as well as they could or should—they usually concoct excuses.

One theorist who is a strong supporter of bilingual education, however, has broached the subject with disarming honesty. In *Mirror of Language: The Debate on Bilingualism*, Kenji Hakuta makes this stunning admission: "There is a sober truth that even the ardent advocate of bilingual education would not deny. Evaluation studies of the effectiveness of bilingual education in improving either English or math scores have not been overwhelmingly in favor of bilingual education. To be sure, there are programs that have been highly effective, but not very many. . . . An awkward tension blankets the lack of empirical demonstration of the success of bilingual education programs. Someone promised bacon, but it's not there.[40]

So how did it get this way?

THE ORIGINS OF BILINGUAL ED

Not every American school at every point in U.S. history has used English as the primary language of instruction. German settlers in Philadelphia operated schools in their native language as early as 1694.[41] As more German immigrants arrived on American shores, German-language instruction spread around the country, especially in the Midwest during the 19th century. Cincinnati operated the most vigorous German-language program in the schools. An 1840 law called on the city "to provide a number of German Schools under some duly qualified teachers for the instruction of such youth as desire to learn the German language or the German and English languages together."[42] Most of the schools were bilingual, and at times they enrolled over half of the city's student population, peaking at more than 18,000 children in 1886.[43] Other city and state governments took a markedly different path. Chicago and Wisconsin, for instance, barred teaching in a language other than English for both public and parochial schools.[44] By 1923, 34 states required elementary instruction in English.[45]

What Cincinnati, Chicago, and Wisconsin all shared in common, however, was the idea of local control. The people of Cincinnati were free to make their own decisions about language in the schools of Cincinnati. The people of Chicago also were allowed to rule their schools, even though they made a fundamentally different choice. Today, bilingual education has been forced on hundreds of school districts by the federal government. During the 1970s and 1980s, it cruised over local control like a steamroller. Bilingual education became widespread not because school districts wanted it—although some did, to be sure—but because federal bureaucrats thought they knew what was best for non-English-speaking kids. There was a certain logic to what they did, but they were motivated primarily by a blind faith in native-language instruction.

In 1960, the United States appeared to face an educational crisis among its 7 million Hispanic residents. Many of them were native-born, but Spanish remained their dominant language. Up to half of all Mexican American and Puerto Rican children entering the first grade during this period could not speak English. The majority of these children were thrown into "sink or swim" classes in which they struggled to pick up a new language without any special assistance. A handful flourished in this environment, but far too many did not. Some of them were simply labeled retarded and shipped off to classes for the mentally disabled. Estimates of Hispanic dropout rates were imprecise but a few liberal estimates ranged as high as 80 percent.[46] Subsequent research suggested that the dropout problem had more to do with faulty statistics than with a flaw in the American system of education. Much of the data on Hispanics was based on people who had been born and raised in Mexico, rather than those who had gone through American schools.[47] At the time the problem was real and it seemed pressing. Educators, for their part, were not sure how to solve it.

A program in Miami offered a glimmer of hope. After Fidel Castro seized power in Cuba in 1959, thousands of mostly middle-class Cubans fled from communist tyranny. They hurried across the Straits of Florida and swarmed into Dade County, where their children entered the public schools. Because most of these refugees considered themselves exiles who would return home after Castro fell from power within a few years, they wanted their children to learn Spanish. Only that language would prepare them for their future lives in Cuba. So that's what Cuban parents asked the schools to provide—an education that would maintain their children's Spanish-speaking abilities. Starting in the early 1960s, Cuban students in Miami spent half the day learning in English, the other half in Spanish. A 1966 evaluation found that children enrolled in these classes performed no worse and occasionally better than comparable children in monolingual English schools. Educators wondered if a similar approach would help other Hispanic youngsters improve their academic standing.[48]

A more important historical trend was also at work. The push for bilingual education came at the height of a national crusade to guarantee equal protection under the law for all Americans, regardless of their skin color or ethnic heritage. The country was in the mood to right its wrongs and to try its hand at creating economic and educational opportunities for minority groups by passing new laws, often on the federal level. The most compelling arguments for expanded civil rights were made in favor of blacks, who were victims of state-sponsored discrimination well into the 1960s, especially in the South. School desegregation was a major part of the civil rights agenda. In the Supreme Court's landmark ruling in the 1954 *Brown* v. *Board of Education* case, Chief Justice Earl Warren built his argument around a notion of self-esteem. He wrote that "To separate [children] from others of similar age and qualifications solely because of their race generates a feeling of inferiority as to their status in the community that may affect their hearts and minds in a way unlikely ever to be undone."[49]

The *Brown* decision marked the beginning of the end of schoolhouse segregation, something that had affected Hispanic children only at the margins.[50] By granting legitimacy to arguments based on self-esteem, it inadvertently opened the door for a new kind of classroom regimentation—one that Hispanic activists eagerly supported. If segregated black children suffered from a battered psychology, they asked, then couldn't low self-esteem also help explain the poor academic performance of Mexican-American children? American public schools, after all, tried to exorcise their Hispanic heritage, especially their language. And what could be more damaging to a child's self-esteem? "In its effort to 'assimilate' all its charges," said one Mexican-American activist in 1968 during congressional testimony on bilingual education, "the American school assaulted . . . the cultural identity of the child . . . it developed in the child a haunting ambivalence of language, of culture, of ethnicity, and of personal self-affirmation." The National Education Association agreed. It contended that too many educators wanted Hispanic children to grow up as Anglos: "This he cannot do except by denying himself and his family and his forbears, a form of masochism which no society should demand of its children."[51]

Here was a difficult political trick for Hispanic activists—how to capitalize on the moral urgency of the civil rights movement but reverse its inspiring logic of integration. The drive for desegregating the schools was essentially about bringing different races together in the classroom. Spanish-language training, however, would set groups apart. Yet the bilingual education advocates pulled it off. According to the day's conventional wisdom, Hispanic children needed to have their language and culture affirmed in the classroom. If only Hispanic children were taught in their native tongue and about their native culture, went the thinking, their dropout rate would shrink, their test scores would rise, and the education gap would vanish. Separation became the vogue. "I think we have discarded the philosophy of the melting pot," said Congressman James H. Scheuer of New York. "We have a new concept of the value of enhancing, fortifying, and protecting [people's] differences, the very differences that make our country [so] vital."[52]

Just as the walls of legal segregation came tumbling down for African-American children, Congress laid the groundwork for a new de facto segregation of Hispanic students. In 1968, it passed the Bilingual Education Act as Title VII of the Elementary and Secondary Education Act—a $7.5 million program to help poor Mexican-American children become literate in English. Senator Ralph Yarborough, a liberal Democrat from Texas, first introduced the legislation in 1967. The goal, he said, was "not to keep any specific language alive. It is not the purpose of the bill to create pockets of different languages through the country . . . not to stamp out the mother tongue and not to try to make their mother tongue the dominant language, but just to try to make those children fully literate in English."[53] It seemed harmless, but the precise wording was so vague that it meant different things to different people. In fairness, many lawmakers thought that they were voting for a program that would help children learn English. But their careless approach actually had created a constituency of bureaucrats, teachers, and political operatives dedicated to native language preservation. Once enacted, bilingual education would become a rallying cry. According to Linda Chavez, "Within two years of Senator Yarborough's modest proposal to help Hispanic children learn English, bilingual education had become the symbol of ethnic solidarity for Hispanic activists."[54] Bilingual education was not just a method, but a strongly held belief. Its devotees harbored intense feelings in support of it. As Diane Ravitch has noted, "career bilingual educators are committed to their method as a philosophy, not as a technique for language instruction. The difference is this: Techniques are subject to evaluation, which may cause them to be revised or discarded; philosophies are not."[55]

Like so much of the civil rights legislation that came out of the 1960s, federal sponsorship of bilingual education would grow in size and scope over the years. A deadly combination of judicial activism and bureaucratic decree even turned bilingual education into a federally mandated right. This development traces back to the 1964 Civil Rights Act, which prevented schools from discriminating on the basis of national origin. In 1970, the Office of Civil Rights (OCR) in the Department of Health, Education, and Welfare issued new rules to cover school districts with student enrollments containing more than 5 percent Hispanic or other national-origin minority groups. These school districts would have to offer affirmative steps to help non-English-speaking children gain access to an education. If they refused to comply, they put all of their federal funding in jeopardy.

The OCR guidelines came under Supreme Court scrutiny in the 1974 *Lau* v. *Nichols* case. A group of Chinese-American parents had filed suit against the San Francisco school district for excluding their children from receiving the special language assistance that the district provided to some but not all of its Chinese student population. In its decision, the court said any student without English-speaking ability was entitled to help. "There is no equality of treatment merely by providing students with the same facilities, textbooks, teachers, and curriculum; for students who do not understand English are effectively foreclosed from any meaningful education," it declared. The Court did not endorse any particular approach to teaching non-English-speaking students, but its enforcers did. OCR used the ruling in 1975 to create a set of "Lau remedies" for what it now called "language minority" children, borrowing the new name rather obviously from the civil rights movement. OCR rejected ESL instruction for elementary and middle-school students and instead insisted on a full-blown program of native-language maintenance. ESL is a necessary component of bilingual education, said the new guidelines, but an ESL program by itself "*is not* appropriate."[56] Children who came from a home in which English was not the primary language had to have a bilingual education—even if the children themselves spoke English. The Lau remedies thus handed schools the task of determining every child's home language, preferred language, and first language. As Chavez notes acidly, "Whether children from such homes understood English and could benefit from an English-language school curriculum was more or less irrelevant under the Lau remedies."[57] The Lau remedies, ironically, are not law and have never been published in the *Federal Register.*[58]

Only a handful of districts actively challenged the new bilingual orthodoxy, and OCR required each of them to demonstrate that another methodological approach was superior. Most simply went along with the orders handed down from Washington. Between 1975 and 1980, OCR negotiated some 500 plans with local school districts to require bilingual education.[59] Several states made bilingual education even more pervasive when they passed their own laws in support of the program. The courts became involved, too. One federal court ruled that Hispanic students in New Mexico were entitled to bilingual education under the equal protection clause of the 14th Amendment to the Constitution. In New York, a federal district court struck down a program that provided ESL instruction for Hispanic children on the grounds that they needed to learn more about their culture. Other courts were instrumental in writing consent decrees between school districts and ethnic activists who demanded bilingual education.[60]

By 1974, federal bilingual education programs had expanded to serve nearly three hundred forty thousand students with more than $58 million.[61] That same year, Congress renewed and broadened its support of bilingual education. The key change involved income levels. Previously, only low-income children were eligible to receive federal funds for bilingual education. Now, middle-class Hispanic children, many of whom spoke only English, were covered. Senator Ted Kennedy was a driving force behind the reauthorization. "When the United States is the fifth largest Spanish-speaking country in the world and when a near majority of people in this hemisphere speak Spanish," he said, "surely our educational system should not be designed so that it destroys the language and the culture of children from Spanish-speaking backgrounds."[62] By 1978, the federal government was spending $135 million each year on bilingual education.[63]

THE BILINGUAL BOONDOGGLE

When the first performance reviews of bilingual education came in, bilingual education was beginning to look like a major disappointment. In 1978, the American Institutes for Research (AIR), under contract from the government, released a comprehensive study of all the Spanish-language bilingual programs that had been operating for at least four years. Its work covered eleven thousand five hundred students in 286 classrooms. Its chief findings ravaged the bilingual education establishment: Most of the children enrolled already spoke English, those who did need to learn English were not learning it, and most of the programs were designed to preserve the students' native language rather than prepare them for mainstream classes. Less than one-third of the students placed in bilingual courses were there because they needed English language instruction, and only 16 percent of them were monolingual in Spanish. A survey of program directors showed that 86 percent of them admitted to keeping students in bilingual classes after they had learned English. Some evidence suggested that the bilingual students were slightly more proficient in mathematics, but on an absolute scale they were still far behind national norms. The only academic subject in which they clearly outperformed their mainstreamed peers was Spanish. In short, the report showed that bilingual education programs were perverting the intent of policymakers who had envisioned students receiving a helpful transition into English-language classes, preventing the rapid acquisition of English, and holding children back from academic achievement.[64]

Noel Epstein got to the heart of the matter in a monograph published in 1977 by George Washington University. Bilingual education, he said, promoted "the idea that the federal government should finance and promote pupil attachments to their ethnic languages and histories."[65] This was a radical departure from the past, when foreign languages in the schools were entirely a product of local control. But now outsiders were all too often dictating the means by which school districts would educate their students. In his conclusion, Epstein quoted a question that anthropologist Margaret Mead asked after studying Pacific Islanders during the 1950s: "How often has our Western attempt to preserve native dress, old customs, different styles of architecture, to respect native laws and customs, been only a thin disguise over an un-willingness to admit a people, newly entering into our way of life, to full participation in the culture which we claim to value so highly?"[66] Were American policymakers dooming non-English-speaking chil-dren—especially Hispanics—to a dead-end education?

More evidence would soon suggest that they were. In 1981, Keith Baker and Adriana de Kanter—both career employees with the De-partment of Education—evaluated more than 300 studies of bilingual education from around the world in the most extensive review of liter-ature on the subject ever undertaken. "The case for the effectiveness of transitional bilingual education is so weak that exclusive reliance on this instructional method is clearly not justified," they concluded. The vast majority of the studies were fundamentally flawed and ruled scien-tifically unsound by the authors. Of the ones Baker and de Kanter ac-cepted, 11 showed positive outcomes in teaching English for students enrolled in bilingual education, 15 showed no difference, and 5 showed a negative effect.[67] They argued for more local control of language in-struction. "The literature makes a compelling case that special pro-grams in schools can improve the achievement of language-minority children. There is no evidence, however, that any specific program should be either legislated or preferred by the federal government."[68]

Interest began to spread outside of educational circles. In 1981, Pres-ident Ronald Reagan departed from the prepared text of a speech: "It is absolutely wrong and against American concept to have a bilingual ed-ucation program that is now openly, admittedly dedicated to preserv-ing their native language and never getting them adequate in English so they can go out and into the job market."[69] In 1985, the Heritage Foundation's *Policy Review* magazine labeled federal oversight of the country's bilingual education programs to be one of the ten worst reg-ulations in American government.[70]

The bilingual education establishment essentially ignored these con-cerns and became more entrenched. During congressional hearings in 1978, John C. Molina, director of the Office of Bilingual Education, proved impervious to any evidence that contradicted his total faith in bilingual education. "You can't evaluate a bilingual education pro-gram," he said. "It is a philosophy and management."[71] Evaluations, therefore, should serve the political purpose of advancing the cause of native-language instruction. If they do not meet this standard, they are suppressed. Education consultant Robert E. Rossier, for example, accused the Los Angeles school district of having "detoured, hidden, and actually aborted studies that would compare other methods with bilingual instruction."[72] The results of these studies apparently would have raised concerns about what bilingual education actually does. Antonio J. Califa, the head of OCR during the Carter administration, didn't even want to discuss bilingual education as bilingual education: "It's not even appropriate to classify these as bilingual regulations," he said. "A better description is equal educational opportunity regulations."[73]

Much to the chagrin of bilingual education activists, hearings in 1978 on the Bilingual Education Act paid some attention to the new critiques of bilingual education, especially the AIR study. In its reauthorization, Congress placed several new restrictions on how federal dollars could be used to support bilingual education, including a provision limiting the English-speaking children who could be enrolled in non-English programs to 40 percent. Yet the rate at which school districts actually complied with these new requirements is an open question. Bilingual education remained a rising juggernaut. State governments became more supportive of native-language maintenance. By 1983, 12 of them had mandated bilingual education and 12 others permitted it.[74] In the late 1980s, 30 states expressly permitted native-language instruction.[75]

Nobody knows how much money is spent each year on bilingual education because the sources of education funding around the country are so diffuse—more than 9 out of every 10 education dollars are spent on the state and local level. Language-minority students clearly cost more money to educate, since they receive special instruction and their teachers are often paid a higher salary than those who deal with English-only students. The American Legislative Exchange Council (ALEC) says that bilingual education cost $5.5 billion nationwide in the 1991–92 school year, but this figure is probably too high. ALEC looked at the total sum of educating language-minority students, not the differential cost.[76] Students always cost money, no matter what language they speak. The relevant economic question is this: How much more money does it cost to send children through a native-language maintenance program? No group or individual has attempted to make an accurate estimation. Organizations that might have the capability and resources to collect the necessary data—such as the bilingual teachers union—have a vested interest in not publicizing the fact that bilingual education students come with a high price tag. The figure is clearly staggering. The federal government alone spent roughly $250 million on bilingual education in 1995.[77] By the end of fiscal year 1995, the federal government had underwritten $3.5 billion worth of bilingual education since its inception.[78] In 1997, President Bill Clinton and Congress increased the annual appropriation to more than $300 million each year.

Money, however, is not the primary consideration. The real question is how well English learners are learning English today. Unfortunately, in some places the evidence is quite troubling.

GOTHAMGATE

Public schools in New York City provide one of the most stunning examples of an entire school system failing to help its non-English-speaking students adjust to life in the United States. The citywide bilingual education program and its willful inability to teach English quickly and effectively is almost entirely to blame. It is as if the Tower of Babel were rebuilt in Manhattan and the schools chancellor had rented office space in it.

Consider the following statements, each taken from a sworn affidavit used in a lawsuit filed by Hispanic parents against the city schools:

- "My son is confused between English and Spanish. I am unhappy with what he has learned in the bilingual education program," said Maria Cruz.[79]

- "I personally met one of [my grandson's] teachers in the bilingual program who did not speak any English. We and other people we know were pressured into keeping our children in bilingual education by school officials. We were told that because my grandson has a Spanish last name, he should remain in bilingual classes," said Ada Jimenez.[80]

- "My son is in the third grade in a bilingual special education program. . . . My son cannot read or write in English or in Spanish," said Juana Zarzuela.[81]

- "When my son was in third grade in the bilingual program, his teacher told me that he spoke neither English nor Spanish. He repeated third grade, this time in an all-English class. He is now learning well in the English third-grade class," said Maria Espinal.[82]

Each of these parents has sued the New York City schools over the sorry state of the language program. These Hispanic parents believe, in the finest tradition of Americanization, that public schools ought to teach students how to speak, read, and write in English. The fact that their children are essentially sentenced to the program is disturbing. The carefree attitude taken by school administrators is even more so. Worst of all, however, the problem is confined essentially to Hispanics. Children with Hispanic surnames are treated differently than other students.

Spread across five boroughs and 32 semi-autonomous districts, the city's schools enroll more than 1 million children. Students speak at least 167 languages.[83] It is not difficult to find a single schoolhouse that contains children from 50 countries. But these massive numbers and incredible diversity are not why the city serves its immigrant students poorly. In fact, this current challenge is not intrinsically different than the one New York schools faced during the last great wave of immigration. Today, the schools are much less concerned with whether children learn English and much more devoted to the idea of native-language maintenance.

A New York State law says that "English shall be the language of instruction" in public schools. The state does permit a three-year transitional program of bilingual education so that students can gain their footing before moving into regular classes. It also allows an extension of this three-year limit "with respect to individual pupils . . . to a period not in excess of six years." A series of complicated court orders, consent decrees, OCR rulings, and state board of education decisions, however, have flouted the state's intentions. They have effectively pushed enormous numbers of Hispanic students into bilingual education programs with slight reference to the children's linguistic abilities or needs. Today, New York City students with Hispanic surnames who score below the 40th percentile on a standardized English test are automatically enrolled in bilingual programs. The problem is that on this type of exam, student scores do not show how much knowledge they have of English, but rather how much knowledge they have *relative to other students.* If 100 students take the exam, 40 of them must score below the 40th percentile—even if they perform well on an absolute scale. Thus, New York City essentially guarantees that large numbers of Hispanic-surnamed students are assigned to the bilingual program, no matter what language they speak or how well. Many of them actually are more comfortable with English than Spanish. Some are barely conversant in what is now dubbed their native language.[84]

Being assigned to the bilingual program is like receiving a life sentence. "Children get locked in," said Lourdes Arroyo, a bilingual educator in East Harlem.[85] They rarely manage to escape. When the nonprofit Public Education Association issued its Consumer Guide to middle schools in Brooklyn, it condemned the practice of bilingual education again and again. One school "repeatedly places native English speakers in bilingual classes because they have Hispanic surnames. When parents attempt to take their children out of bilingual education, many bilingual teachers and school administrators accuse them of not respecting their cultural heritage." During the 1993–94 academic year, less than 1 percent of this school's students actually tested out of the bilingual program.[86] At another nearby middle school, "parents say they are unable to have their children removed from the bilingual program and returned to regular education classes even though parents have the right to do so."[87] In an editorial, the *New York Times* compared the city's regime of bilingual education to a prison.[88]

A longitudinal study of limited-English students conducted by the city's Board of Education highlights the ineffectiveness of bilingual education. Students enrolled in ESL courses, which emphasize English acquisition, worked their way into mainstream classes much more rapidly than children placed in the bilingual program. Among students who entered the schools in kindergarten, almost 80 percent of ESL students and just over half of bilingual education students moved into regular classrooms within three years. Among students who entered in the second grade, exit rates were two-thirds and 22 percent, respectively. The pattern is clear: ESL offers much better opportunities than bilingual education to graduate to English-language instruction. It also offers a greater chance of success. ESL graduates regularly outperformed bilingual education graduates after they were placed in regular classes. Yet the school system continues to insist on bilingual education, at least for many of its Hispanic youngsters.[89] Worse yet, education officials have treated parents' skepticism with nothing but contempt. When a group called Mothers of Multicultural English (MOME) organized in New York City to demand that their children receive an education in English, rather than be placed in a bilingual program, school board member Luis Reyes blasted them as a bunch of ignorant yahoos. MOME, he said, is "a carbuncle on the ass of progress."[90]

Bilingual education has an equally bad track record outside of New York City. A study in Connecticut found that only 6 percent of eleven thousand bilingual education students graduated after they were deemed to be proficient in English.[91] In a comprehensive examination of research data, Christine H. Rossell and Keith Baker have shown that bilingual education programs are almost never better for children— and often worse—than doing nothing at all. A 1997 National Research Council report found that teaching LEP children in their native language has no long-term benefits and teaching kids to read in English first does not have negative consequences.[92] In other words, most kids are no worse off for entering a sink or swim environment than a program focusing on their native language.[93] In early 1996, a group of Los Angeles parents protested bilingual education by keeping their children out of school. "A lot of us want our kids to learn Spanish so they can write to their grandpas," said Lenin Lopez, one of the boycotters. "But I want my children to learn English so they won't have the problems that I've had."[94]

One common complaint among parents who have children in bilingual education programs surrounds the quality of teachers. Many do not speak English very well themselves, leading to worries over how well they can teach it to their charges. Some school districts, citing a labor shortage, have recruited employees in Mexico, Puerto Rico, and Spain.[95] *Phi Delta Kappan* magazine reports that "the Mexican government has a substantial presence in educational programs in many parts of the U.S." Much of this influence comes by way of Spanish-language textbooks and other instructional materials. In 1993, Mexico presented Los Angeles public schools with a gift of forty thousand Spanish-language textbooks.[96] According to a study by the General Accounting

Office, one school district even uses material from Cuba—a country with which the United States does not even have diplomatic relations.[97] But the foreign influence also involves personnel. More than two dozen Mexican teachers participate in Chicago's bilingual-education programs, for example. Mexican educators are regular participants at conventions sponsored by the National Association of Bilingual Education (NABE), as well as conventions put on by NABE's California and Texas branches.[98] At a recent meeting for the Texas Association of Bilingual Education, both the Mexican and American flags adorned the stage. Attendees, who were mainly school teachers and administrators, stood as the national anthems of both countries were sung. Not everybody in the crowd agreed with this behavior. "I stood, out of respect, when the Mexican anthem was played," said Odilia Leal, the bilingual coordinator for Temple Independent School District. "But I think we should just sing the U.S. anthem. My father, who was born in Mexico, taught me that the United States, not Mexico, is my country," she said.[99] This dissenting view, however, is a minority opinion among bilingual education radicals. At NABE's 1995 annual conference, Eugene Garcia, head of bilingual education at the U.S. Department of Education, declared that "the border for many is nonexistent. For me, for intellectual reasons, that border shall be nonexistent."[100]

For most people, of course, borders still have meaning. Immigrants come to the United States—crossing borders to get here—because it is the United States. They strive to succeed in it, and they desperately want their children to prosper. They understand that this means learning English. They may not always agree on the proper way of teaching it to them, but every day the empirical case for maximum exposure to English at a young age becomes stronger. The best news for Americanizers, however, is that bilingual education may already have seen its high water mark. Its dangerous influence may soon begin to recede. And a Pennsylvania school district provides a compelling example of how Americanization can return to the classroom.

THE LITTLE TOWN OF BETHLEHEM

School superintendent Thomas J. Doluisio was puzzled. His Bethlehem, Pennsylvania, district had an elaborate program of Spanish-language classes for its large population of Spanish-speaking children. Proponents of bilingual education said that this would help Hispanic children adjust when they moved on to English-only classes, which they were supposed to do after three years. But it was not working. Hispanic students lagged behind their peers in test scores, reading levels, and graduation rates.[101]

"Our college-track courses were lily-white," said Doluisio. "Our remedial courses were filled with Puerto Rican kids. And the ability to speak English explained most of the difference."

What went wrong?

Doluisio found out in a 1992 meeting with his district's elementary-school principals. The short answer: seven years. That is how long it was taking a typical student in the bilingual program to move into regular classes taught in English. Bethlehem had effectively established an English-second policy, thanks to educators who considered native-language training of primary importance.

"I was flabbergasted," says Doluisio, who became head of the school district in 1986. But more than that, he was angry. And then he got busy.

Within a year, Doluisio led a stunning transformation of Bethlehem's language policy. His district became one of only a handful in the country to reverse course on bilingual education. Bethlehem's Spanish-speaking students are immersed in English-speaking classrooms, where they hear almost nothing but English. The school switched policies only after a bitter struggle that divided the community along racial and ethnic lines. Thanks to Doluisio's leadership, the benefits of English immersion are starting to show and the naysayers are starting to change their minds. Bethlehem provides a stirring example of how other school districts can challenge the bilingual education orthodoxy—and win.

The Bethlehem Area School District is Pennsylvania's fifth largest, serving thirteen thousand children. About 10 percent of its students cannot speak English well, and of these, 86 percent speak Spanish in their homes. Most of these kids are Puerto Rican, although immigrants from Central and South America make up a growing part of the Spanish-speaking population.

Before the 1993–94 school year, Bethlehem was fully committed to bilingual education and its goal of teaching students in their native language before they moved into regular classrooms. English-speakers and immigrant children who did not speak Spanish attended their neighborhood schools. But the school district essentially segregated its Spanish-speaking students, bussing them to one of two elementary schools. Marvine Elementary, north of the Lehigh River, took kindergarten through second grade. Donegan Elementary, on the south side of town, took third through fifth grade. There was little time for English at these segregated schools. Spanish was the language of the classroom, the lunchroom, and the playground.

Most bilingual educators say that native-language instruction is the surest road to English fluency, since it makes for an easier transition. But this defies common sense, according to Doluisio. "You can't teach kids how to swim by giving them a lecture at the side of the pool," he says. "They've got to get wet, and maybe even take in a little bit of water. Our job as educators is to keep them afloat, to make sure they don't go under."

After learning about bilingual education's dismal exit rates in Bethlehem, Doluisio began to investigate the program more intently. He quickly uncovered more outrages. "There were kindergartners—five-year-olds who were at the perfect age to start learning a new language—who did not hear a single word of English all day long," says Doluisio. "I probably should have known that this sort of thing was going on, but nobody told me. I had to discover it for myself."

The more he learned, the less he liked. "I really believe in my heart that we were hurting these kids," says Doluisio. "I started to see a connection between bilingual education and Latino dropout rates. Not a total connection, to be sure. But definitely a connection."

As soon as Doluisio decided that bilingual education was a problem, he set out in search of a solution. He asked the district's bilingual-education director to assemble a committee to study the issue. But the majority of its members were advocates of the status quo. When it reported back to the school board in the fall of 1992, the committee said that the bilingual program was healthy and even suggested expanding it. Doluisio flew into a rage. "For the first time in my career I rejected a report that had come out of my own administration," he says.

The superintendent launched a personal crusade against this kind of complacency. He studied the literature on bilingual education carefully. "I soon learned that in this field you can find research to back up just about any political point you want to make—especially if you support bilingual education," he says. But some of the scholarship raised significant doubts.

Rosalie Pedalino Porter's scathing expose, *Forked Tongue:The Politics of Bilingual Education,* influenced him especially. Porter is a strong proponent of "time on task"—the idea that the amount of time spent learning something is the best predictor of educational achievement. In other words, students must practice English constantly if they are to learn it well. "Nothing in my fifteen years in this field—from firsthand classroom experience to concentrated research—has begun to convince me that delaying instruction in English for several years will lead to *better* learning of English and to a greater ability to study subject matter taught in English," writes Porter, who now heads the READ Institute in Amherst, Massachusetts.[102]

Doluisio examined this and other research, and decided that Bethlehem's language policy needed a complete overhaul. He convinced the school board to schedule a series of public meetings devoted to bilingual education—and to discuss its possible repeal. Community interest was so great that the board had to hold its gatherings in the Liberty High School auditorium, the district's largest. The debate split along racial and ethnic lines early on. Many Latino parents believed that the removal of bilingual education would jeopardize their children's education. Some of Doluisio's non-Hispanic supporters did not help matters when they stepped up to the microphone and made derogatory comments about Puerto Ricans. "These meetings were very heated. They were very emotional. I had to have cops in the back of the room to make sure that there was no trouble," said Doluisio. At one point, a group of Latino activists physically surrounded the school board and, led by a priest from out of town, engaged in a prayer to save Bethlehem's bilingual education program. The Pennsylvania Department of Education also criticized Doluisio's efforts. Myrna Delgado, the state's bilingual education coordinator, urged the school board to vote against the superintendent.

The tenor of the hearings weighed heavily on Doluisio, especially the ugly way in which race and ethnicity intruded. It appeared that all the Latinos were on one side, all the Anglos on another. "This was an extremely unpleasant time for me, and for everybody," says Doluisio. About midway through the controversy, however, a group of Hispanic parents contacted him. They were professionals, led by Luis A. Ramos of Pennsylvania Power and Light. "We hoped to make it clear that Latinos want their children to learn English, and that the superintendent was heading in the right direction," says Ramos, whose two children have attended Bethlehem schools. "Their support really gave me the courage to forge ahead," says Doluisio.

In February 1993, the school board voted to abolish bilingual education and adopt a districtwide plan for English immersion. The board clearly stated its goal of having "all language minority students in the district become fluent in the English language in the shortest amount of time possible to maximize their opportunity to succeed in school."[103] Everybody would attend neighborhood schools, including Spanish-speaking children, and students who required special help would receive ESL instruction several times a week. Spanish-speaking kids would spend the bulk of their time in regular classrooms listening to teachers who, in most cases, spoke virtually no Spanish. "It was our belief that if the Chinese and Russian kids could do well in a regular classroom without bilingual education, then so could the Spanish-speakers," said Rebecca Bartholomew, the principal of Lincoln Elementary.

Lincoln was one of several schools that suddenly had to confront a sizable population of students who did not speak English very well. The school board said that the immersion program had to be in place by the following September, leaving only seven months to implement a completely new plan for teaching children with limited English skills. The move upset bilingual teachers, who believed wholeheartedly in the theory of native-language maintenance. Immersion met with a lot of resistance from non-bilingual teachers as well. They were accustomed to dealing with children who would understand their most basic instructions. "In the first week of the new program, we had homeroom teachers who would tell their class to 'line up'—and half the class wouldn't understand," said Ann Goldberg, who runs the immersion program for Bethlehem. "It was really tough going at first."

"A lot of regular classroom teachers felt really incompetent, since the switch to immersion was so rapid and so complete," said Carole Schachter, an ESL teacher at Donegan who also taught in the bilingual program. "They could barely communicate with many of their students," she said. A number of teachers remain critical of the switch and especially of Doluisio, but they prefer anonymity. A 1996 program evaluation showed that almost all LEP students were making progress and many had been mainstreamed.[104]

Hispanic parents are gradually beginning to approve of the new policy. One who likes the switch is Margarita Rivas. A native of Puerto Rico, she was at first concerned about how well her four children would do in school if they did not hear much Spanish. Then, she changed her mind: "It's very important that they know how to speak English well in this country," she says. "Now they speak English better than Spanish, and they are helping me and my husband improve our English."

After the immersion program had been in place for one year, Bethlehem surveyed the parents of its Spanish-speaking students. The forms went out in two languages, since many of the parents speak no English. The results were remarkably positive. Eighty-one percent of the respondents said that their children had "progressed well academically" in the English-immersion setting. Only 7 percent said that they "did not make progress." Another 82 percent rated the new program as "good" or "very good," 12 percent called it "adequate" or "satisfactory," and only 1 percent deemed it "poor."[105]

The approval ratings have continued to remain high.[106] "My daughter is getting a good education here," says Sayda Castaneda, an immigrant from Honduras. "I don't want my daughter to forget her first language, but English is spoken in the United States."

The teachers have started to come around as well. "I was against immersion in the beginning, but I'm not nearly as critical now," said Jean Walker, a fourth-grade teacher at Donegan who has taught in Bethlehem schools for 24 years. "I didn't think I'd be able to communicate, but these kids learned English faster than I thought they would. I like immersion now. It's not perfect, but I like it," she said. A survey showed that Walker is not alone—62 percent of Bethlehem teachers said that students were making "substantial progress" in learning English after being in the program for one year. Only 13 percent said students made "little" or "no progress."[107]

Rita Hatton, a Cuban-born teacher with 20 years experience in Bethlehem, still has some reservations about immersion. A veteran of the bilingual program and now an ESL teacher at Freemansburg Elementary, she worries that her kids will lose their Spanish fluency. But she also sees rapid gains among her English learners. "At the start of the school year, some of them only spoke two or three words of English," she said. "Now they can speak it, read it, and write it pretty well." In fact, English is far and away the dominant language in her classroom. Donna West, an ESL teacher at Marvine, came to Bethlehem after the immersion program was adopted, but she had taught previously for six years in a Brownsville, Texas, bilingual program. "I like the immersion model much better," she said. "In Brownsville, the kids simply weren't becoming proficient in English. They started a lot of kids in Spanish, but they need English when they're young."

Doluisio was officially condemned at the 1994 convention of the National Association of Bilingual Education. His detractors accuse him of being driven by politics, even of riding a tide of anti-immigration sentiment. He says that his goal is to help immigrants succeed by raising expectations for their performance. "For years it was like we expected our Latino kids to learn differently, that they could not cut it in mainstream classes with the native English speakers or the kids from Asia or Poland," says Doluisio. "The results were like a self-fulfilling prophecy. But today we're saying that Latino kids are just as capable as any other group of students."

Chapter 9

AMERICANIZATION
ON THE JOB

"When I first came to America, nobody taught me how to speak English. I had to do it on my own," says Luigi Solimeo, the Italian-born owner and operator of a busy McDonald's restaurant in Flushing, New York. "I wish I had the opportunity back then to work at McDonald's. This place is a real melting pot," he adds.

Solimeo runs one of the most hectic McDonald's franchises in the New York City area. An entrance to the subway—the last stop for the No. 7 train—is a few steps from his front door and 25 bus routes let off passengers nearby. More than two thousand customers order meals here each day. The lines are always long and the seating crowded. "I can't imagine a better place to learn English," says Solimeo.

Solimeo employs 60 workers and seven managers. Most of them are immigrants, their native languages include Chinese, Korean, Spanish, Vietnamese, and Tamil (spoken in Sri Lanka). For many, McDonald's is their first job in the United States. Language barriers can be tricky for employers, but Solimeo gets by. More than that, he has a plan. He sponsors English lessons for his workers—two hours each week, with their time on the clock. Classes are held in a cramped employee lounge and in a larger space at a local senior citizens center. Solimeo also tells his managers that on-the-job English training is one of their responsibilities. Finally, he places new employees on crew shifts with more experienced compatriots. "I try to help people learn English as fast as possible. When they see that their own people have done it—sometimes the friend or relative who helped get them a job here—they want to improve themselves," he says. "We're always working toward a 100 percent English environment. That takes a lot of effort and support, and I'm doing everything I can to make it happen."[1]

A job at McDonald's—or almost any other fast-food restaurant—is regularly derided as a burger-flipping road to nowhere. That's a myth; more than half of all McDonald's corporate managers and franchise owners started out working on a crew. One out of every eight Americans has held a position at McDonald's.[2] "It's the first place kids go after babysitting and mowing lawns," says Jane Hulbert, a company spokeswoman.[3] In other words, there may be nothing more American than working beneath the golden arches. For immigrants, McDonald's is a great place to learn about basic American work habits: filling out an employment application, showing up on time, taking care of a uniform, functioning on a team, keeping things clean, dealing with customers, operating a computerized register, making change, and speaking English. Over time, they may develop more advanced skills, like checking stock levels and placing orders for the restaurant. Many native-born Americans take these abilities for granted, but millions of immigrants have had to learn each of them after their arrival and in the workplace. "We teach people team building, time management, basic math, even how to assimilate," says Allan Huston, chairman of Pizza Hut, another company that promotes Americanization on the job.[4]

PAVED WITH GOLD

The workplace is a crucible of assimilation for immigrants. Just as schools are probably the most important institutions of assimilation for immigrant children, jobs are probably the most important for adults. Most of them, after all, come to the United States looking for work. They want to improve their material condition, and they usually succeed. Something else happens, too. As they assimilate economically, they assimilate socially. In fact, social assimilation helps underwrite economic assimilation. Whether immigrants find employment mopping floors at the lowliest fast-food joint or developing antibiotics at a giant pharmaceutical corporation, their work teaches vital social and cultural skills and allows them to build human capital particular to the United States. The workplace is actually one of the most effective institutions of assimilation in American life—and probably the one least in need of Americanization-style resuscitation. It is also one place in which the government has not given itself a big role in artificially preserving the native cultures of immigrants. The most significant threat to on-the-job assimilation comes from the welfare state and its ability to keep some immigrants away from the world of work. In addition, some arms of the federal government unwisely have chosen to harass and prosecute employers who implement English-only work rules.

Despite these bad influences, there is much good news about workplace assimilation. Individual immigrants typically need several years to get on their feet, but over time and in the aggregate they become just as productive as native-born Americans. Employers are generally sensitive to the needs of their foreign-born workers. The job opportunities they provide are enormous services in themselves. They allow immigrants to earn incomes and offer a chance for them to learn about their new home. Many businesses go even further and sponsor language classes, in the best tradition of the Americanization movement.

The idea of achieving economic success in America has embedded itself in the consciousness of people around the world. In traditional Gaelic culture, *caisleáin óir*—"castles of gold"—lie to the west. Irish peasants in the 19th century began to project these visions onto the New World, especially after family remittances began pouring in.[5] The Chinese have called America *Gum Shan*—"Mountain of Gold"—ever since the Gold Rush drew thousands of Chinese to California in the 1850s.[6] *El Norte* still holds the promise of El Dorado in the Mexican imagination.[7] Striking it rich requires hard work, and very few immigrants come to the United States counting on a life of complete luxury. Some of them might, of course. "I came to America because I had heard the streets were paved with gold," remarked an Italian immigrant in 1903, "and I found three things. One: The streets were not paved with gold. Two: The streets were not paved at all. Three: I was expected to pave them."[8] Whatever their expectations, among the first things immigrants do after arrival is look for jobs.

Jobs are the number one motivation cited by immigrants themselves for making the trip. According to a *USA Today/CNN* poll of immigrants, 93 percent think that "People who work hard to better themselves can get ahead in this country." A similarly big majority, 82 percent, think that immigrants have more job opportunities in the United States than in their birth countries, and 86 percent say that their children will have more chances to work in America.[9] These attitudes translate into optimism about the economic future. In the 1995 Fannie Mae National Housing Survey, 53 percent of immigrants thought that their families' financial situation will improve in the short term, compared to 39 percent of all adults.[10] This striking sense of hopefulness bears out Thomas Sowell's claim that "Migrations tend to be selective, rather than random, in terms of skills and ambition, as well as in origins and destinations."[11] In the United States, this selection process tends to choose immigrants who are optimists, risk takers, and entrepreneurs. People who volunteer to uproot themselves from their birth countries and travel hundreds or thousands of miles across borders and oceans to succeed in America are a special breed.

Just as immigrants appreciate the value of work in their lives, so do Americans generally. They rank job skills as the most important criteria in admitting legal immigrants—more important than either saving them from political or religious persecution, allowing them to live with American relatives, or taking advantage of money they may have to invest. They also agree that immigrants "work very hard." Almost three-quarters of the public say that Asian immigrants fit this description. Nearly two-thirds say the same about Hispanic immigrants.[12] These beliefs have a firm basis in fact. The labor force participation rate among working-age male immigrants is slightly higher than that of the native population: 89 percent for immigrants and 87 percent for natives. The rate for Asian immigrants is 88 percent. And at 91 percent, working-age Mexican immigrants have the highest male labor force participation rate of any racial or ethnic group, foreign-born or native-born.[13] Immigrants make up about 10 percent of the entire American labor force and account for about 13 percent of its new entrants.[14] Between 30 and 40 percent of the annual growth in the size of the U.S.

labor force comes from recent immigrants.[15] "Work, work, work, church, school, and more work. That is the life of Haitians in this country," says Haitian immigrant Tony Garcon, a country club cook who arrived in 1980.[16] Garcon may not realize it, but he speaks for more than just Haitians.

Immigrants don't make much money when they start life in America, but their prospects improve over time. This is a key point because economic assimilation is fluid, not static. Immigrants who arrive today will not be the same group of people in five years. They will have improved their ability to speak English as well as their knowledge of the American labor market. Perhaps some of them will have gone to school. Whatever the case, the longer they live in the United States, the better they become at competing in its economy. The cultural and linguistic barriers to economic success are steep at first. Sometimes they force immigrants into unfamiliar occupations. It is not uncommon to meet a taxicab driver with a degree from a foreign university. What is uncommon, however, is to meet a taxicab driver with a degree from a foreign university who wants to drive a cab for the rest of his days. Jobs teach immigrants about America and provide those who are motivated with the means to move up and on.

The mean income in 1989 for working-age men born in the United States was $32,057, according to the 1990 Census. Among the most recent working-age male immigrants—those who arrived in 1985 or later—it was $19,966, or just 62 percent of the native level. They don't stay that low forever. The income of immigrants who came between 1975 and 1984 was $24,086. For those who entered between 1965 and 1974, it was $31,140—after living in the United States for about two decades, they had earned virtually the same income as natives. Going back further in time raises immigrant incomes even higher. The 1960–64 wave took home $35,945 in 1989. The 1950–59 cohort raked in $38,833. Pre-1950 arrivals earned $41,705. The earlier immigrants are generally older than the more recent ones, but the pattern persists even when age is held constant: The longer they stay, the higher the pay. Earnings increase sharply at first, then more slowly as the years pass. Immigrant household incomes follow a somewhat shorter path, reaching parity with natives after about 10 years.[17]

Despite these positive indicators, the question of immigrant quality percolates beneath the surface of any discussion of economic assimilation. How do today's immigrants compare to those in the past? It's an old question that often contains the presumption that the latest wave of newcomers—whether they are the Irish of the 1840s, the Poles of the 1890s, the Mexicans of the 1960s, or the Vietnamese of the 1990s—just don't stack up as well as immigrants once did.

The modern-day declinist argument runs like this: The education levels and wages of immigrants—relative to the native population—dropped between 1940 and 1980. (It recovered slightly during the 1980s.) In 1940, recent male immigrants had three-quarters of a year more schooling than native-born men. Two decades later, this edge had slipped to about four-tenths of one year. By 1980, the immigrants actually trailed the natives by about two-thirds of a year. Earnings followed the same downward path. George Borjas, a leading economist in this camp, blames most of the decline on the changing makeup of the immigrant population after 1965, when a new wave of low-skilled immigrants from undeveloped countries gained admission to the United States under the law of family preferences.[18]

There is more to the story. Long-term trends indicate that immigrant education levels are, in an absolute sense, rising. In 1960, about one-third of new immigrants had less than 8 years of schooling and just over 15 percent had 16 years or more. Today, only a quarter of recent immigrants have less than 8 years and about 30 percent have at least 16 years.[19] Native education levels over the same period rose a bit more quickly. This explains why so many critics of immigration speak of the increasing gap between native and foreign-born education levels. Each side of the immigration debate has used these numbers to make self-serving claims about the quality of today's newcomers. The truth is that both natives and immigrants have improved in recent decades, though at different paces.

There is another consideration, too. Immigrant education levels look bad in comparison to natives when 1940 becomes the historical standard, as Borjas and others choose to make it. Better baselines are available, however. The period immediately before and after the Second World War was extraordinary for many reasons. As far as immigration is concerned, it marks an era when few people actually migrated to the United States. Those who did tended to be European war refugees—primarily white-collar professionals with the financial means to escape. Their ranks included 12 Nobel prize winners and such intellectuals as Albert Einstein, Walter Gropius, Thomas Mann, Paul Tillich, and Bruno Walter.[20] Today's immigrants do not resemble this cohort so much as the huddled masses that arrived at the turn of the 20th century. Indeed, immigrant education levels relative to natives are similar during both periods. In absolute levels, of course, today's arrivals are much better off.[21]

Although many recent immigrants have low levels of education, many of them have climbed to the upper reaches of academic achievement. The foreign-born are twice as likely as the native-born to hold a Ph.D., for instance.[22] And these degrees are often in demanding fields such as math, science, and engineering. According to the 1993 National Survey of College Graduates, 23 percent of U.S. residents with a doctorate in science or engineering were immigrants, as were 28 percent of the doctoral scientists and engineers engaged in research and development.[23] More than one in four (26.4 percent) of the U.S. patents awarded in 1988 and 1994 were created by immigrants working alone or collaborating with U.S.-born coinventors.[24] Because of this phenomenon, the foreign-born are becoming an increasingly important part of the American high-technology economy.

Many immigrants, however, remain poorly educated and unskilled. This would not necessarily be a problem were it not for the existence of the welfare state and its ability to sap newcomers of their work ethic. When the Ellis Island generation of immigrants arrived in the United States, after all, they may have been poor—"Give me your tired, your poor," reads the Emma Lazarus poem—but they were not greeted by an array of failed antipoverty programs that often mire their recipients in the swamp waters of dependency. Many of them needed help from time to time, and they would find it in their families and communities. Religious groups and relief organizations also came to the rescue. If nothing seemed to work out, immigrants could turn around and return to their country of origin—not the happiest of stories, but hardly shameful.

Today, immigrants are slightly more likely than the native-born to use public assistance: 5.8 percent versus 4.5 percent, according to the

1996 Current Population Survey of the Census Bureau.[25] This is due mainly to dramatic overuse among two subgroups: refugees and the elderly. Together, they make up 21 percent of immigrants, but 41 percent of immigrant welfare users. Refugees are forced onto welfare rolls when they arrive in the United States as a matter of federal policy. This makes a certain amount of sense because refugee policy is driven almost entirely by humanitarian concerns and the refugees themselves have not always had much time to prepare for their departure. Whatever the rationale, at 13.1 percent they are almost twice as likely to use welfare as nonrefugee immigrants.[26] Elderly immigrants also have special access to welfare. They can take advantage of Supplementary Security Income (SSI), a cash assistance program for seniors. In 1994, nearly 738,000 noncitizens received SSI—a 580 percent increase over the 127,900 who used it just 12 years earlier.[27]

By factoring out refugees and the elderly, the welfare gap between immigrants and natives shrinks substantially. When the Urban Institute compared working-age, nonrefugee immigrants to working-age natives, it found that the welfare rates in 1994 were almost identical: 5.3 percent for the immigrants versus 5.1 percent for the natives. Despite this, welfare use among this group has risen since it was measured in the 1990 Census. Back then, working-age, nonrefugee immigrants were actually less likely than working-age natives to use welfare: 2.5 percent to 3.7 percent.[28] It is not yet clear whether this rise represents an emerging trend or merely the result of special circumstances peculiar to the early 1990s. These numbers bear watching.

Perhaps even one immigrant on welfare—or at least one noncitizen on welfare—is too much. Immigration is a privilege, not a right. The United States should not feel obligated to provide generous public aid to noncitizens. The problem is not that welfare for the foreign-born costs a lot of money, but that it corrodes the values that help immigrants achieve economic success in the United States. One of the most valuable qualities immigrants bring to America is their willingness to work. Many of them may be poor, but do not think of themselves as poor. They are not looking for handouts. Poor immigrants in 1994 were a good deal less likely to use public assistance than poor natives: 16 percent versus 25 percent.[29] Yet the welfare state and the culture of dependency it promulgates can easily turn striving have-nots into struggling do-nothings. The last thing the United States needs is to import a generation of people and hand them membership cards for the permanent underclass. This is the wrong kind of Americanization.

In the summer of 1996, Congress took a positive step when it passed a welfare reform law that imposes new restrictions on public aid to noncitizens. Under it, legal immigrants who have not naturalized are denied food stamps, SSI, and federal cash support for the poor, elderly, and disabled. Furthermore, state governments have the ability to limit cash welfare, Medicaid, and other forms of public assistance. Facing an election in November, President Clinton signed the bill despite vocal opposition from left-wing allies. In approving the legislation, however, he singled out the provisions for noncitizens as ones he would like to see repealed in the near future. The 1997 budget agreement restored many benefits to noncitizens, but did attempt to make distinctions between people who were in the country when the welfare law passed and those who have come since or will arrive in the future.[30] It is too early to gauge the permanence or the impact of these changes.

Perhaps no amount of wrangling over economics and welfare can reveal the whole picture of how immigrants actually fare. The most important question is not how much money they make or how many years they have gone to school, but how well they Americanize. Assimilation is about more than numbers and rates. Income and education form a part of the Americanization equation, but hardly the whole thing. No one can assign a dollar figure to the value of knowing how to speak English, at least not easily. And yet learning English is one of the central benefits of employment for immigrants.

LEARNING ENGLISH ON THE JOB

Miguel Angel Rivera came to the United States from El Salvador in 1984 and worked at a series of Chinese restaurants around Baltimore. "I didn't speak any English when I came here," he says. "I didn't need to know it because I was washing dishes and bussing tables." But he soon realized that he had to learn English if he ever wanted to become a waiter and earn tips. "You have to know English if you're going to work the floor. I started doing that and picked it up from the customers," he says. Rivera's job became a crash course in the English language. Although he has only one year of formal education—at the age of 16 in El Salvador—today he speaks fluent English. He also owns and operates Restaurante San Luis, which specializes in Chinese and Salvadoran cuisine. He opened it in a building that had been vacant for two decades. It took him years to save enough money for start-up costs, but he considers owning a small business crucial to his family's future. His customers are mostly a mix of Hispanic immigrants and native-born Anglos. "I have no problem communicating with any of them," he says.[31]

Economic assimilation ultimately hinges on social assimilation. As immigrants increase their knowledge of the American labor market and develop skills particular to it—these can include anything from the simple lessons of a McDonald's restaurant to a complex understanding of semiconductor physics—their lot improves. For most immigrants, the ability to speak English is the key to economic success. It is accessible to virtually all newcomers, regardless of their linguistic background, and probably opens more employment opportunities than any other skill that they are likely to acquire in the United States. As the case of Miguel Angel Rivera shows, it turns dishwashers into waiters and waiters into restaurant owners. One study shows that immigrants who speak English fluently earn 17 percent more income than those who do not.[32] A more recent one by the same authors suggests that the difference is 20 percent.[33] This may be a low estimate. Research on Southeast Asian refugees has found that fluent English speakers earned an average hourly wage of $14.82, compared to $5.16 for those who spoke just a few words.[34] One of the earliest investigations into this question found that native Spanish speakers who do not speak English could count on earning 15 to 40 percent less income than native Spanish speakers who were also fluent in English.[35] On top of all that, non-English speakers face limited shopping and housing opportunities, factors which may result in higher prices paid for goods and services. No matter what the actual payoff, learning English makes economic sense.

Although their children may receive the benefit of a public education, most adult immigrants learn English by osmosis—talking to people who already know it, watching television, and going to movies. Those who have no regular interaction with people who speak English may never learn it. Immigrants are much more likely to learn English if they do not live in communities filled with compatriots, for example. According to the 1990 Census, in counties with the highest concentrations of immigrants from one country, only 11 percent of the foreign-born are fluent in English. In diverse counties, English fluency among immigrants averages 74 percent.[36] It follows that informal, on-the-job interaction with native English speakers plays an important role in helping newcomers learn English, as in the case of Rivera. Some newcomers take formal approaches and enroll in English as a Second Language (ESL) courses that are often available through the adult education branches of public school districts in areas with many immigrants. In fact, ESL learners made up 51 percent of all people enrolled in adult education programs in 1992, and they received 76 percent of the hours of instruction. Virtually all of them were foreign-born.[37] The classes generally attract hordes of students and overenrollment is a chronic problem in many areas. Today's adult education system is an outgrowth of the Americanization movement's efforts to teach English to adult immigrants in the early part of the 20th century. It succeeded in part because of business backing and the belief that an English-speaking workforce would be more productive.

Employers continue to have an interest in an English-speaking workforce, especially when workers are likely to come into contact with customers and managers who do not speak their language. Many businesses have become active in helping their foreign-born staff learn the language. ESL is particularly popular in the hotel industry, as well as in customer service departments and in manufacturing. Thousands of individual ESL teachers subcontract with companies to provide English-language training to immigrant workers. Their services range from literacy-level courses for people who do not know any English to accent-reduction sessions for immigrant doctors and other professionals who interact heavily with the native-born. Several entrepreneurial ESL instructors have formed their own companies, such as California's LinguaTec and On-Site English, to cater to this market.

The Fender Guitar Company in Corona, California, offers English training in a company conference room. "We wanted to help our employees cope in the society they live in," says Doug Mills, vice president and general manager for guitar operations. "We want a better educated worker. We want to make them valuable employees at Fender and keep them happy with their jobs here," he says.[38] Many companies that have offered workplace ESL have done it with the help of federal job-training dollars. Others, however, pay out of pocket to boost their bottom line. Helping immigrants learn English, they say, makes workers more productive, improves customer relations, reduces accidents, lessens turnover, and allows companies to fill vacancies through internal promotion rather than external recruiting. "These workers used to check their brains at the door, and now they are being asked to think and give their opinion," says Vicki Efird, who teaches English to employees of Wilton Connor Packaging, a North Carolina company that packages Duracell batteries, Saran Wrap, and other products.[39]

Workplace ESL uses a different curriculum than regular ESL classes. At Fairfax Hospital in Fairfax, Virginia, Myrna Tarrant teaches her class—whose students come from three different language backgrounds and include receptionists, food preparers, cleaning staff, and operating room aides—about English pronunciation, grammar, and dictation by emphasizing vocabulary and circumstances unique to hospitals. A lesson on the present progressive tense, for example, features a clinic waiting room. Other handouts focus on medical treatment; parts of the body; and ailments, symptoms, and injuries. For homework, students must write five questions they might ask a patient.[40] "We offer the course as a benefit to employees," says Mary Anne Leitch, the hospital's employee program coordinator. "It helps them assimilate."[41]

Some businesses offer accent-reduction programs for employees who want them. Bell Atlantic, for example, lets its telecommunications personnel enroll in these courses.[42] Such training is popular among foreign-born professionals who must communicate with precision. "A person can be very competent in his field and assume that others understand him. He may have no idea that he isn't communicating clearly," said Shellie Bader, a speech therapist who runs L.A. West Speech Communication, a firm that specializes in accent reduction. "I thought I was speaking fluent English, but when I was talking with patients, they couldn't understand certain words," said Asadollah Shahideh, an allergist at William Beaumont Hospital in Royal Oak, Michigan. Since enrolling in a program offered by the hospital, he says, "I've improved a lot."[43]

Some employers choose to treat language like a dress code—they simply require English of their workers. "We insist on English around here," says Armand Dipalma, the owner of Dalma Dress Manufacturing Company in New York City. He oversees 40 workers from about a dozen different countries making upscale ladies dresses and evening wear, including pieces worn by Barbara Bush and Hillary Clinton. "I can't have two Greek girls speaking to each other across two Spanish-speakers. The Spanish girls will think they're being talked about," he says. "We don't need that kind of problem."[44] Dipalma is not the kind of boss who would fire somebody over a few stray words, but he also thinks that maintaining an English policy in his shop keeps everybody working on the same team and prevents disruptions. The employees seem content, and turnover is low. "I like working here," says Tonia Sylla, a Liberian immigrant and a sewer at Dalma since 1984.[45]

Yet the Equal Employment Opportunity Commission (EEOC), a federal civil rights agency, see things a bit differently. If a disgruntled Dalma employee were to complain about the language policy to the EEOC, Dipalma might be in trouble. In April of 1994, the EEOC forced the New York retailer Wallach's Inc. to pay more than $30,000 to a worker who claimed that an English-only rule had forced her to quit her job.[46] Indeed, the agency views many English workplace rules as violations of the 1964 Civil Rights Act and its ban on national-origin discrimination. According to EEOC guidelines written in 1970 and still in place today, English rules "create an atmosphere of inferiority, isolation, and intimidation based on national origin which could result in a discriminatory working environment." The EEOC permits language standards only if an employer can justify them as a "business necessity."[47] It has developed 22 pages of detailed rules and examples describing when it thinks employers should and should not be allowed to require English on the job.[48] The agency has sued 13 employers over the last decade; 10 of them have abandoned their English rules as a result.[49] An unknown number of language lawsuits proceed without EEOC involvement.

Although the EEOC rules are not popular with employers, they have many cheerleaders among ethnic and civil rights activists. "When you deny someone the right to speak another language you are depriving them of a key part of their heritage," said Ed Chen, a lawyer for the American Civil Liberties Union.[50] Perhaps, except that workers are always free to find jobs elsewhere if they have domineering supervisors. Kathryn K. Imahara of the Asian Pacific American Legal Center, however, goes even further. She compares English rules to slavery, telling the *Business and Society Review* that "there is nothing new about efforts to suppress use of another language. Southern plantation owners in the 18th century stamped out the use of African dialects by their slaves."[51]

The courts have not offered much guidance on the question of how much authority employers have over the language of their employees. In the public sector, they apparently have next to none. The Ninth Circuit Court of Appeals gave state employees the right to use whatever language they please in performing their official duties. A medical malpractice claims adjuster in Arizona wanted not only to conduct interviews in Spanish, but also to file her reports in that language—even though she knew that her supervisor could not read them. The court said that "Language is by definition speech, and the regulation of any language is the regulation of speech." More to the point, perhaps, it said that its ruling acted out of a concern "for the diverse and multicultural character of our society."[52]

Private sector employers have been given a bit more leeway, but there is still a good deal of confusion—and expensive litigation—over what kind of language rules businesses can make for their workers. Spun Steak, a small meatpacking company in San Francisco, wrote an English work rule in 1990 after its president heard complaints from a black and an Asian employee who allegedly overheard racist remarks spoken in Spanish by a pair of Hispanic colleagues. In response, management issued a new policy: "Only English will be spoken in connection with work. During lunch, breaks, and employees' own time, they are obviously free to speak Spanish if they wish."[53] About 60 percent of Spun Steak employees spoke Spanish as their first language and English fluency was not a hiring requirement.[54]

An employee sued, saying that the new work rule violated her civil rights. A federal judge agreed and declared the rule illegal. But the Ninth Circuit overturned this decision. The Supreme Court let the ruling stand in 1994, even though the Clinton administration had urged it to reverse the decision because language in the workplace is "an issue of great national importance to national origin minorities."[55] The

EEOC, for its part, essentially chose to ignore the ruling because the Ninth Circuit has jurisdiction over only nine states.[56] In every other state, the EEOC continues to enforce a bureaucratic guideline that the Supreme Court implicitly has repudiated.

The EEOC's interference with work rules requiring English, as well as the court's vague and contradictory interpretations of their legality, is not a front-burner issue for the typical American employer. Most businesses that enforce language policies probably will never have to face investigations or lawsuits. Employees who initiate lawsuits may use the issue as nothing more than a way to attack old bosses for what are actually separate grievances. The simple fact that public-sector institutions have entered the picture in this fashion is troubling. Employers ought to have the right to monitor their workers' on-the-job behavior. If they decide, rightly or wrongly, that an English rule is a business necessity for them, then they ought to be given the benefit of any doubt. Mistreated workers will look for positions elsewhere, and no employer will want to drive away capable and experienced help over petty matters. The problem is that governmental agents are doing more to restrain effective organs of assimilation than encourage them. In the heyday of the Americanization movement, employers worked in cooperation with the government to encourage immigrants to learn English. Now they are on their own. Perhaps that would be enough—if the government in turn would leave them alone.

HANDS-ON AMERICANIZATION: TWO CASE STUDIES

As a private agent of assimilation, the workplace is one of the most effective institutions of Americanization. But it can work on immigrants in very different ways. The adaptation experience of a Mexican-born construction worker will appear to have little in common with that of a doctor raised in Pakistan. Although they head toward similar end points—economic well-being, English-speaking ability, a commitment to the American way of life—the paths that take them there cover different terrain. To show how employment can accommodate Americanization in varying ways, two case studies conclude this chapter. The first examines blue-collar assimilation in a small Kansas community with a large foreign-born population. The second looks at Silicon Valley, the heart of the U.S. technology industry and a magnet for highly educated immigrants.

Hacking It on the Kill Floor: Case Study 1

Garden City, Kansas, is the last place in America where you would expect to find immigrants. A four-hour drive west of Wichita, this town of twenty-seven thousand sits almost exactly halfway between the Atlantic and Pacific Oceans. A steady flow of settlers following the Santa Fe Trail rolled past this place on the Arkansas River during the second half of the 19th century. Their 125-year-old wagon ruts are still visible in a few spots where farmers haven't plowed them away. Railroads came next, then a highway. "Anybody who has made the coast-to-coast journey across America, whether by train, or by car, has probably passed through Garden City," wrote Truman Capote, "but it is reasonable to assume that few travelers remember the event."[57] Capote's own occasion for visiting—and remembering—came while he researched *In Cold Blood,* his best-selling account of the 1959 Clutter family murder. The locals don't like to talk much about that incident, but it has become an instant point of reference for outsiders.

Today Garden City is a destination. Its settlers are primarily Mexican immigrants and Southeast Asian refugees attracted by the prospect of jobs in the world's largest meatpacking plant, owned by IBP and located a few miles northwest of town. Monfort, a division of ConAgra, also runs a factory just to the southeast. Together, the two companies directly employ almost five thousand people and indirectly support thousands of others who work in nearby feed lots, agriculture manufacturing, and irrigation. They have the capacity to slaughter ten thousand cattle each day and buy $2 billion in livestock each year. Thanks to such high levels of productivity, the city population has increased by one-third over the last 12 years. "Most of that growth is a result of the meat industry," says Robert M. Halloran, city manager since 1987 and a resident since 1974.[58]

The IBP plant opened in 1980 as part of an industrywide move away from unionized packing cities and into the rural towns of right-to-work states. Sioux City, Dakota City, and Garden City replaced Chicago, St. Louis, and Des Moines as centers of the trade. Southwest Kansas became particularly attractive in the 1960s because of an agricultural development called center-pivot irrigation. It allowed farmers to tap the Ogallala Aquifer and grow cattle feed.[59] This combination of water and feed grain revolutionized the regional economy. Feed yards sprang up everywhere. Garden City residents suddenly found themselves living in a cow town.

The newly crowned cow town lacked only one thing when IBP arrived: a labor supply. Unemployment hovered around 3 percent as the company started to hire 2,850 employees for the plant. "At first, IBP tried to recruit all our people from Nebraska and Iowa," said Duane West, a retired lawyer and former city commissioner. "But the simple fact is that this is hard, tough work, and farm boys just didn't want it."[60]

Immigrants did. They flocked to the area, eager to accept jobs with few takers. That seemed appropriate, as the meatpacking industry has relied on immigrant muscle since slaughterhouses dominated Chicago's southside at the turn of the century. Back then, native-born workers avoided the plants for the same reasons they do today. Upton Sinclair's socialist novel *The Jungle* was not far off the mark when it described the toil of Packingtown laborers in 1906: "There are learned people who can tell you out of the statistics that beef boners make forty cents an hour, but, perhaps, these people have never looked into a beef boner's hands."[61] Sinclair is best known for his account of how greedy capitalists shipped contaminated meat to unsuspecting consumers, but these passages are only several pages of a full-length book. *The Jungle* is basically the story of a Lithuanian immigrant's struggle to survive in a world he does not understand.

Immigrants are naturals for meatpacking factories because working in one does not demand much in the way of English-speaking ability. Jobs on the kill floor—the place where living cattle become boxed beef in less than an hour—are low-skilled and routine. They require virtually no verbal communication with other workers. Training for a spot on the disassembly line usually consists of little more than watching somebody perform the task for a day or two and then taking over. Teacher and student do not have to speak with each other. Even if they want to, the loud and constant drone of chains and saws makes conversation difficult. Many employees actually wear earplugs to keep down the noise.

The other aspect of meatpacking factory labor that suits immigrants, of course, is the hard and unpleasant work. "That meatpacking work is pure hell," says Suzanne Murphrey, who teaches English as a Second Language in Garden City.[62] In the words of University of Kansas anthropologist Donald Stull, it involves "killing, bleeding, skinning, gutting, sawing, boning, cutting, trimming, shrink-wrapping, boxing, and loading hundreds of cattle an hour."[63] Job titles on the kill floor sound no more appealing. They include knockers, shacklers, bleeders, tail rippers, flankers, rumpers, pregutters, gutters, and back-splitters, to name just a few.[64] "There are a lot of jobs that regular Americans won't do," says Steve Orozco of Garden City's Job Service Center. "This is one of them."[65]

A job on the kill floor of a meatpacking factory is the most dangerous occupation in America, with annual injury rates as high as 39 percent.[66] Workers wield large knives that they sharpen constantly. Some are expected to make five separate cuts on a carcass every 15 seconds for eight hours a day, six days a week. The floors are wet with water and blood and even the most experienced hacks can slip and cut themselves badly. Kam Virachack, a Laotian refugee, once worked as a trimmer for IBP. He describes the day his father, Khamla, hurt himself on the job in 1989: "He slipped on the floor and got his foot stuck in the conveyor belt. Everyone tried to pull him out but nobody could do it. They had to stop the whole belt. His foot was mangled. He couldn't walk for six weeks, but he hopped into work the next day so that he wouldn't lose his job."[67] Workers wear protective gear, but virtually everyone who has spent time on the line has a few scars to prove it. Even so, almost nothing can guard against carpal tunnel syndrome, in which repetitive motion causes painful nerve damage that can require surgery. It is a major cause of disability among workers. Members of the line crew often fall victim to what they commonly call butcher's wrist.

The plants provide limited opportunities for interaction between immigrants, natives, or different ethnic groups. According to some reports, the companies deliberately put Mexicans on the morning shift, and Southeast Asians on the afternoon shift. IBP and Monfort deny this, and it's a matter of genuine dispute even among workers as to whether segregation actually occurs. One team of researchers detected some occupational clustering, but concluded that "Although workers from one ethnic group or nationality often work in close proximity, there is no evidence that this represents a conscious policy on the part of management. New hires are placed in jobs according to vacancies and prior experience."[68] The industry's profit margins are so low—less than 1 percent of all sales become profit—that supervisors need to fill gaps in their lines much more quickly than a policy of separation would allow.[69] Off the line, some ethnic mingling appears to go on in the cafeteria. People who work near each other often sit together without respect to ethnicity.[70]

Nobody on the kill floor considers his job a lifetime vocation. "There aren't many people aspiring to work in a meat plant," says Stull, who studies the meat business and has lived in Garden City. "The jobs there make you strong and then they make you old," he says.[71] Still, many immigrants use the industry as a stepping-stone to greater things. IBP salaries begin at $7.00 per hour and can rise to $10.35 per hour for the most difficult jobs—either one a good wage in southwest Kansas. "The work is physically demanding, but if you can get three or four family members earning that kind of money, it's easy to save up, buy a home, and move on," says Nancy Harness, coordinator of refugee services at Garden City's Adult Learning Center. She gives a few examples of people who have done just that. Many of the local Vietnamese, she says, move down to Texas to buy shrimping boats and run their own small businesses.[72]

"Jobs in the plants are really tough," says Donald To, a former IBP head dropper who escaped from Vietnam by boat in 1979 and arrived in Kansas the next year at the age of 17. "It's the last place I would want to work, but it can be a good way to start making a living in America," he says. While working 48 hours each week in the plant, To held a second job, earned his high school equivalency diploma, and studied at the local community college. He became licensed as a life insurance salesman in 1993 and is now an independent representative for American Family Insurance. He uses his Vietnamese language skills to tap clients that other agents cannot reach, though his client list includes nonimmigrants as well.[73] To proudly wears a ring that signifies his membership in the Life Diamond Club, American Family's award for leading the state in writing premiums. "He's a top-level producer," says

Lyle Dodson, To's district manager. "He has an incredible work ethic."[74]

Even as To spent every day at IBP thinking about how to escape from it, some immigrants have moved into management at the plants. With such a large non-English-speaking workforce, meat companies have promoted bilingual employees into supervisory positions. Tony Thaya, a Laotian refugee who came to the United States in 1980, avoided a job on the line by putting his education to work. He had earned an associate's degree as an electrician from Fresno Community College in California before coming to Garden City in 1993. Now he works four 12-hour shifts at Monfort each week as a scale technician and electrical maintenance man. Thaya thinks about opening a computer store someday. He has created printer fonts in Laotian script already and sold them to IBP for its employee manual.[75]

The immigrants' upward mobility is reflected in Garden City's general prosperity. "Those immigrants spend a lot of money here," says Ernie Ortiz, owner of the El Conquistador restaurant for the last 15 years and a Garden City native.[76] "Some of our best customers are Mexican Americans," says R. Kent Nanninga, co-owner of Western Motor, a local car dealership. "The Southeast Asians have been especially good because they can't drive across the border. They need cars almost as soon as they get here," he adds.[77] City manager Halloran can attach some numbers to this consumer phenomenon: "In 1982, 18,000 people lived here and we instituted a half-cent city sales tax that generated about one-half million dollars in revenue," he says. "This year, we're about 50 percent bigger in terms of population but the same sales tax will produce triple the revenue. Immigrants definitely have something to do with that." Halloran's only complaint is that many of the plant workers only stay for two or three years before moving elsewhere—often to better jobs in other cities and, in the case of Hispanic immigrants, sometimes back to Mexico or Central America. Despite this, immigrant purchasing power in Garden City is substantial and remains an emblem of their economic and social assimilation.

The Garden City experience may seem unique, and to a certain extent it is. But so are all the stories of immigrants with varied backgrounds living in different cities all over the country. They are all bound by the near-universal expectation that life in the United States is a life of labor. Americanization affects them gradually, helping them adapt to the United States and become more comfortable living in their new home. Perhaps what is most striking about the immigrant working class is its contrast to the native-born underclass. As sociologist William Julius Wilson has observed, impoverished and uneducated Mexican immigrants in Chicago show relatively few signs of social pathology—unemployment, crime, welfare dependency, and drug use—that have come to mark the city's native-born underclass.[78] The same is true for dozens of other blue-collar immigrants, whether they are Pakistani cab drivers, Salvadoran dishwashers, Haitian cooks, Mexican construction workers, Vietnamese shrimpers, Chinese garment sewers, or Laotian meatpackers.

Assimilation Superhighway: Case Study 2

Silicon Valley has no skyline, unless you count downtown San Jose—which you shouldn't do because the heart of America's technology industry actually lies several miles to the north in Santa Clara, Sunnyvale, and Mountain View. Companies here build out, not up. Their low-lying buildings sprawl across hundreds of acres, sometimes occupying ten or more structures. Few are taller than two stories, so it's easy to drive by on I–880 or US–101 and fail to see any of them. If you're not looking, they're not there.

The same might be said of the thousands of immigrants who work here. "In our business, immigrants are so common that their presence doesn't even register mentally," says Ken Wirt, vice president of marketing at Diamond Multimedia, a leading producer of computer graphics boards. "I never think about where they come from, or whether they are first generation or second generation," he adds.[79] Linda Shaw, Diamond's manager of human resources, puts it another way: "I feel funny calling them 'they.' Around here, it's 'we.'"[80]

Statements like these are common throughout the industry. They point toward highly skilled immigrants' almost total integration into the American technology business. There are no hard data on how many immigrants work in the industry—it is illegal to ask employees where they're from—but the management at several of the largest cutting-edge companies informally estimate that one-third of their workers with Ph.D.'s are foreign-born. In fact, immigrant engineers are a much more common sight than female ones. "Just look around this cafeteria," says Barbara Beck, vice president for human resources at Cisco Systems, as she gazes across a crowded, ethnically mixed, and integrated room at lunchtime. "We've got a real melting pot here," she adds. Since the late 1980s, Cisco Systems has gone from being a start-up company with fewer than 40 employees to a multi-billion dollar networking giant with thousands of people on payroll. Five of Cisco's 20 vice presidents are immigrants. "They're making a difference here," says Beck.[81]

Immigrants hold vital positions at dozens of other firms as well. "How important are immigrants to my company?" asks T. J. Rodgers, president and CEO of Cypress Semiconductor, a $400 million company that builds high-speed computer chips. "Four of my 10 vice-presidents are immigrants. They are responsible for overseeing 1,200 of 1,700 employees. Our whole company is probably 30 percent immigrant at all levels, from manufacturing to engineering. So I'm not exaggerating to say that we would be out of business without immigrants."[82]

Another building on the Cypress campus is the company's research and development wing. Next to the office of Tony Alvarez—the division's vice president and an immigrant from Cuba—is a map of the world posted on a cubicle wall. Dozens of pins stick out of the map, each one representing an employee's place of birth. Most come from different cities in the United States, but perhaps half the pins lie outside American borders. Home countries include China, Ghana, India, Panama, Philippines, Russia, Taiwan, Zimbabwe, and many others. "Without immigrants, you could cut the wealth of Silicon Valley by a factor of 100. And that's a conservative estimate," says Alvarez.[83]

That estimate certainly applies to Intel, an industry leader with a workforce in the tens of thousands. Its microprocessors include such well-known brand names as Pentium and Pentium Pro and operate in at least 150 million personal computers. Somebody buys an Intel-based computer twice every second.[84] Sitting atop this chipmaking empire is Andy Grove, the third employee Intel ever hired, its current CEO, and an immigrant from Hungary.[85] "He is probably second only to Bill Gates of Microsoft in terms of his importance to the computer industry," said Ron K. Unz, president of Wall Street Analytics, a software firm in Palo Alto.[86] *Forbes* magazine recently dubbed Grove "the industry's best manager."[87] Although Grove is extraordinary, he is not alone. Other technology companies founded or headed by immigrants include Applied Materials, AST, Borland International, Kingston Technology, and Sun Microsystems.

Landing a job at a company like Intel often requires a Ph.D. in physics, engineering, or computer science. "We're always looking for the best and brightest people in a few narrow technical fields," says Coeta Chambers, a human resources professional at Intel.[88] Companies recruit this sort of person right out of American graduate schools, where foreigners on student visas earn the finest education the world has to offer. Nearly half a million foreign students attend college in the United States, and nearly half of these study at the graduate level.[89] In 1990, they accounted for 62 percent of the engineering doctorates awarded in American universities. They received math, physics, and computer science degrees at similar rates. The National Science Foundation reports that immigrants hold 23 percent of all science and engineering doctorates in the United States.[90] According to the 1990 Census, an immigrant is twice as likely as a native to hold a Ph.D.

Silicon Valley companies reach into this labor pool because their job market is so big and the number of qualified applicants so few. Demand outweighs supply. "We regularly have more than 1,000 openings," says Heidi Wilson, a human resources specialist at Sun Microsystems.[91] Federal law prohibits employers simply from making a job offer to a foreign-national until they gain special certification from the Department of Labor. This is to ensure that outsiders do not come into the United States and steal jobs from Americans or depress their wages. The American Immigration Lawyers Association calls this "one of the most complex of all immigration-related procedures."[92] Employers must show that they need a certain foreign worker's skills and abilities, that they have tried to recruit citizens and permanent legal residents for the position by running advertisements and notifying their other employees of the opening, that the candidate's salary will be no less than the prevailing wage, and that the candidate will not replace a striking worker. After completing this process, the company must then prove to the INS that the job in question requires a professional, college-educated worker and that the candidate fulfills this need. As a result of these regulations, companies have a compelling incentive to hire from within the country. Yet Intel keeps a staff of seven devoted to this kind of visa procurement. Coeta Chambers of Intel estimates that it costs her company $8,000 to $10,000, not including legal fees, for every immigrant it sponsors. "If we can find a citizen to do the job, we definitely hire that person first," says Rajesh Parekh, chief technology officer at Sun Microsystems and an Indian immigrant. "Hiring noncitizens is a big hassle because of all the regulations, the lawyers, the waiting period, the paperwork. But if someone is really good, we will go out of our way to bring that person here," he says.[93]

Surviving in this environment requires a knowledge of English. "It's the lingua franca of high-tech," says Diamond Multimedia's Wirt. "Most of the technology business in any country is done in English," adds Parekh of Sun Microsystems. Foreign-born students in American graduate schools typically have grappled with this reality before arriving in the United States. Many have earned degrees from top institutions in their home countries, like Tsinghua University in Beijing, known as China's MIT, or the Indian Institutes of Technology, also modeled after a certain school in Massachusetts. Textbooks and research materials in advanced subjects such as theoretical physics and semiconductor technology are not available in dozens of languages—if you want to study in these areas, in many cases you must do so in English.

Foreign-born students often reverse the standard immigrant practice of learning to speak first, with reading and writing coming later, if at all. Instead, they learn to read English very well from books but make poor speakers, mainly because they have few occasions to practice before arriving in the United States. "I used physics to learn English, not the other way around," says Gang Bai, a chip designer at Intel and a Chinese immigrant. "My physics class became my English class," he says.[94] In fact, a common complaint heard among university undergraduates taking coursework in math, engineering, or the sciences is that their teaching-assistant instructors—the same foreign-born students working toward Ph.D.'s and jobs in the computer industry—are very smart people but lousy oral communicators. "When I first came to America, I knew technical English," says Jose Arreola, a Mexican-American engineer at Cypress who earned his Ph.D. from the University of Florida in 1978. "I had to learn regular English from friends, teachers, and television."[95] That's a necessity for most foreign-born students. "If you cannot communicate in English, you won't survive the graduate programs," says Bai.

Even so, language can present challenges. The same job pressures that convince companies to recruit foreign-born workers also affect their selection process. They have a glut of openings and only a handful of qualified applicants, which means that sometimes they must hire immigrants with second-rate English. "We don't run into tons of language problems here. But let's face it, a lot of jobs emphasize working on computers and not speaking to other people," says Anant Agrawal, vice-president for engineering at Sun and an immigrant from India. Tracy Hoyt, an independent job recruiter with 15 years of experience in the technology industry, says that most companies insist on English-speaking abilities. But language can become more of an obstacle to advancement than to employment. "Sometimes I tell clients to go home and watch Sesame Street because it will help them learn English and move to the next level in their careers," she says.[96]

Corporate cultures also can have an important influence on how immigrants assimilate. They help introduce immigrants to organizational modes not familiar to them in their homelands. If a certain set of traits mark American business—decentralization, a rough egalitarianism, and flexibility in their approach to rules, for example—then a corporate culture will teach them.[97] In the process, immigrants learn about the United States. "America is like Intel because success is merit-based, it's not about where you come from," says Intel's Bai. "Your race doesn't matter, only your success," he adds. Cypress Semiconductor maintains a distinct corporate culture aimed at aggressive growth. Managers are told to make sure that potential employees have the right "cultural fit" before offering them positions.[98] This fit is defined most precisely in a memo, sent out to new employees, that outlines the company's core values, purpose, and mission. One writer says that these core values can become "scrawled in the blood" of managers.[99] They may seem to have an almost ethereal quality to them—"Cypress is about winning" or "We never let success go to our heads"—but they all drive toward a common purpose of "working together in tight coordination to reach specific goals."[100]

Cypress culture rubs onto immigrants in positive ways. "As a core value, 'winning' is very American," says chip designer Danny Ryan, an Irish immigrant. "It's as American as 'keeping up with the Joneses.'"[101] Jose Arreola agrees. "Our core values are valuable to immigrants. They are about winning, honesty, integrity, and hard work. They teach about successful behavior at Cypress but have broader application. Immigrants can take them anywhere," he says. The values evolved over 10 years of experience and were designed with the help of many Cypress employees. New hires now have to attend a seminar in Cypress culture training shortly after joining the company. Vice-president Alvarez says that Americanization is too ambitious a goal for the core values, but that they probably do help immigrants integrate into society. "We don't have mini-societies here. It's inconsistent with the company values," he says.

AMERICAN DREAM

If you want a cheap ride from LaGuardia International Airport in Queens to midtown Manhattan, step outside the door near baggage claim and look for Mohammed Burki (a pseudonym). Better yet, just stand by and wait for him to scamper up and offer you a lift for $35 plus tolls. That's more than a regular cab charges, but Burki will bargain. A smart customer can bring him down to $15 or so—a very good rate.

After striking a deal, Burki hurries his passengers over to a shiny black Lincoln Towncar and speeds away with an alarming disregard for yellow lights, left-turn-only lanes, and the curses of other drivers. He shuttles travelers back and forth like this every day and there's not a moment to lose. More business waits for him at the terminal.

Burki immigrated from Pakistan a little more than three years ago. He left behind his wife and two children to join members of his extended family in New York City. "It's hard being away from them, but coming to America is a good idea for us," he said in heavily accented English, a language he could not speak before arriving here. Today he could ace the language section of the citizenship test he plans to take in two years, when he's eligible to try it.

His uncle initially helped him find a job working the counter of a drug store, but he's happier behind the wheel of his gypsy cab. "I make more money now," said Burki. He's not greedy, just pragmatic. When his wife and children join him in a few years, Burki plans to take his savings and open a store. "I know a lot of Pakistanis who own 7-Elevens. That's what I would like to do. Maybe in Minneapolis. A lot of Pakistanis live there now," he said. "Yes, I think that is my American dream."[102]

Chapter 10

AN AMERICANIZATION
MANIFESTO

There is nothing new about Americanization. It is as old as the republic itself. In fact, this book does not say much that has not been said before, and often better, by other writers. Consider its message a reminder: Assimilation must accompany immigration. And as Dr. Johnson tells us, "People need to be reminded more often than they need to be instructed."

This idea—assimilation must accompany immigration—may seem obvious. Who needs to be reminded of truisms? And yet the very question of assimilation has left many Americans wondering about today's newcomers. They fear that immigrants are not becoming Americans, and they see the political debate about immigration polarized between left-wing multiculturalists and right-wing nativists. Multiculturalists say that immigrants should not have to assimilate. They advance an unsettling agenda of racial and ethnic entitlements, cheapened naturalization standards, foreign-language voting, and bilingual education. Nativists say that immigrants cannot assimilate. They wrap themselves in particularist definitions of American nationhood, issue bleak predictions about the future, and seem to derive a strange satisfaction from their talk of decline. With these two sides so dominant in the country's conversation about immigrants, hardly anybody says a word in defense of Americanization.

All of this understandably rubs Americans the wrong way. Their initial political reaction may be to say "Keep 'em out!" One sure way to fix the assimilation crisis, after all, is to cut off the supply of newcomers. If we are not going to Americanize immigrants, we should not let them in at all, the thinking goes. But this is, at best, only a partial solution that creates its own set of problems. What about assimilating the roughly 25 million immigrants who are already here? Do we just give up on them? Moreover, even if immigration were to be reduced sometime in the future, it is unlikely to be eliminated altogether. There will always be immigrants in need of Americanization, even in years to come, even if they number just 200,000 or 300,000. Must we forget them? And what about the proud American tradition of being a nation of immigrants? Is the United States suddenly to abandon a key part of its Americanizing heritage because some political extremists have decided to make a lot of noise about multicultural education? The United States historically has done a very good job of helping immigrants become Americans. Why not revive this important tradition?

WHAT AMERICA DOES WELL

Perhaps Americans must be reminded that their country always has done certain things very well. From creating an unsurpassed political structure to performing peaceful transitions of power, from maximizing personal freedom to promoting equality under the rule of law, from nurturing ingenuity to advancing material prosperity, the United States has no equal. In John Winthrop's famous phrase, America shines like a city on a hill, a city that cannot be hid, a model polity for others around the globe to emulate. Its political principles have cultivated a land of voluntary joiners, a people uniquely fit for looking after themselves and their neighbors, a people united in their devotion to self-government. It is a place where folks can bury the past, a place where the sins of the fathers do not pass on to the children, a place where people can remake themselves by picking up and moving westward—or, at least in the 1990s, to the sunbelt. It is a country of spaces so vast that it hardwires humility into the American spirit and helps make Americans among the most religious, but not fanatic, people on the planet. America is a nation of inventors and tinkers who take thousands of little steps on the path of technological progress every day. Individual effort can reap enormous rewards and admiration, but rarely jealousy. Americans do not resent Horatio Alger, they want to share in his success. They hope to live their own American dream, and do not begrudge people who have lived theirs.

Of all the things America does well, one of the things it does best is Americanize. Its faith in the natural, magnetic power of immigrant adaptation and assimilation has allowed millions of foreigners to become Americans by the dint of their own effort and the generosity of the American people. This is something no other country in the world can claim. Ronald Reagan makes the point nicely in a passage from his autobiography. "I brought up a thought that had been expressed to me in a letter from a recent immigrant to America: Americans, he said, come from every corner of the world, but once they are in America, they are assimilated in a way that is unique in the world," writes Reagan. "An immigrant can live in France, he said, but not become a Frenchman; he can live in Germany but not become a German; he can live in Japan but not become a Japanese; but anyone from any part of the world can come to America and become an American."[1]

Virtually everybody admits that Americanization worked remarkably well in the past. To suggest that something went wrong at Ellis Island is to question one of the deepest American traditions, almost akin to lamenting the decision of the 13 colonies in 1776 or wishing that the South had won the Civil War. The history of Americanization is one in which Americans ought to take a certain amount of pride, as it is an accomplishment that no other group of people can claim. But more than pride, it should serve as a lesson in what is possible. The success of Americanization provides the answer to the assimilation challenges that immigration poses to the United States in all times and all places. Why should it not work again today?

It can work again, but success will not happen by itself. Especially today, with the ideal of assimilation in disrepute among many elites on both the left and the right, Americanization needs powerful advocates and a compelling agenda. There is, thankfully, a reservoir of strength available to would-be Americanizers: the vast majority of ordinary

Americans, who believe in the importance of assimilation. They may disagree—in fact they do disagree, mightily—regarding the value of immigration to the United States, its economic consequences, and whether legal immigration should continue and at what level. But they agree that once legal immigrants arrive in the United States and intend to stay, they should Americanize. They should dedicate themselves to the American proposition. They should learn to speak English, especially the children. And they should become citizens, swearing off foreign allegiances and committing themselves wholly to their new country.

Americanization has succeeded historically because Americans confidently have asserted themselves as a people who stand for a certain set of principles outlined in their nation's founding documents. They have understood that they can share their national identity with immigrants, but that before it can happen immigrants must assimilate into the American way of life. Unlike today, there used to be very little squeamishness about what a phrase like *the American way of life* meant. At bottom, it meant attachment to the Founders' ideas about equality, liberty, and government. In practical terms, this meant that immigrants in the United States should live by its laws, lead productive lives, learn English, become citizens, and, somewhere along the way, dedicate themselves to the uniquely American proposition. To say these things bluntly is not intolerant, as multiculturalists claim. Neither is it pie-in-the-sky idealism, as nativists argue. It is quite simply the American way of life. Asking immigrants to assimilate into it is not something that should make Americans feel guilty. They should not have to apologize for what, in the final analysis, is an extraordinary example of magnanimity.

The Americanization movement of the early 20th century provides a blueprint for how the United States ought to react to the millions of new immigrants who came over the last 20 or 30 years, as well as those who will soon arrive. Despite all of its eventual failings, the movement's tactics, strategies, and specific ideas about how to incorporate the foreign-born population have much to recommend. The most pressing duty of modern Americanizers, of course, is to restore the good name of Americanization. The original Americanizers were quite talented at advancing their agenda in a positive fashion. Ultimately, Americanization is something that immigrants should want to pursue because they see its benefits and consider it desirable. It cannot be force-fed. To regain the energy and strength it had at the start of the 20th century, Americanization will have to spring out of the individual efforts of American citizens, not government decrees. Politicians must forsake the venomous cult of group rights. Teachers must commit themselves to helping immigrant children learn English. INS officers must make sure that naturalization applicants are worthy of citizenship. Employers must help their foreign-born workers adapt to their new country. Americans everywhere should do these things in the name of an upbeat Americanization that always encourages immigrants. Done well on this individual level, Americanization will succeed again.

THE AMERICANIZATION AGENDA

Public institutions must do their part, too. In fact, there are several areas in which the government, through proper legislation and action, can make Americanization more effective. In most areas, this means shrinking government authority that in recent years has expanded in ways that actively discourage or inhibit immigrant assimilation. Here are ten public policy suggestions that could fill out an Americanization agenda for the turn of the century—nine goals to pursue and one trouble spot to avoid. They represent practical, commonsense ideas that the vast majority of ordinary Americans could easily endorse. Although they may be deemed radical because they would mark a profound change from the status quo, they are in reality only a return to truer principles of American nationhood. The only radicals are the people who refuse to support Americanization.

Embrace Colorblind Law

Racial preferences rank among the most divisive government policies in the United States. Almost nothing in our political life stirs more resentment than color consciousness in public employment, contracting, university admissions, mortgage applications, political districting, and dozens of other areas. Racial preferences violate the fundamental American principle that rights belong to individuals, not to groups. Perhaps there was a time when black Americans deserved a temporary program of affirmative action. That case is increasingly difficult to sustain in the

1990s. It always has been impossible to sustain with respect to immigrants, no matter what their skin color.

Unlike U.S.-born blacks, of course, the foreign-born could never claim a centuries-long history of systematic discrimination in the United States. Taiwanese-born entrepreneurs should not be allowed to profit from business set-asides for minorities. Wealthy Cuban-American kids should not get an edge in college acceptances over the children of working-class whites. Immigrants should be treated as individuals striving to earn a better life for themselves and their families, rather than as members of claimant groups in need of race-based political patronage. In fact, the government should aggressively move away from all forms of racial classification.

Race and ethnicity should be understood as private concerns rather than as public dilemmas. Not even the Census Bureau, benign as it may seem, should sort Americans by race. This may cause social scientists to scream and holler—"How will we do our research?" they will plead—but the principle of colorblind law is much more important than their journal articles. Immigrants must understand that their new attachments as Americans dedicated to a proposition must trump the old group-based loyalties into which they were born. Embracing colorblind law is the surest way our public institutions can do that.

Pull the Plug on Bilingual Education

Americanization is not just for adults. It can influence the children of immigrants, too. Because of this, schools play an important role in the assimilation process. When they do not help these kids learn English as well as possible, however, they have failed at what might be one of their most important tasks. Schools must insist on effective English acquisition. One of the biggest obstacles to that goal is the bilingual education establishment. Modern Americanizers must cut its lifeline.

For starters, the federal government should halt its spending on bilingual education. First and foremost, this would mean that bureaucrats at the Department of Education could no longer micromanage the language policies of states and localities. Second, it would also end direct federal support for educational practices light on English acquisition and heavy on native-language maintenance. Finally, it would prevent federal research grants from going to the education and linguistics professors who concoct fancy theories to support the current, corrupt regime of bilingual education.

State governments should pursue a similar English-first strategy. They should grant local school districts as much freedom as possible to design their own techniques for teaching non-English-speaking children. They should monitor results rather than methodology, concerning themselves with how well local programs help children learn English instead of with pedagogy. In this survival-of-the-fittest atmosphere, strategies emphasizing English immersion will naturally rise to the top and native-language maintenance programs will perish.

Finally, governments at all levels must ensure the rights of students and parents. In too many school districts, officials enroll Hispanic children in bilingual education programs simply because they are Hispanic, not because they need special assistance. This pernicious ethnic classification condemns certain children to a subpar education. It is also a violation of their civil rights. In addition, parents need to have full knowledge of how their children are being taught English. They should have to sign off on any program that separates their children from mainstream classrooms. Furthermore, parents should have the right to remove their children from bilingual education programs, no matter how bitterly school officials object. Parents generally know much better than bureaucrats what is in their children's best interests.

English-First in the Voting Booth

Foreign-language ballots are an unfunded mandate thrust on localities by a federal government that does not seem to care if its requirements are costly and impractical. Worse than that, however, its requirements are demoralizing. They tell the vast majority of foreign-born citizens who have struggled to learn English to naturalize (and gain the vote) that learning English is not important. Congress should amend the Voting Rights Act to stop the Department of Justice from coercing local communities to print election materials in foreign languages. There should be no federal rules regarding the language in which elections are held. This does not mean that immigrant voters who still have difficulty communicating in English would not be without recourse. There is a long tradition in the United States of ethnic newspapers— often printed in languages other than English—providing political guidance to readers in the form of sample ballots and visual aids that explain how to vote. It would surely continue.

Replace "One Person, No Vote" with "One Person, One Vote"

It is hard to believe that citizens and noncitizens receive equal weight in congressional apportionment schemes. It is even harder to believe that citizens and illegal aliens receive equal weight. But both groups do. The case against illegal aliens is easy to make. These people have broken the law to enter and stay in the United States. Tourists and business travelers do not count in congressional apportionment. Neither should illegal immigrants.

The case against noncitizens generally is a bit tougher to make, since the bulk of them are law-abiding people who pay their taxes. Yet it is nearly as important. Adults who cannot vote in federal elections should not count in congressional apportionment because there is no way that they can be guaranteed representation. Politicians who claim to speak on their behalf are not accountable to them. This is antidemocratic. Noncitizen representation creates a system of modern-day rotten boroughs of politicians who lord over their districts and proclaim to speak on behalf of people whose voices cannot be heard through the political process. Worse yet, it diminishes the idea of citizenship by blurring the line between citizen and noncitizen. Immigrants who have not naturalized have chosen on their own accord to remain apart from their American political community. That is their decision, and they can still lead happy lives in the United States in spite of it. But they should be under no illusion that they have any kind of influence over the political decisions this country makes. Citizenship is not a right, it is a privilege. To receive its benefits, immigrants must naturalize. Congress should therefore pass a law that only citizens count toward congressional apportionment.

Strengthen the Naturalization Process

Citizenship is a cornerstone of Americanization, and every immigrant should be encouraged to naturalize. In this day of dumbed-down standards, however, the INS has to make sure that it does not weaken the requirements that immigrants currently must fulfill to become full members of the American political community. In fact, the INS should strengthen the standards that already exist. Citizenship applicants already must pass a test on U.S. history and government, but the tests are administered so haphazardly throughout the 33 INS districts that some immigrants who pass in one district would fail in another. To guarantee fairness, the INS should introduce a set of national standards for naturalization exams. This would also provide an opportunity to make the current tests more meaningful. Tests should measure immigrants' actual understanding of U.S. history and government, rather than their knowledge of trivial data. The exams should not necessarily become more difficult. Passing them should be challenging, but also achievable.

More important than revamping the tests, the INS should establish partnerships with local groups to promote formal citizenship instruction. Students who enroll in citizenship-education courses at community colleges or with religious organizations, for example, could have their applications expedited.

Finally, Congress should eliminate the English-language exemption that it grants to certain immigrants. Under current law, legal permanent residents who are 50 years old and have lived in the United States for 20 years do not have to demonstrate the ability to speak, read, and write in English. Immigrants who are 55 and have lived in the United States for 15 years receive the same treatment. Naturalization should treat all applicants equally. Granted, it is more difficult for elderly people to learn a new language than it is for youngsters, but opening even a single loophole sets a bad precedent. Naturalization standards should apply to everybody across the board. Those who fail to meet them always can try again. Those who pass should be congratulated for having met a mark set for all.

Permit English Work Rules

Employers know better than bureaucrats how to manage their employees. Despite this, the federal government has seen fit to sanction many private companies that require their workers to speak English on the job. Congress should put an end to this practice with a law that specifically permits employers to regulate the language their employees use when they are working, just as it allows them to impose dress codes and test for illegal drugs. The workplace is a crucible of assimilation. There is hardly a better place for foreign-born adults to learn English and develop the habits and skills they need to compete in the American economy. Employers have a definite business interest in advancing this kind of Americanization. The government should step out of their way.

To the extent that it should have any role in this matter, Congress may want to consider granting tax credits to companies that provide English as a Second Language courses for their employees. This is clearly some of the best job training around.

Deny Welfare to Noncitizens

Noncitizens who fall on hard times should not expect other taxpayers to support them. If they require financial assistance, they should seek it from family, friends, and private charities. The problem with noncitizens receiving welfare is not that these services cost too much but that they encourage an undesirable way of life. The United States should not encourage immigrants to assimilate into a culture of public dependency. One of the greatest assets immigrants bring to America is their remarkable work ethic. What a tragedy if liberal welfare policies rob them of this precious and admirable quality.

The 1996 welfare reform law goes a long way toward meeting the goal of no welfare for noncitizens, although it is far too soon to tell how effective it will be. When President Clinton signed the welfare bill, he specifically said that he objected to the restrictions on noncitizens and would try to have them lifted. In 1997, Clinton and Congress restored some benefits to legal immigrants who had been living in the United States when the reforms were passed. These remaining restrictions must be enforced with vigilance, because immigrants who arrive on our shores with nothing have a lot to teach this country about hard work and thrift. We should be loath to tell them that these virtues do not much matter.

Finally, one area that welfare reform has not addressed is public assistance to refugees. It makes sense to provide financial assistance to refugees because they often have not had much time to plan for their arrival. Yet there is no excuse for the high rates of long-term welfare use among them. They have a difficult time kicking the habit. Congress should discuss reforming refugee aid and think about providing refugees with loans rather than handouts. Also, Congress should completely privatize the delivery of refugee welfare services. Private groups, especially religious organizations, have much better records than public agencies of helping refugees find jobs and adjust to life in the United States. Their influence in this area ought to expand.

Forbid the Cultural Defense

Courts must reject the idea that some foreign-born criminals should receive lenient treatment because they come from different cultures and may not understand American legal customs. This so-called cultural defense defies the basic principle of equal justice under the rule of law. The cultural defense has not yet become widespread, but it has encouraged prosecutors in some jurisdictions to reduce charges against immigrants who might otherwise face convictions for murder, rape, and other crimes. Cultural relativism has no place in the American legal system.

Reduce Illegal Immigration

Legal immigrants generally outnumber illegal immigrants each year by a 2-to-1 or 3-to-1 margin. Roughly five or six times as many foreign-born Americans live in this country legally than illegal aliens. Despite this, a 1993 poll showed that more than two-thirds of Americans think that most of the immigrants who have come into the United States in recent years have done so illegally.[2] This misperception undoubtedly has diverted much of the country's political energy away from immigrant policies such as Americanization and toward illegal immigration control.

The INS has done a spectacularly poor job of controlling the U.S. border, especially in southern California. Much of its failure is due to a Congress that continues to burden the agency with jobs it cannot perform well, including drug interdiction and employer sanctions. A good share of blame lies on the INS's own shoulders, however, as the agency continues to operate under almost scandalous management. Whatever the sources of this breakdown, the federal government must do a better job of preventing illegal immigration. Of course, a free and prosperous country like the United States will always attract people desperate enough to risk their lives and break our laws to get here. In an odd way, we should hope that these sorts of people always have reason to come. But that does not mean we should just shrug them off. High levels of illegal immigration erode the country's confidence in legal immigration. If we cannot even control our borders, some ask, then how are we going to advance the complicated, long-term process of assimilation? The answer is that we must do both, and that we must do the first in part so that more people have faith in our ability to do the second.

Warning: Avoid the Trap of Official English

The problem with many of the proposals to make English the official language of the United States is that they fail to address severe language problems spawned by bad public policy, such as bilingual education and foreign-language voting ballots. Odd as it may seem, some of the most popular official-English bills in Congress address neither of these areas. They simply declare English official, leaving bilingual education and foreign-language ballots untouched. This is silly. Nobody knows as well as non-English-speaking immigrants that English is the common language of the United States. Telling them so with a law that fails to remove any of the hurdles to English acquisition is patronizing, even insulting. Done this way, official English tricks voters into thinking that one of their concerns is being addressed, and at the same time it winks to the political activists who support bilingual policies and tells them not to worry, nothing will change. Perhaps this is why so many politicians like the neutered form of official English. The lesson here is that it is much more important to create pro-English public policies and repeal anti-English ones than it is to make grand statements that do not affect the lives of immigrants except to inspire negative feelings.

Taken together, these nine suggestions round out an Americanization strategy that may not solve all of the country's assimilation problems, but would certainly make assimilation easier for millions of people. They are pragmatic ideas that most Americans would support. They would also accomplish something much larger than the successful assimilation of immigrants.

LAST, BEST HOPE

The original Americanizers in the early 20th century understood that the successful Americanization of immigrants required a measure of national self-confidence among the native-born. "We shall never have an Americanized foreign-born population until we have an Americanized native-born population—nationalized and giving definitely of its thought, time, and strength to making a better America for everybody," said Frances Kellor in 1916.[3] In other words, members of the host society must have a solid understanding of who they are as a people before they can hope to share and transmit this understanding to newcomers. And herein lies what is perhaps the greatest challenge—and opportunity—facing a new Americanization movement.

There has been a rumor in America that the United States has lost its greatness, that its best days are in the past, that the future holds no promise. As Arthur Herman has shown in *The Idea of Decline in Western History*, professional doomsayers in recent years have benefited from a bull market in pessimism. "The sowing of despair and self-doubt has become so pervasive that we accept it as a normal intellectual stance—even when it is directly contradicted by our own reality," writes Herman.[4] The political scientist Paul Kennedy provides a perfect example of this mind-set. In his influential *Rise and Fall of Great Powers,* Kennedy says that the time has come for the United States to sell itself short. "The task facing American statesmen over the next decades . . . [will be] to 'manage' affairs so that the relative erosion of the United States' position takes place slowly and smoothly," writes Kennedy, who made this forecast two years before the Berlin Wall toppled and the world was left with a single, unchallenged superpower.[5] And yet Kennedy is considered a seer of our country's future.

Little wonder Americans occasionally entertain notions of national self-doubt, and have been so reluctant to advocate a new round of Americanization for the current wave of immigrants. Americanization, of course, requires national certitude. The United States may become "an impossible place to live in by the end of the century," writes one of our gloomiest prognosticators, because of recent immigration.[6] If today's Americans are truly gripped by such pessimism, then it would be unreasonable to expect them to tell immigrants that they both can and must become Americans. Their encouragements would be lies. And if the United States cannot muster the strength it needs to say a few modest things that it has said to immigrants many times before—follow our laws, lead productive lives, learn English, become citizens—

then maybe the rumor of decline is, sadly, not a rumor. Perhaps the magnificent glory days of the United States have come and gone. Perhaps Americans must go the way of the Romans and await a Gibbon to tell the story of their decline and fall. Perhaps they must follow the British and step aside to watch some other people climb to greatness. Perhaps Kennedy is right.

Of course, he is not; and surely through the national project of Americanization, the United States can regain its sense of self. A conscious effort to help make new Americans will have value that goes far beyond helping immigrants. It will Americanize all of us, and restore the kind of patriotic self-confidence that encouraged a group of colonists to sign the Declaration of Independence more than 200 years ago. In 1862, Abraham Lincoln called America "the last, best hope of earth" during our country's darkest hour. The outcome of the Civil War was far from clear. It could have gone either way, and some kind of permanent separation between north and south seemed likely. And yet Lincoln did not talk about managing the "relative erosion" of America's greatness. He did not complain that the United States might become "an impossible place to live in." He spoke with resolve on the necessity of preserving the union: "The way is plain, peaceful, generous, just—a way which if followed the world will forever applaud and God must forever bless."[7]

The same might be said of Americanization. It, too, is plain, peaceful, generous, and just. It even speaks to the question of union. If the United States is to remain whole, it must Americanize its immigrants. And in Americanizing our immigrants, we will remind ourselves of what a blessing it is to be American.

NOTES

Introduction

1. David M. Potter, *The Impending Crisis, 1848–1861* (New York: Harper and Row, 1976), pg. 479.

Chapter 1. Americanization and Its Enemies

1. Patrick J. McDonnell and Robert J. Lopez, "L.A. March Against Prop. 187 Draws 70,000," *Los Angeles Times,* October 17, 1994, pg. Al; Patrick J. McDonnell and Robert J. Lopez, "Some See New Activism in Huge March," *Los Angeles Times,* October 18, 1994, pg. Bl; L. Erik Bratt, "Flag Savior: For Brave Act, Student Hailed as Hero, Patriot," *San Diego Union-Tribune,* November 4, 1994.
2. The speaker was Randolfo Acuna, a professor of Chicano Studies at California State University. See Craig Hymowitz, "The Birth of a Nation," *Heterodoxy,* January 1995, pg. 4.
3. *Newsweek,* August 9, 1993, pg. 19.
4. Rita Simon and S. H. Alexander, *The Ambivalent Welcome* (Westport, Conn.: Praeger, 1993).
5. "Immigration," *American Enterprise,* January–February 1994, pgs. 97–99. For a detailed examination of polling data, see Thomas J. Espenshade and Katherine Hempstead, "Contemporary American Attitudes toward U.S. Immigration," *International Migration Review* 30, no. 2 (Summer 1996), pgs. 535–70.
6. Arthur M. Schlesinger, Jr., *The Disuniting of America: Reflections on a Multicultural Society* (New York: W. W. Norton & Company, 1992), pgs. 17, 18.
7. *Newsweek,* August 9, 1993, pg. 19.
8. *Newsweek,* July 10, 1995, pgs. 26, 27.
9. All of these numbers are derived from the Immigration and Naturalization Service's 1995 *Statistical Yearbook.* The annual average of 750,000 is based on the years 1990–95 and does not include people amnestied under the 1986 Immigration Reform and Control Act.
10. Immigration and Naturalization Service, *Statistical Yearbook,* 1994 (Washington, D.C.: Government Printing Office, 1994), pg. 25.

11. James M. McPherson, *Battle Cry of Freedom: The Civil War Era* (New York: Oxford University Press, 1988), pg. 606. See also Ella Lonn, *Foreigners in the Union Army and Navy* (New York: Greenwood Press, 1951). It is interesting to note that although immigrants accounted for a larger share of the military population than the general population, the percentage of foreign-born men in the services was actually smaller than the percentage of foreign-born men of military age in the Union. See also Stuart Anderson, *In Defense of a Nation: The Military Contributions of Immigrants* (Washington, D.C.: Empower America and the American Immigration Law Foundation, 1996).

12. Bureau of the Census, *The Foreign-Born Population: 1996,* P20–494, March 1997. The percentage of foreign-born people in the general population is bound to rise in coming years, or at least for as long as the United States admits large numbers of legal immigrants.

13. Martha Farnsworth Riche, "We're All Minorities Now," *American Demographics,* October 1991.

14. Quoted in John O'Sullivan, "America's Identity Crisis," *National Review,* November 21, 1994, pg. 76.

15. Quoted in Wendy Lin, "Choosing the Right Language of Learning," *Newsday,* October 16, 1991, pg. 26.

16. Stephen Small, "The Foul Language of Oppression," *Weekly Journal,* May 27, 1993, pg. 15. Ellipsis in original.

17. Paul Simon, *The Tongue-Tied American: Confronting the Foreign Language Crisis* (New York: Continuum, 1980), pg. 11. The quotes, in full, read as follows: *Commissioner of the Common Schools of New York City, 1896:* "I consider it the paramount duty of public schools, apart from the educational knowledge to be instilled into our pupils, to form American citizens of them . . . obliterating from the very earliest moment all the distinguishing foreign characteristics and traits, which the beginners may bring with them, as obstructive, warring, and irritating elements."

    Adolf Hitler, Mein Kampf: "It is impossible to understand why millions of people . . . must learn two or three foreign languages only a fraction of which they can make use of later and hence most of them forget entirely; for a hundred thousand pupils who learn French, for example, barely two thousand will have a serious use for this knowledge later, while ninety-eight thousand . . . will not find themselves in a position to make practical use of what they once learned. They have . . . devoted thousands of hours to a subject which later is without value and meaning for them . . . So in reality, because of the two thousand people for whom the knowledge of this language is profitable, ninety-eight thousand must be tormented for nothing and made to sacrifice valuable time."

18. Michael Walzer, *What It Means to Be an American* (New York: Marsilio Publishers Corp., 1996), pg. 11.

19. Nathan Glazer, "Is Assimilation Dead?" *Annals of the American Academy of Political and Social Science,* November 1993, pg. 123.

20. Juan M. Garcia-Passalacqua, "The United States: Ethnocentric or Pluralistic?" *Washington Post,* June 7, 1996, pg. A23. For a response, see Gerald Solomon and Toby Roth, "Equal Partners, Common Bonds," *Washington Post,* July 4, 1996, pg. A29.

21. According to the 1990 Census, 78 percent of native-born Hispanics speak Eng-

lish very well. Those who don't are almost certainly the children of immigrants. They will presumably improve their English as they grow older.

22. John Isbister, *The Immigration Debate: Remaking America,* (West Hartford, Conn.: Kumarian Press, 1996), pg. 206.

23. Isbister, pg. 194.

24. Paul Hollander, *Anti-Americanism* (New York: Oxford University Press, 1992), pg. 41.

25. Quoted in Hollander, pgs. 61 and 63.

26. Hollander, pg. 468.

27. Vice-President Al Gore, Address to the Institute of World Affairs, Milwaukee, Wisconsin, January 6, 1994.

28. Clyde Wilson, "As a City Upon a Hill," in *Immigration and the American Identity: Selections from Chronicles: A Magazine of American Culture, 1985–1995* (Rockford, Ill.: The Rockford Institute, 1995), pg. 29.

29. Chilton Williamson, Jr., *The Immigration Mystique: America's False Conscience* (New York: Basic Books, 1996), pg. 198.

30. Williamson, pg. 67.

31. Williamson, pg. 200.

32. Williamson, pg. 199.

33. Williamson, pg. 198.

34. Peter Brimelow, *Alien Nation: Common Sense about America's Immigration Disaster* (New York: Random House, 1995), pg. 216.

35. Brimelow, pg. 10.

36. Brimelow, pg. 264.

37. Williamson, pg. 117.

38. Samuel Francis, "Prospects for Racial and Cultural Survival," *American Renaissance* 6, no. 3 (March 1995), pg. 5.

39. Francis, pgs. 6–7.

40. Williamson, pg. 201.

41. Ron K. Unz, "Political Scapegoats," *Policy Review,* Fall 1994, pg. 38.

42. Stephen Moore, "Return of the Nativists," *American Spectator,* June 1996, pg. 27.

43. U.S. Commission on Immigration Reform, *Legal Immigration: Setting Priorities,* June 1995, pg. 175. See also U.S. Commission on Immigration Reform, *Becoming an American: Immigration and Immigrant Policy,* September 1997; Barbara Jordan, "The Americanization Ideal," *New York Times,* September 11, 1995, pg. A15.

44. "Two States of Mind about Those Southern Neighbors," *The Economist,* July 13, 1996, pg. 25.

Chapter 2. *The American Idea*

1. William Bradford, *Of Plymouth Plantation 1620–1647,* ed. Samuel Eliot Morison (New York: Alfred A. Knopf, 1994), pgs. 59–60. For a compelling narrative of the pilgrims' voyage and the early days of Plymouth Colony, see Arthur Quinn, *A New World: An Epic of Colonial America from the Founding of*

Jamestown to the Fall of Quebec (Boston: Faber and Faber, 1994), pgs. 80–116. See also Kate Caffrey, *The Mayflower* (New York: Stein and Day, 1974), especially pgs. 91–141; and Henry Bamford Parkes, *The American Experience: An Interpretation of the History and Civilization of the American People* (New York: Vintage Books, 1959), pgs. 26–34.

2. Bradford, pg. 75.

3. Quoted in Samuel Eliot Morison, "The Mayflower Compact," *An American Primer,* ed. Daniel J. Boorstin (Chicago: University of Chicago Press, 1966), pg. 24.

4. Diane Ravitch, ed., *The American Reader: Words that Moved a Nation* (New York: HarperCollins, 1990), pg. 3.

5. Bernard Bailyn, *Voyagers to the West: A Passage in the Peopling of America on the Eve of Revolution* (New York: Alfred A. Knopf, 1986), pg. 25.

6. Bernard Bailyn, *The Peopling of British North America: An Introduction* (New York: Vintage Books, 1988), pg. 16.

7. In 1751 Benjamin Franklin had this to say about the German influence in Pennsylvania: "Why should Pennsylvania, founded by the English, become a Colony of Aliens, who will shortly be so numerous as to Germanize us instead of our Anglifying them, and will never adopt our Language or Customs, any more than they can acquire our Complexion." Quoted in Roger Daniels, *Coming to America: A History of Immigration and Ethnicity in American Life* (New York: HarperCollins, 1990), pgs. 109–10.

8. Quinn, pg. 189.

9. Daniels, pgs. 66–68.

10. Thomas Paine, *Common Sense* (Oxford: Oxford University Press, 1995), pg. 22.

11. Quoted in Maldwyn A. Jones, *American Immigration* (Chicago: University of Chicago Press, 1960), pg. 79.

12. J. Hector St. John de Crèvecoeur, *Letters from an American Farmer* (New York: New American Library, 1963), pgs. 63–64.

13. Thomas Jefferson, *The Papers of Thomas Jefferson,* vol. 1, ed. Julian P. Boyd (Princeton, N.J.: Princeton University Press, 1950), pgs. 495–96; Charles Cotton Wilson, *The New Order of the Age* (Los Angeles: WPA Education Program, 1941); Richard S. Patterson and Richard Dougall, *The Eagle and the Shield* (Washington, D.C.: Department of State, 1978), pgs. 510–14; *The Great Seal of the United States* (Washington, D.C.: Department of State, 1986).

14. G. K. Chesterton, *What I Saw in America* (London: Hodder and Stoughton, 1923), pg. 7.

15. Dennis J. Mahoney, "The Declaration of Independence as a Constitutional Document," in *The Framing and Ratification of the Constitution,* eds. Leonard W. Levy and Dennis J. Mahoney (New York: Macmillan Publishing Company, 1987), pgs. 55–68.

16. Robert A. Goldwin, *Why Blacks, Women, and Jews Are Not Mentioned in the Constitution, and Other Unorthodox Views* (Washington, D.C.: The AEI Press, 1990), pg. 14. Goldwin also points out that words indicating race such as *black* and *white* appear nowhere in the Constitution, including its amendments. (Slaves were referred to as "other Persons" [Article 1, Section 2] or "Person held

to Service or Labour" [Article 4, Section 2].) Words that appear only in amendments include *slavery, race,* and *color.* See pg. 10.

17. Abraham Lincoln, *Selected Speeches and Writings* (New York: Vintage Books/Library of America, 1992), pg. 145.

18. John O'Sullivan, "Nationhood: An American Activity," *National Review,* February 21, 1994, pg. 37.

19. John O'Sullivan, "America's Identity Crisis," *National Review,* November 21, 1994, pg. 37.

20. C. S. Lewis, *The Abolition of Man* (New York: Macmillan Publishing Company, 1955), pg. 34.

21. D. W. Brogan, *The American Character* (New York: Vintage Books, 1956), pgs. 23, 154.

22. Bernard Bailyn, *The Ideological Origins of the American Revolution,* enlarged ed., (Cambridge: Harvard University Press, 1992), pg. 321.

23. Glen E. Thurow, *The Transformation of American Citizenship* (Claremont, Calif.: Center for the American Constitution of the Claremont Institute, 1990), pgs. 3–4.

24. Quoted in Jones, pg. 79.

25. Quoted in Hans Kohn, *American Nationalism: An Interpretive Essay* (New York: Macmillan Co., 1957), pg. 133.

26. Matthew Spalding, "From Pluribus to Unum: Immigration and the Founding Fathers," *Policy Review,* Winter 1994, pgs. 35–41.

27. Quoted in Frank George Franklin, *The Legislative History of Naturalization in the United States: From the Revolutionary War to 1861* (Chicago: University of Chicago Press, 1906), pg. 101.

28. Luella Gettys, *The Law of Citizenship in the United States* (Chicago: University of Chicago Press, 1934), pgs. 9–27.

29. U.S. Constitution, Amendment XIV, Section 1.

30. There was no such thing as an illegal immigrant in 1868, so this is a rich example of a constitutional principle coming to have a meaning in the late 20th century that its authors more than a century earlier did not foresee. Several politicians, led by California Governor Pete Wilson, have suggested not awarding citizenship to children born in the United States to parents who are illegal aliens. These politicians argue that illegal immigrants are not "subject to the jurisdiction" of the United States, as the Fourteenth Amendment requires, and so their children are not eligible for citizenship. Changing the law to disallow citizenship in these cases would take either a simple act of Congress or a complicated amendment to the U.S. Constitution. Legal scholars are currently in dispute.

31. Sir William Holdsworth, *A History of English Law,* 2d ed., vol. 9 (London: Methuen & Co., 1938), pgs. 76–77.

32. *Oxford English Dictionary,* 2d ed. (New York: Oxford University Press, 1989).

33. "I will return a perfect courtier; in the which my instruction shall serve to naturalize thee, so thou wilt be capable of a courtier's counsel and understand what advice shall thrust upon thee." William Shakespeare, *All's Well that Ends Well* (New York: Washington Square Press, 1965), pgs. 213–16.

34. Holdsworth, pgs. 76–77, 89–90.

35. Spalding, pgs. 36–37.

256 Notes for Chapter 3

36. James H. Kettner, *The Development of American Citizenship, 1608–1870* (Chapel Hill: University of North Carolina Press, 1978), pgs. ix, 10.
37. U.S. Constitution, Article 1, Section 8: "The Congress shall have Power. . . . To establish a uniform Rule of Naturalization."
38. Daniels, pgs. 114–15. Jefferson, for his part, had wanted to get rid of the residency requirement altogether. See Franklin, pgs. 97–116.
39. William S. Bernard, "Immigration: History of U.S. Policy," in *Harvard Encyclopedia of American Ethnic Groups,* ed. Stephan Thernstrom (Cambridge: Harvard University Press, 1980), pgs. 488–89.
40. Reed Ueda, "Naturalization and Citizenship," in *Harvard Encyclopedia of American Ethnic Groups,* ed. Stephan Thernstrom (Cambridge: Harvard University Press, 1980), pgs. 737, 740.
41. Daniels, pg. 266.
42. John Palmer Gavit, *Americans by Choice* (1922; reprinted, Montclair, N.J.: Patterson Smith, 1971), pg. 26.
43. Reed Ueda, *Postwar Immigrant America: A Social History* (Boston: Bedford Books of St. Martin's Press, 1994), pg. 119.
44. David H. Bennett, *The Party of Fear: The American Far Right from Nativism to the Militia Movement,* 2d ed. (New York: Vintage Books, 1995), pg. 112.
45. John Higham, *Strangers in the Land: Patterns of American Nativism 1860–1925,* 2d ed. (New York: Atheneum, 1963), pg. 13.
46. Quoted in Daniels, 270. Lincoln did not have many kind words for the Know-Nothings. In an 1855 letter, he wrote: "I am not a Know-Nothing. That is certain. How could I be? How can any one who abhors the oppression of negroes be in favor of degrading classes of white people? Our progress in degeneracy appears to me to be pretty rapid. As a nation, we began by declaring that '*all men are created equal.*' We now practically read it "all men are created equal, *except negroes.*' When the Know-Nothings get control, it will read 'all men are created equal except negroes, *and foreigners, and catholics.*' When it comes to this I should prefer emigrating to some country where they make no pretense of loving liberty—to Russia, for instance, where despotism can be taken pure, and without the base alloy of hypocrisy." See Lincoln, pgs. 105–6.
47. Quoted in David M. Kennedy, "Can We Still Afford to Be a Nation of Immigrants?" *Atlantic Monthly,* November 1996, pg. 52.
48. Bernard, pg. 489.
49. Quoted in Ueda, "Naturalization," pg. 739.
50. Ueda, *Postwar Immigrant America,* pgs. 27–30.
51. Higham, pg. 214; and Daniels, pg. 266.
52. Ueda, "Naturalization," pg. 746; Ueda, *Postwar Immigrant America,* pg. 52.
53. Daniel J. Boorstin, *Hidden History* (New York: Vintage Books, 1989), pg. 65.

Chapter 3. The Rise of Americanization

1. The term *bread and roses* comes from a 1912 poem by James Oppenheimer, which was inspired by a Lawrence striker who carried a banner that read "We

want bread and roses too." Bread represented basic needs and roses represented a small amount of comfort. The best source on Lawrence and the 1912 strike is Donald B. Cole, *Immigrant City: Lawrence, Massachusetts, 1845–1921* (Chapel Hill: University of North Carolina Press, 1963). See also Eartha Dengler, *Lawrence, Massachusetts: The Strike of 1912* (Lawrence, Mass.: Immigrant City Archives); Eartha Dengler, Katherine Khalife, and Ken Skulski, *Lawrence, Massachusetts: Images of America* (Dover, New Hampshire: Arcadia Publishing, 1995); Maurice B. Dorgan, *Lawrence Yesterday and Today (1845–1918)* (Lawrence, Mass.: Dick & Trumpold, 1918), pgs. 66–74.

2. Cole, pg. 179.
3. Cole, pgs. 10–11.
4. Bill Cahn, *Mill Town* (New York: Cameron & Kahn, 1954).
5. Quoted in Cole, pgs. 9–10.
6. Quoted in Barbara Miller Solomon, *Ancestors and Immigrants: A Changing New England Tradition* (New York: John Wiley & Sons, 1956), pg. 199. See also Cole, pg. 10.
7. Quoted in Cole, pg. 190.
8. Cole, pgs. 12–13.
9. Thomas K. McCraw, "The Progressive Legacy," in *The Progressive Era,* ed. Lewis L. Gould (Syracuse, N.Y.: Syracuse University Press, 1974), pg. 182.
10. Allan Nevins and Henry Steele Commager, *A Pocket History of the United States,* 5th ed., (New York: Washington Square Press, 1967), pg. 287.
11. John Higham, *Strangers in the Land: Patterns of American Nativism 1860–1925,* 2d ed. (New York: Atheneum, 1963), pg. 54.
12. Higham, pgs. 54–55.
13. Higham, pgs. 106, 107.
14. Quoted in Higham, pg. 168.
15. Jacob Riis, *How the Other Half Lives: Studies among the Tenements of New York* (1890; reprinted, New York: Hill and Wang, 1957), pgs. 2–3.
16. Reed Ueda, "Naturalization and Citizenship," in *Harvard Encyclopedia of American Ethnic Groups,* ed. Stephan Thernstrom (Cambridge, Mass.: Harvard University Press, 1980), pgs. 743–44.
17. Immigration Restriction League, "The U.S. Must Restrict Immigration," in *Immigration: Opposing Viewpoints,* ed. Teresa O'Neill (San Diego: Greenhaven Press, 1992), pg. 231.
18. IRL, pg. 233.
19. Prescott F. Hall, "The New Immigrants Threaten America's Racial Stock," in *Immigration: Opposing Viewpoints,* ed. Teresa O'Neill (San Diego: Greenhaven Press, 1992), pg. 108.
20. Hall, pg. 114.
21. Hall, pgs. 109–10.
22. Cole, pgs. 195–96.
23. Jeanne Schinto, *Huddle Fever: Living in the Immigrant City* (New York: Alfred A. Knopf, 1995), pg. 154. Note: Despite this, there is a state historical park devoted to Lawrence's immigrant history, including special treatment of the 1912 strike.

24. Theodore Roosevelt, "Americanism," in *Immigration and Americanization: Selected Readings*, ed. Philip Davis (Boston: Ginn and Company, 1920), pg. 658.

25. Higham, pg. 245.

26. Franklin K. Lane, "What America Means," in *Immigration and Americanization: Selected Readings*, ed. Philip Davis (Boston: Ginn and Company, 1920), pg. 615.

27. "The National Conference on Immigration and Americanization," *The Immigrants in America Review* 2, no. 1 (April 1916), pg. 45.

28. William S. Bernard, ed., *Americanization Studies: The Acculturation of Immigrant Groups into American Society*, 10 vols. (1920 to 1924; reprinted, Montclair, N.J.: Patterson Smith, 1971).

29. Edward George Hartmann, *The Movement to Americanize the Immigrant* (New York: Columbia University Press, 1948), pgs. 269–70.

30. Peter Roberts, *The Problem of Americanization* (New York: Macmillan Company, 1920), pg. 39.

31. Louis D. Brandeis, "True Americanism," in *Immigration and Americanization: Selected Readings*, ed. Philip Davis (Boston: Ginn and Company, 1920), pgs. 639–40.

32. Alexis de Tocqueville, *Democracy in America*, vol. 1 (New York: Vintage Books, 1945), pgs. 250–53.

33. Hartmann, pgs. 28–29, 36.

34. Hartmann, pg. 38.

35. Hartmann, pgs. 39–41.

36. Hartmann, pgs. 51–53.

37. Hartmann, pgs. 46–47, 56.

38. Hartmann, pgs. 30–31.

39. Higham, pgs. 239–41; Hartmann, pg. 70. For more on the life of Frances A. Kellor, see John J. Miller, "Miss Americanizer," *Policy Review*, May–June 1997, pg. 64.

40. Quoted in Hartmann, pg. 66.

41. Quoted in Hartmann, pg. 90.

42. Hartmann, pg. 92.

43. Hartmann, pgs. 99–100.

44. Hartmann, pgs. 100–104.

45. Quoted in Higham, pg. 110.

46. Israel Zangwill, *The Melting-Pot* (New York: Macmillan Company, 1909), pgs. 198–99. Note: Several stage directions are dropped from this excerpt, for the purpose of brevity.

47. Quoted in Arthur Mann, *The One and the Many: Reflections on the American Identity* (Chicago: University of Chcago Press, 1979), pg. 100.

48. Quoted in Mann, pg. 118.

49. Quoted in Mann, pg. 108.

50. Ralph Waldo Emerson, *Journals of Ralph Waldo Emerson*, vol. 7, ed. Edward Waldo Emerson and Waldo Emerson Forbes (Boston: Houghton Mifflin, 1912), pg. 116.

51. J. Hector St. John de Crèvecoeur, *Letters from an American Farmer* (New York: The New American Library, 1963), pgs. 63–64.

52. George Washington, Writings, vol. 34, ed. J.C. Fitzpatrick (Washington, D.C.: Government Printing Office, 1990), pg. 23.

53. Herman Melville, *Redburn* (New York: Penguin, 1976), pg. 238.

54. Frederick Jackson Turner, "The Significance of the Frontier in American History," in *An American Primer,* ed. Daniel J. Boorstin (New York: The New American Library, 1968), pg. 557.

55. Philip Gleason, "American Identity and Americanization," in *Harvard Encyclopedia of American Ethnic Groups*, ed. Stephan Thernstrom (Cambridge: Harvard University Press, 1980), pg. 38.

56. F. James Davis, *Who is Black? One Nation's Definition* (University Park: Pennsylvania State University Press, 1991), pg. 166. See also Joel Williamson, *New People: Miscegenation and Mulattoes in the United States* (New York: New York University Press), 1984.

57. Douglas J. Besharov and Timothy S. Sullivan, "One Flesh," *The New Democrat,* July–August 1996, pg. 19.

58. David M. Heer, "Intermarriage," in *Harvard Encyclopedia of American Ethnic Groups,* ed. Stephan Thernstrom (Cambridge: Harvard University Press, 1980), pgs. 515–19.

Chapter 4. The Fall of Americanization

1. "110,000 to March in Today's Great Patriotic Parade," *New York Times,* July 4, 1918, pg. 1.

2. "Day-Long Pageant Pictures America United for War," *New York Times,* July 5, 1918, pg. 1.

3. Ibid.

4. Ibid.

5. "Peace by Sword Only; Will Not Be Sheathed for Compromise, President Says," *Washington Post,* July 5, 1918, pg. 1.

6. Edward George Hartmann, *The Movement to Americanize the Immigrant* (New York: Columbia University Press, 1948), pg. 207.

7. Woodrow Wilson, "Address at Convention Hall," in *Immigration and Americanization: Selected Readings,* ed. Philip Davis (Boston: Ginn and Company, 1920), pgs. 611–14.

8. Hartmann, pg. 164.

9. John Higham, *Strangers in the Land: Patterns of American Nativism 1860–1925,* 2d ed. (New York: Atheneum, 1963), pg. 216.

10. Higham, pgs. 161–62.

11. Quoted in Higham, pgs. 164–65.

12. Higham, pgs. 189–90.

13. Quoted in Higham, pg. 186. In 1920, Georgia elected Watson to the U.S. Senate. He served in the Senate until his death in 1922.

14. Higham, pgs. 196–97.

15. *The Clamorous Era 1910–1920* (Alexandria, Va.: Time-Life Books, 1970), pg. 235.

16. Quoted in Higham, pg. 197.

17. Higham, pg. 208.

18. Quoted in David H. Bennett, *The Party of Fear: The American Far Right from Nativism to the Militia Movement*, 2d ed. (New York: Vintage Books, 1995), pg. 184.

19. Higham, pg. 215.

20. William Preston, Jr., *Aliens and Dissenters: Federal Suppression of Radicals, 1903–1933* (New York: Harper & Row), 1963.

21. Quoted in Higham, pg. 214.

22. Frances A. Kellor, "What Is Americanization?" *Yale Review* 8, no. 2 (January 1919), pg. 290.

23. Ralph Linton, "Nativistic Movements," *American Anthropologist* 45, no. 2 (April–June 1943), pgs. 230–40; Anthony F. C. Wallace, "Revitalization Movements," *American Anthropologist* 58, no. 2 (April 1956), pgs. 264–81; Stanley Coben, "A Study in Nativism: The American Red Scare of 1919–20," *Political Science Quarterly* 79, no. 1 (March 1964), pgs. 66–67.

24. Quoted in Bennett, pg. 193.

25. Quoted in Bennett, pg. 193.

26. Quoted in Bennett, pg. 195.

27. Higham, pgs. 259–60.

28. Higham, pg. 248.

29. Kellor, pg. 294.

30. Higham, pgs. 271–72.

31. Madison Grant, *The Passing of the Great Race,* 4th rev. ed. (New York: Charles Scribner's Sons, 1921), pg. 16.

32. Grant, pg. xxxi.

33. Quoted in Higham, pg. 273.

34. Quoted in Tom Bethell, "*Roe's* Disparate Impact," *The American Spectator,* June 1996, pg. 18.

35. Grant, pgs. 50–51.

36. Quoted in Bennett, pg. 221.

37. Quoted in Higham, pg. 254.

38. Calvin Coolidge, "Whose Country Is This?" *Good Housekeeping,* February 1921, pg. 14.

39. Quoted in Higham, pg. 317.

40. Thomas J. Archdeacon, *Becoming American: An Ethnic History* (New York: The Free Press, 1983), pg. 175.

41. Immigration and Naturalization Service, *1993 Statistical Yearbook,* pg. 25.

42. Horace M. Kallen, *Culture and Democracy in the United States* (New York: Boni and Liveright, 1924), pg. 139 n1.

43. Sidney Ratner, "Horace M. Kallen and Cultural Pluralism," in *The Legacy of Horace M. Kallen,* ed. Milton R. Konvitz (Rutherford, N.J.: A Herzl Press Publication (Associated University Presses), 1987), pg. 48.

44. Reprinted in Kallen, pgs. 67–125. See also Horace M. Kallen, "Democracy versus the Melting Pot," *The Nation,* February 18 and 25, 1915.

45. Kallen, pg. 132.
46. Kallen, pg. 61.
47. Kallen, pg. 116.
48. Kallen, pg. 63.
49. Kallen, pg. 126.
50. Kallen, pg. 99.
51. Kallen, pg. 139.
52. Philip Gleason, "American Identity and Americanization," in *Harvard Encyclopedia of American Ethnic Groups*, ed. Stephan Thernstrom (Cambridge: Harvard University Press, 1980), pg. 43.
53. Kallen, pg. 104.
54. Kallen, pgs. 124–25.
55. Quoted in Ratner, pg. 51.
56. Kallen, pg. 94.
57. Kallen, pg. 119.
58. Higham, pg. 109; Kallen, pg. 119.
59. Kallen, pg. 190.
60. Kallen, pg. 121. Italics in original.
61. Arthur Mann, *The One and the Many: Reflections on the Amerian Identity* (Chicago: University of Chicago Press, 1979), pgs. 141–42.
62. Cole, pgs. 202, 203.
63. P. P. Claxton, "Americanization," in *Immigration and Americanization: Selected Readings*, ed. Philip Davis (Boston: Ginn and Company, 1920), pgs. 621–22.
64. Ueda, "Naturalization," pg. 745.
65. Lawrence H. Fuchs, *The American Kaleidoscope: Race, Ethnicity, and the Civic Culture* (Hanover, New Hampshire: Wesleyan University Press (University Press of New England), 1990), pg. 66.

Chapter 5. Americanization's Resurgence and Undoing

1. I am indebted to K. Scott Wong of Williams College for this anecdote. It appears in his paper, "Finally Americans? Chinese Americans at Mid-Century," presented at the University of California at San Diego, May 24, 1996.
2. William Wei, *The Asian American Movement* (Philadelphia: Temple University Press, 1993), pg. 22.
3. Wei, pg. 8.
4. Wei, pg. 45.
5. Roger Daniels, *Coming to America: A History of Immigration and Ethnicity in American Life* (New York: HarperCollins, 1990), pgs. 294–95.
6. Daniels, pg. 296.
7. The most important immigration-related political issue to emerge during the 1930s involved the plight of German Jews and the neglect they suffered from President Franklin D. Roosevelt and the United States. The state department and other organs of government made it exceedingly difficult for Jews to flee Nazi Germany and find refuge in the United States. It is important to recognize two points here. First, the full implications of Hitler's anti-Semitism and the Holo-

caust would not be understood until after Roosevelt's death and the final days of the Second World War. Second, American indifference to the Jews underscores the point that immigration was *not* a burning political concern during the 1930s.

8. Oscar Handlin, *Race and Nationality in American Life* (Garden City, N.Y.: Doubleday Anchor Books, 1957), pg. 145.

9. Annie E. S. Beard, *Our Foreign-Born Citizens: What They Have Done for America,* 3rd ed. (New York: Thomas Y. Crowell Company, 1939).

10. Francis J. Brown and Joseph S. Roucek, eds., *Our Racial and National Minorities: Their History, Contributions, and Present Problems* (New York: Prentice-Hall, 1937).

11. Brown and Roucek, pg. 763.

12. Philip Gleason, "American Identity and Americanization," in *Harvard Encyclopedia of American Ethnic Groups,* ed. Stephan Thernstrom (Cambridge: Harvard University Press, 1980), pg. 45.

13. Brown and Roucek, pg. 303.

14. Brown and Roucek, pg. 265.

15. Brown and Roucek, pg. 448.

16. William Carlson Smith, *Americans in the Making: The Natural History of the Assimilation of Immigrants* (New York: D. Appleton-Century Co., 1939), pg. xii. Italics in original.

17. Smith, pg. 116.

18. Smith, pg. 119. Italics in original.

19. Smith, pg. 117.

20. Marcus Lee Hansen, "The Problem of the Third Generation Immigrant," Augustana Historical Society, Rock Island, Illinois, 1938), pg. 6. See also Marcus Lee Hansen, "The Third Generation in America: A Classic Essay in Immigrant History," *Commentary* 14, no. 5 (November 1952), pgs. 493–94.

21. Carl Wittke, *We Who Built America: The Saga of the Immigrant* (New York: Prentice-Hall, 1939), pg. 518.

22. Ruby Jo Reeves Kennedy, "Single or Triple Melting Pot? Intermarriage Trends in New Haven," *American Journal of Sociology* 49, January 1944, pgs. 331–39; Will Herberg, *Protestant-Catholic-Jew* (New York: Doubleday, 1955).

23. Francis J. Brown and Joseph S. Roucek, eds., *One America: The History, Contributions, and Present Problems of Our Racial and National Minorities,* rev. ed. (New York: Prentice-Hall, 1945), pg. vi.

24. John Higham, *Send These to Me: Immigrants in Urban America,* rev. ed. (Baltimore: Johns Hopkins University Press, 1984), pg. 59.

25. Margaret Mead, *And Keep Your Powder Dry: An Anthropologist Looks at America* (New York: William Morrow and Company, 1942), pg. 49.

26. Quoted in Fuchs, pg. 360.

27. Gleason, pg. 47.

28. James T. Patterson, *Grand Expectations: The United States, 1945–1974* (New York: Oxford University Press, 1996), pgs. 15–18.

29. Gunnar Myrdal, *An American Dilemma: The Negro Problem and Modern Democracy,* vol. 1 (New York: Harper Brothers Publishers, 1944), pg. xix. Italics in original.

30. Myrdal, pg. 48.

31. For a short but interesting biographical sketch of Handlin, see Barbara Miller

Solomon, "A Portrait of Oscar Handlin," in *Uprooted Americans: Essays to Honor Oscar Handlin,* eds. Richard C. Bushman, et al. (Boston: Little, Brown and Company, 1979), pgs. 1–8.

32. Oscar Handlin, *The Uprooted: The Epic History of the Great Migrations that Made the American People* (Boston: Little, Brown and Company, 1951), pg. 3.
33. Handlin, *The Uprooted,* pg. 285.
34. Milton Rugoff, "Pathways to the Land of Promise," *New York Times,* October 7, 1951, sec. 7, pg. 6.
35. Handlin, *The Uprooted,* pg. 305.
36. Handlin, *The Uprooted,* pgs. 306–7.
37. Frederick C. Jaher, *Oscar Handlin's The Uprooted: A Critical Commentary* (New York: American R.D.M. Corporation, 1966), pg. 50.
38. Gleason, pg. 50.
39. Thomas J. Archdeacon, *Becoming American: An Ethnic History* (New York: The Free Press, 1983), pg. 186.
40. Horace M. Kallen, *Cultural Pluralism and the American Idea* (Philadelphia: University of Pennsylvania Press, 1956), pg. 12.
41. Kallen, pg. 44.
42. Kallen, pg. 97.
43. Lyndon Baines Johnson, *Public Papers of the Presidents,* Book II (Washington, D.C.: U.S. Government Printing Office, 1966), pgs. 1038–39.
44. Richard Hofstadter, *The Paranoid Style in American Politics and Other Essays* (New York: Vintage Books, 1967), pgs. 3–40.
45. David H. Bennett, *The Party of Fear: The American Far Right from Nativism to the Militia Movement,* 2d ed. (New York: Vintage Books, 1995), pgs. 409–75.
46. Oscar Handlin, "The Immigration Fight Has Only Begun," *Commentary,* 14, no. 1 (July 1952), pg. 3.
47. Reed Ueda, *Postwar Immigrant America: A Social History* (Boston: Bedford Books of St. Martin's Press, 1994), pg. 52.
48. Immigration and Naturalization Service, *Statistical Yearbook, 1994* (Washington, D.C.: Government Printing Office, 1994), pg. 27.
49. Handlin, *Race and Nationality in American Life,* pg. x.
50. John F. Kennedy, *A Nation of Immigrants* (New York: Harper and Row, 1964).
51. Quoted in Daniels, pg. 340.
52. Daniels, pg. 340.
53. Johnson, pg. 1039.
54. The single best source is Hugh Davis Graham, *The Civil Rights Era: Origins and Development of National Policy 1960–1972* (New York: Oxford University Press, 1990).
55. Terry Eastland, *Ending Affirmative Action: The Case for Colorblind Justice* (New York: Basic Books, 1996), pg. 43.
56. Nathan Glazer and Daniel P. Moynihan, *Beyond the Melting Pot: The Negroes, Puerto Ricans, Jews, Italians, and Irish of New York City* (Cambridge: M.I.T. Press, 1963), pg. 290.
57. Glazer and Moynihan, pg. 290.
58. Glazer and Moynihan, pg. 291.
59. Glazer and Moynihan, pg. 16. Italics in original.

60. Glazer and Moynihan, pg. v.
61. Rudolph J. Vecoli, "*Contadini* in Chicago: A Critique of *The Uprooted*," *Journal of American History* 51, no. 3, (December 1964), pgs. 404–17.
62. Vecoli, pg. 404.
63. Vecoli, pg. 417.
64. Murray Friedman, "Overcoming Middle Class Rage," in *Overcoming Middle Class Rage*, ed. Murray Friedman (Philadelphia: Westminster Press, 1971), pg. 375.
65. Rudolph J. Vecoli, "Ethnicity: A Neglected Dimension of American History," in *Overcoming Middle Class Rage*, ed. Murray Friedman (Philadelphia: Westminster Press, 1971), pg. 174.
66. Andrew Greeley, "What Is an Ethnic?" in *Overcoming Middle Class Rage*, ed. Murray Friedman (Philadelphia: Westminster Press, 1971), pg. 239.
67. Murray Friedman, "Is White Racism the Problem?" in *Overcoming Middle Class Rage*, ed. Murray Friedman (Philadelphia: Westminster Press, 1971), pg. 283.
68. Andrew Greeley, *Why Can't They Be Like Us? Facts and Fallacies about Ethnic Differences and Group Conflict in America* (New York: Institute of Human Relations Press, 1969), pgs. 57–58.
69. Quoted in Irving M. Levine and Judith M. Herman, "The New Pluralism," in *Overcoming Middle Class Rage*, ed. Murray Friedman (Philadelphia: Westminster Press, 1971), pg. 276.
70. Quoted in Ronald Radosh, *Divided They Fell: The Demise of the Democratic Party, 1964–1996* (New York: The Free Press, 1996), pg. 138.
71. Harold R. Isaacs, "The New Pluralists," *Commentary*, March 1972, pg. 77. For responses to this compelling review, see "Letters to the Editor: Ethnics and Pluralists," *Commentary*, June 1972, pgs. 8–16.
72. Murray Friedman, "The 'New Pluralism,'" in *Overcoming Middle Class Rage*, ed. Murray Friedman (Philadelphia: Westminster Press), 1971, pg. 230.
73. Quoted in Arthur Mann, *The One and the Many: Reflections on the American Identity* (Chicago: University of Chicago Press, 1979), pg. 37.
74. Mann, pgs. 37–38.
75. W. H. Auden, "I'll Be Seeing You Again, I Hope," *New York Times*, March 18, 1972, pg. 31.
76. Quoted in Peter Binzen, *Whitetown, U.S.A.* (New York: Random House, 1970), pg. 29.
77. Monroe W. Karmin, "Nationality Groups Aim to Vie with Negroes for Government Aid," *Wall Street Journal*, April 24, 1969, pg. 1.
78. Michael Novak, *The Rise of the Unmeltable Ethnics: Politics and Culture in the Seventies* (New York: Macmillan Company, 1972), pg. 229.
79. Robert Alter, "A Fever of Ethnicity," *Commentary*, June 1972, pg. 70. For responses to this essay, including one from Novak, see "Letters to the Editor: Ethnicity," *Commentary*, October 1972, pgs. 10–24.
80. Novak, pg. 32. Italics in original.
81. Michael Novak, *Unmeltable Ethnics: Politics and Culture in American Life*, 2d ed. (New Brunswick, N.J.: Transaction Publishers, 1996), pgs. xiii, xxv.
82. "Letters to the Editor," *Commentary*, pg. 10.

83. "Six Historians Reflect on What Ails the American Spirit," *Newsweek,* July 6, 1970, pgs. 15, 26 as cited in Mann, pg. 1.
84. Quoted in Arnold Beichman, *Nine Lies About America,* rev. ed. (New York: Pocket Books, 1973), pgs. 15, 17.
85. Hansen, pgs. 5–20.
86. Ishmael Reed et al., "Is Ethnicity Obsolete?" in *The Invention of Ethnicity,* ed. Werner Sollors (New York: Oxford University Press, 1989), pg. 227.
87. Richard D. Alba, *Ethnic Identity: The Transformation of White America* (New Haven: Yale University Press, 1990), pg. 20.
88. Alba, pg. 15.
89. Richard D. Alba, "Assimilation's Quiet Tide," *The Public Interest,* Spring 1995, pgs. 3–18.
90. Quoted in Mann, pg. 36.

Chapter 6. The Problem of Group Rights

1. Ali Raza, Statement against Bill No. 1944, April 23, 1991.
2. Michael Barone, *Our Country: The Shaping of America from Roosevelt to Reagan* (New York: The Free Press, 1990), pgs. 26–27.
3. Robert Dahl, *Who Governs?* (New Haven: Yale University Press, 1961), pgs. 32–51.
4. Marcus Lee Hansen, *The Immigrant in American History* (Cambridge: Harvard University Press, 1940), pg. 132.
5. Edward R. Kantowicz, "Politics," in *The Harvard Encyclopedia of American Ethnic Groups,* ed. Stephan Thernstrom (Cambridge: Harvard University Press, 1980), pg. 805.
6. David A. Hollinger, *Postethnic America: Beyond Multiculturalism* (New York: Basic Books, 1995), pg. 23.
7. Nathan Glazer and Daniel P. Moynihan, *Beyond the Melting Pot: The Negroes, Puerto Ricans, Jews, Italians, and Irish of New York City,* 2d ed. (Cambridge: M.I.T. Press, 1970), pg. 222.
8. Doriane Lambelet Coleman, "Individualizing Justice Through Multiculturalism," *Columbia Law Review* 96, no. 5 (June 1996), pgs. 1093–1167; Margaret Talbot, "Baghdad on the Plains," *New Republic,* August 11 & 18, 1997, pgs. 18–22; Patricia Hurtado, "No Jail for Man Who Killed Wife," *Newsday,* April 1, 1989, pg. 3; Myrna Oliver, "Immigrant Crimes; Cultural Defense—A Legal Tactic," *Los Angeles Times,* July 15, 1988, pg. 1.
9. Peter Skerry, *Mexican Americans: The Ambivalent Minority* (New York: The Free Press, 1993), pgs. 330–31.
10. Abigail Thernstrom, *Whose Votes Count? Affirmative Action and Minority Voting Rights* (Cambridge: Harvard University Press, 1987), pg. 15.
11. Thernstrom, pg. 2.
12. Stephan Thernstrom and Abigail Thernstrom, *America in Black and White: One Nation, Indivisible* (New York: Simon & Schuster, 1997), pg. 289.
13. Linda Chavez, *Out of the Barrio: Toward a New Politics of Hispanic Assimilation* (New York: Basic Books, 1991), pgs. 41–42.

14. Quoted in Chavez, pg. 45.
15. Thernstrom, pg. 256.
16. Abigail Thernstrom, "Dole's Pass," *The New Republic,* April 1, 1996, pg. 11.
17. John J. Miller, "English Is Broken Here," *Policy Review,* September–October 1996, pg. 54.
18. John Silber, testimony before the Subcommittee on the Constitution of the Committee on the Judiciary, House of Representatives, April 18, 1996.
19. Quoted in Ashley Dunn, "Bilingual Ballot Law Fails to Help Chinese-American Voters," *New York Times,* August 14, 1994, pg. 39.
20. Dunn, pg. 39.
21. Thomas D. Elias, "English Spurned by Flood of Citizenship Applicants," *Washington Times,* December 30, 1995, pg. A1. There is also a 55/15 rule.
22. Quoted in Miller, pg. 54.
23. See Article I, Section 2.
24. They are Alaska, Delaware, Montana, North Dakota, South Dakota, Vermont, and Wyoming.
25. Dictionary definition of *constituent,* meant in the political sense: one who helps appoint another as his representative, especially by voting in an election. Since relatively few of the people in Roybal-Allard's district can vote, are they really her constituents?
26. Skerry, pg. 337.
27. "The Latino Vote at Mid-Decade," The Tomas Rivera Center in Claremont, Calif., 1996, pg. 2.
28. Michael Barone and Grant Ujifusa, *The Almanac of American Politics 1998* (Washington, D.C.: National Journal, 1997), pgs. 999-1001.
29. Clifford J. Levy, "Court Outlaws New York District Drawn Up to Aid Hispanic Voters," *New York Times,* February 27, 1997, pg. A1.
30. Alfredo Cardenas, interview by author, San Diego, Texas, February 28, 1996.
31. Bebe Zuniga, interview by author, Laredo, Texas, February 28, 1996.
32. Barone and Ujifusa, pgs. 335–37, 342–44.
33. Barry A. Kosmin and Ariela Keysar, "Party Political Preferences of U.S. Hispanics: The Varying Impact of Religion, Social Class and Demographic Factors," *Ethnic and Racial Studies* 18, no. 2 (April 1995), pg. 338.
34. *New York Times,* November 5, 1992.
35. Rodolfo O. de la Garza and Louis DeSipio, "Latinos and the 1992 Elections," in *Ethnic Ironies: Latino Politics in the 1992 Elections* (Boulder, Colo.: Westview Press, 1996), pgs. 30–32.
36. "New American Co-ethnic Voting," *Research Perspective on Migration,* 1, no. 3 (March/April 1997); Linda Chavez, "The Hispanic Political Tide," *New York Times,* November 18, 1996, pg. 17A.
37. Richard L. Berke, "G.O.P. Making Gains among Hispanic Voters," *New York Times,* July 5, 1993, pg. 1.
38. Sam Attlesey, "Bush Naming of Hispanic Both Symbolic, Practical; Nonpartisan Group Says More Latinos Supported Richards," *Dallas Morning News,* December 18, 1994, pg. 44A.
39. Frank Guerra, interview by author, San Antonio, Texas, February 27, 1996.

40. Kosmin and Keysar, pg. 336.
41. Kosmin and Keysar, pg. 346.
42. John J. Miller, "Asian Americans Head for Politics," *The American Enterprise,* March–April 1995, pg. 56.
43. Seth Mydans, "A Vietnamese-American Becomes a Political First," *New York Times,* November 16, 1992, pg. A11.
44. Miller, "Asian Americans Head for Politics"; John J. Miller, "The Conservative Asian American," *The American Enterprise,* February 1997, pg. 14.
45. Carole J. Uhlaner, "Perceived Discrimination and Prejudice and the Coalition Prospects of Blacks, Latinos, and Asian Americans," in *Racial and Ethnic Politics in California,* ed. Byran D. Jackson and Michael B. Preston (Berkeley: IGS Press, 1991), pgs. 339–71.
46. Jennifer Cheeseman Day, *Population Projections of the United States, by Age, Sex, Race, and Hispanic Origin: 1992 to 2050,* Bureau of the Census, P25–1092, November 1992.
47. Stephan Thernstrom, "The Minority Majority Will Never Come," *Wall Street Journal,* July 26, 1990, pg. A16.
48. John J. Miller, "Assimilation Enriches America's Melting Pot," *Insight,* October 3, 1994, pg. 21.
49. U.S. Bureau of the Census, 1990 Census of Population and Housing, Public Use Microdata Samples.
50. Susan Kalish, "Interracial Baby Boomlet in Progress?" *Population Today* 20, no. 12 (December 1992).
51. U.S. Bureau of the Census, 1990 Census of Population and Housing, Public Use Microdata Samples.
52. Greta A. Gilbertson, Joseph P. Fitzpatrick, and Lijung Yang, "Hispanic Intermarriage in New York City: New Evidence from 1991," *International Migration Review* 30, no. 2 (Summer 1996), pgs. 445–59.
53. Gabrielle Sandor, "The 'Other' Americans," *American Demographics,* June 1994, pg. 36.

Chapter 7. The Naturalizers

1. Linda Wai and Dan Childs, interview by author, Arlington, Va., October 27, 1995.
2. William Branigan, "Inspector General to Probe 'Citizenship USA' Program," *Washington Post,* April 29, 1997.
3. John J. Miller, "Citizenship on the Cheap: Politics Pollutes Naturalization Process," *Organization Trends* (Washington, D.C.: Capital Research Center, June 1997), pgs. 1-7.
4. William Branigan, "INS Accused of Giving in to Politics," *Washington Post,* March 4, 1997, pg. 1.
5. Patrick J. McDonnell, "INS May Waive Some Interviews for Citizenship," *Los Angeles Times,* September 1, 1995, pg. B1.
6. Arnold Rochvarg, "Reforming the Administrative Naturalization Process: Reducing Delays while Increasing Fairness," *Georgetown Immigration Law Journal*

9, no. 3 (Summer 1995), pgs. 397–449. For a response, see John J. Miller, "Dumbing Down Naturalization," *Georgetown Immigration Law Journal* 10, no. 1 (March 6, 1996), pgs. 55–57.

7. Georgie Anne Geyer, *Americans No More: The Death of Citizenship* (New York: Atlantic Monthly Press, 1996), pgs. 137–89; Frank Trejo, "Immigration Firm Told to Halt Citizenship Testing," *Dallas Morning News*, June 28, 1996, pg. 1A; John J. Miller, "Contract Killers," *Reason*, February 1997, pgs. 56–58. See also the ABC News program *20/20*, "Selling Out America," July 12, 1996.

8. Harry Pachon, "Prop. 187 Isn't All That's Propelling Latinos to INS," *Sacramento Bee*, May 22, 1995, pg. B7.

9. Joel Kotkin, "Hotheads in California," *New York Times*, October 27, 1995, pg. 29A.

10. Immigration and Naturalization Service, *1993 Statistical Yearbook*, M-367 (Washington, D.C.: Government Printing Office, 1993), pg. 134.

11. U.S. Constitution, Article 2, Section 1: "No person except a natural born Citizen, or a Citizen of the United States, at the time of the Adoption of this Constitution, shall be eligible to the Office of President." In addition, Article 1, Section 2 requires seven years of citizenship before immigrants can serve in the House of Representatives. Article 1, Section 3 requires nine years for the Senate.

12. John Higham, *Strangers in the Land: Patterns of American Nativism 1860–1925*, 2d ed. (New York: Atheneum, 1963), pgs. 111, 237; Edward George Hartmann, *The Movement to Americanize the Immigrant* (New York: Columbia University Press, 1948), pg. 33. See also Jeremy W. Kilar, "'I am Not Sorry,'" *Michigan History Magazine* 79, no. 6 (Nov.–Dec. 1995), pgs. 11–17.

13. Quoted in Hartmann, pg. 36.

14. Quoted in Hartmann, pg. 113, note 13.

15. Quoted in Hartmann, pg. 67.

16. U.S. Commission on Immigration Reform, June 1995, pgs. 175–200.

17. Leon Bouvier, "Embracing America: A Look at Which Immigrants Become Citizens," Center for Immigration Studies (Center Paper 11), 1996.

18. Author calculations based on Immigration and Naturalization Service, *1995 Statistical Yearbook*, pgs. 27, 140.

19. Author calculation using data from Bureau of the Census, *The Foreign-Born Population in the United States*, 1990 CP–3–1.

20. Immigration and Naturalization Service, *1995 Statistical Yearbook*, pgs. 130–39. These rates are actually a bit low because they do not include children who gained citizenship when their parents naturalized.

21. Marion T. Bennett, *American Immigration Policies: A History* (Washington, D.C.: Public Affairs Press, 1963), pg. 343.

22. John Martin, "A Natural Surge in Naturalization," *Immigration Review* 22, Summer 1995, pgs. 9–11.

23. Sam Dillon, "Mexico Woos U.S. Mexicans, Proposing Dual Nationality," *New York Times*, December 10 1995, pg. 16A.

24. U.S. Commission on Immigration Reform, June 1995, pgs. 181–82.

25. Marcus Stern, "The Rush to Citizenship: Citizens-to-Be Stretch INS, Naturalization System Buckling under Backlog," *San Diego Union-Tribune*, April 2,

1995, pg. 1. See also Patrick J. McDonnell, "Applications for Citizenship Soar in L.A.," *Los Angeles Times*, April 10, 1995, pg. 1.

26. Immigration and Naturalization Service, *1995 Statistical Yearbook*, pg. 132.
27. Immigration and Naturalization Service, *1978 Statistical Yearbook*, pg. 83.
28. Immigration and Naturalization Service, *1995 Statistical Yearbook*, pgs. 132, 144–45; author calculations.
29. Bouvier, pgs. 13–15.
30. Zai Liang, "On the Measurement of Naturalization," *Demography* 31, no. 3 (August 1994), pgs. 525–48.
31. Philip Q. Yang, "Explaining Immigrant Naturalization," *International Migration Review* 28, no. 3 (Fall 1994), 449–77.
32. According to Yang, service in the U.S. armed forces increases the odds of naturalization by 320 percent. See ibid., pg. 470.
33. Dowell Myers, "The Changing Immigrants of Southern California," Research Report LCRI–95–04R, School of Urban and Regional Planning, University of Southern California, October 25, 1995. See also Carol Tucker, "Immigrants on the Move," *University of Southern California Chronicle*, November 6, 1995.
34. Yang, pg. 472. Note: Yang holds all variables constant and thus is able to isolate the effect of particular characteristics.
35. Yang, pgs. 470–72.
36. Bouvier, pgs. 35–47.
37. Yang, pg. 472.
38. Greg Gourley, interview by author, Bellevue, Wash., November 21, 1995. See also "U.S. Students Stumble on Citizenship Test," *American Teacher*, October 1995; and Lawrence Hardy, "U.S. Citizenship Test Stumps Native Kids," *USA Today*, July 5, 1995, pg. 4D.
39. Paul L. Williams, et al., *NAEP 1994 U.S. History: A First Look*, Office of Educational Research and Improvement, U.S. Department of Education, November 1995; see also Rene Sanchez, "Knowing the Past May Be History, U.S. Test Reveals; Many American Students Ignorant of Basic Facts," *Washington Post*, November 2, 1995, pg. A1.
40. The problem does not end with high school students. On July 4, 1995, the television program *Dateline NBC* aired a short segment in which it asked Americans questions from the citizenship test. One woman said that there were 49 stars on the flag and a man said that there were 52. Generals Colin Powell, Norman Schwarzkopf, and John Shalikashvili each were identified by separate respondents as the commander-in-chief. The president, however, is the commander-in-chief. According to one man, the Pilgrims first came to America on the *Nina*, the *Pinta*, and the *Santa Maria*, not the *Mayflower*.
41. National Association of Latino Elected Officials Education Fund, "New Citizens in Limbo? One in Three Applicants for U.S. Citizenship Neither Pass Nor Fail," NALEO Background Paper 8, 1988.
42. Robert A. Alvarez, "A Profile of the Citizenship Process among Hispanics in the United States," *International Migration Review* 21, no. 2 (Summer 1987), pgs. 327–51.

43. Joel Brinkley, "At Immigration, Disarray and Defeat," *New York Times,* September 10, 1994, pg. 1.

44. Daniel Sutherland, "Abolish the INS: How Bureaucracy Dooms Immigration Reform," *CEO Policy Brief* (Washington, D.C.: Center for Equal Opportunity, January 1996), pg. 3.

45. From June 1994 to June 1996, the average processing time for a naturalization application was 373 days: General Accounting Office, "Alien Applications: Processing Differences Exist Among INS Field Units," GAO/GGD-97-47, May 20, 1997, pg. 12.

46. John Palmer Gavit, *Americans by Choice* (1922; reprinted, Montclair, N.J.: Patterson Smith, 1971), pg. 124.

47. See for example Joseph N. Boyce, "Hispanic Influx Spurs Legislator to Practice Multiethnic Diplomacy," *Wall Street Journal,* May 7, 1997, pgs. A1, A8.

48. John J. Miller and William Muldoon, "Citizenship for Granted: How the INS Devalues Naturalization Testing," *CEO Policy Brief* (Washington, D.C.: Center for Equal Opportunity, 1996).

49. *Georgetown Immigration Law Journal* 10, no. 1 (March 6, 1996), pg. 12.

50. Ibid., pg. 9.

51. Immigration and Naturalization Service, *United States History, 1600–1987,* M–289, 1987; Immigration and Naturalization Service, *U.S. Government Structure,* M–291, 1987; Immigration and Naturalization Service, "100 Typical Questions," WR–709 2211, July 30, 1993.

52. R. K. O'Neil and G. K. Estes, *Naturalization Made Easy: What to Do and What to Know,* 4th ed. (San Francisco: A. Carlisle & Co., 1913).

53. Ibid., pg. 21.

54. Ibid., pg. 23: "You must not be discouraged if you find after reading the Constitution once or twice that you do not understand it thoroughly. You are not expected to learn in a few months what many lawyers have failed to comprehend in a lifetime."

55. Ibid., pgs. 89–96.

56. Cathrine A. Bradshaw, *Americanization Questionnaire,* rev. ed. (New York: Noble and Noble Publishers, 1930).

57. Ibid., pg. 15. The answer is: "Because he ought to leave enough money to pay for his sickness and burial, and some support for those who are dependent on him."

58. Quoted in Hartmann, pgs. 35–36.

59. Barbara Madsen, interview by author, Federal Way, Wash., November 8, 1995.

60. Greg Gourley, interview by author, Bellevue, Wash., November 7, 1995.

61. Ibid.

62. Ibid.

63. Katherine Long, "BCC Will Make It Easier to Become a U.S. Citizen," *Seattle Times,* September 14, 1995, pg. B1. See also Jen Ellison, "America Still Land of Opportunity for Immigrants," *Redmond Sammamish Valley News,* September 27, 1995; Mike Lee, "Immigrants Inspired by Citizenship Class: BCC Inundated with Calls for No-Hassle Naturalization," *Kirkland Courier,* September 27, 1995, pg. 1.

64. Cheryl Zeh, interview by author, Seattle, Wash., November 8, 1995.

65. Viktor Bozhko, interview by author, Bellevue, Wash., November 9, 1995.

66. Ramon Negrin, interview by author, Bellevue, Wash., November 6, 1995.

67. Scott Winslow, interview by author, Federal Way, Wash., November 8, 1995.

68. Cal Uomoto, interview by author, Seattle, Wash., November 6, 1995.

69. Bob Salisbury, interview by author, Bellevue, Wash., November 9, 1995.

70. *National Standards for Civics and Government* (Calabasas, Calif.: Center for Civics Education, 1994), pg. v.

71. Rex Tung, interview by author, Alexandria, Va., October 19, 1995.

72. Raul Vallejos, interview by author, Alexandria, Va., October 19, 1995.

73. U.S. Department of Justice, Immigration and Naturalization Service, *Citizenship Education and Naturalization Information* (Washington, D.C.: U.S. Government Printing Office, 1987), pg. 40.

Chapter 8. The Failure of Bilingual Education

1. For the purposes of this chapter, immigrant children means both children who literally are foreign-born as well as children who have foreign-born parents. Both groups are likely to face the same linguistic challenges and require similar teaching approaches. Interviews at Willmore were conducted in January 1996.

2. "Children demonstrate a remarkable ability to acquire a second language spontaneously in the absence of explicit instruction. . . . During the initial phase of learning, adults and older children are faster at learning the second language than younger children. In the long run, however, children are more successful learners of a second language." Kenji Hakuta, *Mirror of Language: The Debate on Bilingualism* (New York: Basic Books, 1991), pg. 232.

3. Diane Ravitch, *The Great School Wars: A History of the New York City Public Schools* (New York: Basic Books, 1974), pg. 244.

4. Josué M. González, "Spanish as a Second School Language: Adding Language to the Discourse of Multicultural Education," in *Reinventing Urban Education: Multiculturalism and the Social Context of Schooling,* ed. Francisco L. Rivera-Batiz (New York: Institute for Urban and Minority Education, Teachers College, Columbia University, 1994), pg. 263.

5. Quoted in Daniels, pgs. 109–10.

6. Quoted in Dennis Baron, *The English-Only Question: An Official Language for Americans?* (New Haven: Yale University Press, 1990), pg. 64.

7. Baron, pgs. 87–90.

8. Quoted in Baron, pg. 90.

9. In 1996, the House of Representatives passed a bill declaring English the official language of the United States. The Senate did not vote on the issue and President Clinton threatened a veto.

10. General Accounting Office, "Limited English Proficiency: A Growing and Costly Challenge Facing Many School Districts," GAO/HEHS–94–38, January 28, 1994, pg. 1.

11. General Accounting Office, "School Age Demographics: Recent Trends Pose

New Educational Challenges," GAO/HRD–93–105BR, August 1993, pgs. 42 and 70.

12. U.S. Department of Education, "Chapter 201: Bilingual Education Programs—Discretionary Grants to Local Education Agencies—Part A," *Biennial Evaluation Report—FY 93–94,* CFDA No. 84.003.

13. Dowell Myers, "The Changing Immigrants of Southern California," Research Report No. LCRI–95–04R, Lusk Center Research Institute, University of Southern California, October 1995.

14. Alejandro Portes and Richard Schauffler, "Language and the Second Generation: Bilingualism Yesterday and Today," in *The New Second Generation,* ed. Alejandro Portes (New York: Russell Sage Foundation, 1996), pg. 28.

15. Rubén G. Rumbaut, "The New Californians," in *California's Immigrant Children: Theory, Research, and Implications for Educational Policy,* ed. Rubén G. Rumbaut and Wayne A. Cornelius (San Diego: University of California, Center for U.S. -Mexican Studies, 1995), pgs. 18–19.

16. Frank V. Thompson, *Schooling the Immigrant* (1920; reprinted, Montclair, N.J.: Patterson Smith, 1971), pgs. 2, 4.

17. Hartmann, pgs. 73, 191.

18. Thompson, pg. 16.

19. Thompson, pg. 214.

20. Thompson, pg. 26.

21. U.S. English, "Survey of Voter Attitudes in the United States," August 18–19, 1993. See also Christine H. Rossell and Keith Baker, *Bilingual Education in Massachusetts: The Emperor Has No Clothes* (Boston: Pioneer Institute, 1996), pgs. 161–84.

22. Center for Equal Opportunity, "The Importance of Learning English: A National Survey of Hispanic Parents," September 5, 1996. See also Linda Chavez, "Hispanic Parents Want English Education," *Wall Street Journal,* September 5, 1996.

23. Jim Cummins, *Empowering Minority Students,* Teacher Training Monograph Number 5, Teacher Training Project for Bilingual & English Teachers to Speakers of Other Languages, University of Florida, July 1987, pgs. 25, 26.

24. Richard Bernstein, "In U.S. Schools, a War of Words," *New York Times Magazine,* October 14, 1990, pg. 34.

25. Robert E. Rossier, "Bilingual Education: Training for the Ghetto," *Policy Review,* Summer 1983, pg. 37.

26. Quoted in "The New Apartheid," *National Review,* July 23, 1990, pg. 14.

27. Rosalie Pedalino Porter, *Forked Tongue: The Politics of Bilingual Education* (1990; reprinted, New Brunswick, N.J.: Transaction Publishers, 1995), pg. 60.

28. Porter, pg. 70.

29. Porter, pg. 21.

30. Consuelo Ryan, interview by author, Boston, Mass., February 12, 1996.

31. Elena Rivas, interview by author, Boston, Mass., February 12, 1996.

32. Josefina Rodriguez, interview by author, Boston, Mass., February 12, 1996.

33. Ibid.

34. Archie Walsh, interview by author, Boston, Mass., February 12, 1996.

35. Celina Quirindongo, interview by author, Boston, Mass., February 12, 1996.
36. Interview by author, Boston, Mass., February 12, 1996.
37. Sonyan Wong, interview by author, Boston, Mass., February 12, 1996.
38. Robert E. Rossier, "Second Language Teaching: A Theoretical Baseline for Policy Makers," *READ Perspectives* 1, no. 1 (Autumn 1993), pg. 11.
39. Porter, pgs. 82–83.
40. Hakuta, pg. 219.
41. James Crawford, *Bilingual Education: History, Politics, Theory, and Practice* (Trenton, N.J.: Crane Publishing Co., 1989), pg. 19.
42. Quoted in Joshua A. Fishman, *Language Loyalty in the United States: The Maintenance and Perpetuation of Non-English Mother Tongues by American Ethnic and Religious Groups* (The Hague: Mouton and Co., 1966), pg. 233.
43. Carolyn R. Toth, *German-English Bilingual Schools in America: The Cincinnati Tradition in Historical Context* (New York: Peter Lang Publishing, 1990), pg. 61. See also Louis Viereck, *German Language Instruction in American Schools* (1902, New York: Arno Press, 1978).
44. Fuchs, pgs. 458–59 and 584 n7.
45. Baron, pgs. 144–50.
46. Linda Chavez, *Out of the Barrio: Toward a New Politics of Hispanic Assimilation* (New York: Basic Books, 1991), pg. 10.
47. Abigail Thernstrom, "Language: Issues and Legislation," in *Harvard Encyclopedia of American Ethnic Groups*, ed. Stephan Thernstrom (Cambridge: Harvard University Press, 1980), pg. 620.
48. Chavez, pgs. 10–11. See also Hakuta, pgs. 193–98.
49. Thernstrom, pg. 622.
50. Between 1885 and 1947, for example, it was legal to segregate Indians and "Mongolians" in California public schools. Some districts used this law to separate Mexican-American children from non-Hispanic whites. See W. Henry Cooke, "Segregation of Mexican-American School Children," in *A Documentary History of the Mexican Americans*, ed. Wayne Moquin with Charles Van Doren (New York: Bantam Books, 1971), pgs. 422.
51. Thernstrom, "Language," pg. 622.
52. Quoted in Abigail Thernstrom, "Bilingual Miseducation," *Commentary*, February 1990, pg. 45.
53. Quoted in Crawford, pg. 32.
54. Chavez, pg. 13.
55. Diane Ravitch, *The Schools We Deserve: Reflections on the Educational Crises of Our Time* (New York: Basic Books, 1985), pg. 268.
56. Crawford, pg. 37.
57. Chavez, pg. 15.
58. Rossier, pg. 42.
59. Rochelle L. Stanfield, "Are Federal Bilingual Rules a Foot in the Schoolhouse Door?" *National Journal*, October 18, 1980. See also Chavez, pgs. 15–16.
60. Chavez, pgs. 15–17; Crawford, pgs. 34–35.
61. Thernstrom, "Language," pg. 623.
62. Quoted in Thernstrom, "Language," pg. 624.

63. Thernstrom, "Language," pg. 624.
64. Chavez, pgs. 19–20; Thernstrom, "Language," pgs. 624–25.
65. Noel Epstein, *Language, Ethnicity, and the Schools: Policy Alternatives for Bilingual-Bicultural Education* (Washington, D.C.: Institute for Educational Leadership, George Washington University, 1977), pg. 3.
66. Epstein, pg. 70.
67. Chavez, pgs. 25–27.
68. Keith A. Baker and Adriana A. de Kanter, "Federal Policy and the Effectiveness of Bilingual Education," *Bilingual Education: A Reappraisal of Federal Policy*, ed. Keith A. Baker and Adriana A. de Kanter (Lexington, Mass.: Lexington Books, 1983), pg. 49.
69. Quoted in Hakuta, pg. 207.
70. It was number eight. See Doug Bandow, "The Terrible Ten: America's Worst Regulations," *Policy Review*, Spring 1985, pg. 42.
71. Quoted in Thernstrom, "Language," pg. 625.
72. Rossier, pg. 40.
73. Stanfield.
74. Fuchs, pg. 465.
75. Crawford, pg. 33.
76. American Legislative Exchange Council, "The Report Card on American Education: Bilingual Education in the United States, 1991–92," September 1994.
77. Rene Sanchez, "Federal Math Fails to Keep Pace with the Need to Learn English," *Washington Post*, December 27, 1995, pg. A8.
78. Chester E. Finn, Jr., "Toward Excellence in Education," *The Public Interest*, Summer 1995, pgs. 50–51.
79. Jorge Amselle, ed., *The Failure of Bilingual Education* (Washington, D.C.: Center for Equal Opportunity, 1996), pg. 101.
80. Amselle, pg. 110.
81. Amselle, pg. 107.
82. Amselle, pg. 99.
83. Joseph Berger, "Schools Cope with Influx of Immigrants," *New York Times*, April 15, 1992, pg. B3.
84. Jorge Amselle, "Bilingual Education: A Ten State Report Card, *CEO Policy Brief* (Washington, D.C.: Center for Equal Opportunity, April 1997), pg. 25.
85. Joseph Berger, "School Programs Assailed as Bilingual Bureaucracy," *New York Times*, January 4, 1993, pg. A1.
86. Public Education Association, "A Consumer's Guide to Middle Schools in District 32, Brooklyn," 1996, pg. 3.
87. Public Education Association, pg. 7.
88. Editorial, "New York's Bilingual 'Prison,'" *New York Times*, September 22, 1995, pg. A22.
89. Board of Education of the City of New York, "Educational Progress of Students in Bilingual and ESL Programs: A Longitudinal Study, 1990–1994," October 1994.
90. Quoted in Wendy Lin, "Choosing the Right Language of Learning," *Newsday*, October 16, 1991, pg. 26.

91. "Bilingual-Education Program Needs Work," *Hartford Courant,* November 24, 1994, pg. A12.

92. Diane August and Kenji Hakuta, eds., *Improving Schooling for Language-Minority Children: A Research Agenda* (Washington, D.C.: National Academy Press, 1997).

93. Rossell and Baker, pgs. 45–65. See a lso Christine H. Rossell and Keith Baker, "The Educational Effectiveness of Bilingual Education," *Research in the Teaching of English* 30, no. 1 (February 1996), pgs. 7–74.

94. Quoted in Amy Pyle, "Bilingual Schooling Is Failing, Parents Say," *Los Angeles Times,* January 13, 1996, pg. B1. See also Amy Pyle, "80 L.A. Students Held out of School in Latino Boycott," *Los Angeles Times,* February 14, 1996, pg. B1.

95. General Accounting Office, "Limited English Proficiency," pg. 37.

96. Stephanie Chavez, "Mexico Sending Books, Teachers to L.A. Schools," *Los Angeles Times,* August 3, 1993, pg. 1A.

97. General Accounting Office, "Limited English Proficiency," pg. 38.

98. Robert Miller, "Mexico's Role in U.S. Education—A Well-Kept Secret," *Phi Delta Kappan* 76, no. 6 (February 1995), pg. 470.

99. Linda Chavez, "One Nation, One Common Language," *Reader's Digest,* August 1995, pg. 91.

100. Chavez, "One Nation," pg. 89.

101. All the direct quotes from people in Bethlehem, Pennsylvania, are from interviews by the author, February 7–8, 1996. See John J. Miller, "Muchas Gracias, Mr. Doluisio," *Policy Review,* May/June 1996, pgs. 46–49.

102. Porter, pg. 63. Italics in original.

103. Quoted in Judith Simons-Turner, Mark Connelly, and Ann Goldberg, "The Bethlehem, PA, School District's English Acquisition Program: A Blueprint for Change," *READ Perspectives* II, no. 2 (Fall 1995), pg. 57.

104. Ann Goldberg, "Follow-up Study on the Bethlehem, Pa., School District's English Acquisition Program," *READ Perspectives,* IV, no. 1 (Spring 1997), pgs. 59–94.

105. Simons-Turner, et al., pgs. 87–89.

106. Goldberg, pgs. 75–76.

107. Simons-Turner, et al., pgs. 77–78.

Chapter 9. Americanization on the Job

1. Luigi Solimeo, interview by author, Flushing, NY, November 16, 1995.

2. Barnaby J. Feder, "Dead-End Jobs? Not for These: Immigrants Flourish in the McDonald's System," *New York Times,* July 4, 1995, pg. 45.

3. Julie Cleary, interview by author, New York, NY, November 16, 1995. See also Ben Wildavsky, "McJobs: Inside America's Largest Youth Training Program," *Policy Review,* Summer 1989, pgs. 30–37.

4. Amity Shlaes, "About Those McDonald's Jobs . . . " *Wall Street Journal,* August 15, 1995, pg. A17.

5. Kerby A. Miller, *Emigrants and Exiles: Ireland and the Irish Exodus to North America* (New York: Oxford University Press, 1985), pgs. 134, 486–88, 517.

6. Betty Lee Sung, *The Story of the Chinese in America* (New York: Collier Books, 1971), pg. 1; Lisa See, *On Gold Mountain: The One-Hundred-Year Odyssey of a Chinese-American Family* (New York: St. Martin's Press, 1995), pg. 3.

7. Patrick J. McDonnell, "New Urban Flight—to *El Norte,*" *Los Angeles Times,* September 22, 1993, pg. 1.

8. Quoted in Vicki Goldbert and Arthur Ollman, *A Nation of Strangers* (San Diego: Museum of Photographic Arts, 1995).

9. Maria Puente, "Immigrants Eager to Be Called 'Americans'," *USA Today,* July 5, 1995, pg. 5A.

10. James A. Johnson, "What Immigrants Want," *Wall Street Journal,* June 20, 1995, pg. A18.

11. Thomas Sowell, *Migrations and Cultures: A World View,* (New York: Basic Books, 1996), pg. 4.

12. "Anti-Immigrant Feeling Running High in the USA," *USA Today,* July 14, 1993.

13. Barry R. Chiswick and Teresa A. Sullivan, "The New Immigrants," in *State of the Union: America in the 1990s,* vol. 2: *Social Trends,* ed. Reynolds Farley (New York: Russell Sage Foundation, 1995), pgs. 240–45.

14. Michael Fix and Jeffrey S. Passel, *Immigration and Immigrants: Setting the Record Straight* (Washington, D.C.: Urban Institute, 1994), pg. 34.

15. Charlene Marmer Solomon, "Managing Today's Immigrants," *Personnel Journal,* February 1993, pg. 2.

16. Quoted in William Booth, "'Work, Work, Work': In Little Haiti, Life Is Hopeful but Hard," *Washington Post,* May 19, 1994, pg. A3.

17. Chiswick and Sullivan, pgs. 259–64.

18. George J. Borjas, "National Origin and the Skills of Immigrants in the Postwar Period," in *Immigration and the Work Force: Economic Consequences for the United States and Source Areas,* ed. George J. Borjas and Richard B. Freeman (Chicago: University of Chicago Press, 1992), pgs. 17–47.

19. Julian L. Simon, *Immigration: The Economic and Demographic Facts* (Washington, D.C.: Cato Institute and National Immigration Forum, 1995), pg. 14.

20. Maldwyn Allen Jones, *American Immigration,* 2d ed. (Chicago: University of Chicago Press, 1992), pgs. 241–42.

21. Julian Simon and Ather Akbari, "The Truth about Immigrant 'Quality'," Alexis de Tocqueville Institution, April 1995.

22. Bureau of the Census, *The Foreign-Born Population in the United States: 1990,* CP-3-1.

23. Mark C. Regets, "Immigrants Are 23 Percent of U.S. Residents with S&E Doctorates," Data Brief of the National Science Foundation 1995, no. 15 (November 15, 1995).

24. Philip Peters, "Made in the USA: Immigrants, Patents, and Jobs," Alexis de Tocqueville Institution, March 6, 1996.

25. Bureau of the Census, *The Foreign-Born Population: 1996,* p20-494, March 1997.

26. Michael Fix and Wendy Zimmerman, "When Should Immigrants Receive Public Benefits?" Urban Institute, May 1995, pgs. 4–5.

27. Robert Rector, "A Retirement Home for Immigrants," *Wall Street Journal,* February 20, 1996, pg. A18.
28. Fix and Zimmerman, pg. 5.
29. Fix and Zimmerman, pg. 6.
30. Robert Pear, "Legal Immigrants to Benefit Under New Budget Accord," *New York Times,* July 30, 1997, pg. A17.
31. Miguel Angel Rivera, interview by author, Baltimore, Md., September 13, 1995.
32. Barry R. Chiswick and Paul W. Miller, "Language in the Immigrant Labor Market," in *Immigration, Language, and Ethnicity: Canada and the United States,* ed. Barry R. Chiswick (Washington, D.C.: The AEI Press, 1992), pgs. 229–96.
33. Barry R. Chiswick and Paul W. Miller, "The Languages of the United States: What Is Spoken and What It Means," *READ Perspectives* 3, no. 2 (Fall 1996), pgs. 5–41.
34. Leigh Hopper, "Study: Asian Refugees' English, Income Linked," *Houston Post,* May 24, 1994, pg. A1.
35. Walter S. McManus, William Gould, and Finis Welch, "Earnings of Hispanic Men: The Role of English Language Proficiency," *Journal of Labor Economics* 1, no. 2 (April 1983), pgs. 101–30.
36. Edward P. Lazear, *Culture Wars in America,* Essays in Public Policy No. 71 (Stanford, Calif.: Hoover Institution, 1996), pg. 9.
37. Nicholas B. Fitzgerald, "ESL Instruction in Adult Education: Findings from a National Evaluation," (Center for Applied Linguistics, Washington, D.C.), EDO–LE–95–03, *ERIC Digest,* July 1995.
38. Quoted in Joe Gutierrez, "Company Offers Employees Opportunity to Learn English," *Riverside, (Calif.) The Press-Enterprise,* July 16, 1994.
39. Quoted in Tawn Nhan, "Immigrant Workers Learn English from Colleagues," *Charlotte Observer,* May 29, 1995.
40. Myrna Tarrant, interview by author, Fairfax, Va., October 19, 1995.
41. Mary Anne Leitch, interview by phone, October 24, 1995.
42. Lena H. Sun, "Students' Accent Is on Reducing Theirs," *Washington Post,* December 5, 1995, pg. B1.
43. Jack Wax, "Accent on English," *American Medical News* 33, no. 22 (June 8, 1990), pg. 9.
44. Armand Dipalma, interview by author, New York, N.Y., October 4, 1995.
45. Tonia Sylla, interview by author, New York, N.Y., October 4, 1995.
46. Dottie Enrico, "English-Only Translates to Trouble," *Newsday,* October 9, 1994, pg. 7.
47. Gregory C. Parliman and Rosalie J. Shoeman, "National Origin Discrimination or Employer Prerogative? An Analysis of Language Rights in the Workplace," *Employee Relations Law Journal,* March 22, 1994.
48. U.S. Equal Employment Opportunity Commission, Technical Assistance Program, *National Origin Discrimination: Employment Discrimination Prohibited by Title VII of the Civil Rights Act of 1964, As Amended,* May 1995, pgs. 623–21 to 623–22.

49. Ann Davis, "English-Only Rules Spur Workers to Speak Legalese," *Wall Street Journal,* January 23, 1997, pgs. B1, B6.

50. Roger E. Hernandez, "Court's Ruling Muffles Workers," *Rocky Mountain News,* July 1, 1994, pg. 56A.

51. Norman Sklarewitz, "American Firms Lash out at Foreign Tongues," *Business and Society Review,* September 22, 1992.

52. Linda Chavez, "Multilingualism Getting out of Hand," *USA Today,* December 14, 1994, pg. 13A.

53. David G. Savage, "High Court Lets English-Only Job Rules Stand," *Los Angeles Times,* June 21, 1994, pg. A1.

54. William E. Lissy, "Workplace Language Rules," *Supervision* 54, no. 4 (April 1993), pg. 20.

55. Savage, pg. A1.

56. The states are Alaska, Arizona, California, Hawaii, Idaho, Montana, Nevada, Oregon, and Washington.

57. Truman Capote, *In Cold Blood: A True Account of a Multiple Murder and Its Consequences* (New York: Signet/Penguin Books, 1965), pg. 45.

58. Robert M. Halloran, interview by author, Garden City, Kans., September 28, 1995.

59. Donald D. Stull, Michael J. Broadway, and Ken C. Erickson, "The Price of a Good Steak: Beef Packing and Its Consequences for Garden City, Kansas," in *Structuring Diversity: Ethnographic Perspectives on the New Immigration,* ed. Louis Lamphere (Chicago: University of Chicago Press, 1992), pg. 39.

60. Quoted in Deborah Sontag, "New Immigrants Test Nation's Heartland," *New York Times,* October 18, 1993, pg. 1A.

61. Upton Sinclair, *The Jungle* (New York: The New American Library of World Literature, 1960), pg. 17.

62. Quoted in Alan Montgomery, "Kansas Melting Pot: Garden City Adapts as City's Immigrant Population Grows," *Hutchinson News,* September 24, 1995, pg. 1.

63. Donald D. Stull, "Knock 'em Dead: Work on the Killfloor of a Modern Beef-packing Plant," in *Newcomers in the Workplace: Immigrants and the Restructuring of the U.S. Economy,* ed. Louise Lamphere, Alex Stepick, and Guillermo Grenier (Philadelphia: Temple University Press, 1994), pg. 49.

64. Stull, pgs. 57–62.

65. Steve Orozco, interview by author, Garden City, Kans., September 29, 1995.

66. Stull, pg. 74.

67. Kam Virachack, interview by author, Garden City, Kans., September 29, 1995.

68. Stull, et al., pg. 52.

69. Stull, et al., pg. 38.

70. Stull, et al., pg. 54; Stull, pg. 67.

71. Donald D. Stull, interview by phone, September 1995.

72. Nancy Harness, interview by author, Garden City, Kans., September 28, 1995.

73. Donald To, interview by author, Garden City, Kans., September 28, 1995.

74. Lyle Dodson, interview by phone, October 23, 1995.

75. Tony Thaya, interview by author, Garden City, Kans., September 29, 1995.

76. Ernie Ortiz, interview by author, Garden City, Kans., September 29, 1995.

77. R. Kent Nanninga, interview by author, Garden City, Kans., September 28, 1995.

78. William Julius Wilson, *When Work Disappears: The World of the New Urban Poor* (New York: Alfred A. Knopf, 1996), pgs. 51–52.

79. Ken Wirt, interview by author, San Jose, Calif., September 26, 1995.

80. Linda Shaw, interview by author, San Jose, Calif., September 26, 1995.

81. Barbara Beck, interview by author, San Jose, Calif., September 25, 1995.

82. T. J. Rodgers, interview by author, San Jose, Calif., September 26, 1995.

83. Tony Alvarez, interview by author, San Jose, Calif., September 26, 1995.

84. Robert D. Hof, "Intel Unbound," *Business Week,* October 9, 1995, pg. 148.

85. Andrew S. Grove, "Immigration Pays," *Wall Street Journal,* January 8, 1996, pg. A18.

86. Ron K. Unz, interview by author, San Jose, Calif., September 25, 1995.

87. "Microchip Wealth," *Forbes ASAP,* October 9, 1995, pg. 92.

88. Coeta Chambers, interview by author, Santa Clara, Calif. September 25, 1995.

89. "Foreign Students: Who They Are," *New York Times,* January 4, 1995, pg. A17.

90. Mark C. Regets, "Immigrants Are 23 Percent of U.S. Residents with S&E Doctorates," *Data Brief* (Science Resources Studies Division of the National Science Foundation), November 15, 1995. See also Jagdish Bhagwati and Miland Rao, "Foreign Students Spur U.S. Brain Gain," *Wall Street Journal,* August 31, 1994; George Gilder, "Geniuses from Abroad," *Wall Street Journal,* December 18, 1995; and Paul Desruisseaux, "A Record Number of Foreign Students Enrolled at U.S. Colleges Last Year," *Chronicle of Higher Education,* December 6, 1996, pgs. A64–A66.

91. Heidi Wilson, interview by author, Washington, D.C., September 12, 1995.

92. Brochure published by American Immigration Lawyers Association, "Permanent Residence from a Job Offer: The Labor Certification."

93. Rajesh Parekh, interview by author, Menlo Park, Calif., September 25, 1995.

94. Gang Bai, interview by author, Santa Clara, Calif., September 25, 1995.

95. Jose Arreola, interview by author, San Jose, Calif., September 26, 1995.

96. Tracy Hoyt, interview by author, Los Gatos, Calif., September 26, 1995.

97. W. Richard Scott, *Organizations: Rational, Natural, and Open Systems* (Englewood Cliffs, N.J.: Prentice-Hall, 1987), pgs. 129–34.

98. T. J. Rodgers, "The Science of Interviewing," *Harvard Business Review,* July-August 1990, pg. 88.

99. Joseph L. McCarthy, "Mr. Rodgers' Neighborhood," *Chief Executive,* January-February 1995.

100. Welcome memo from T. J. Rodgers.

101. Danny Ryan, interview by author, San Jose, Calif., September 26, 1995.

102. Interview by author, New York, N.Y., April 1994.

Chapter 10. An Americanization Manifesto

1. Ronald Reagan, *An American Life,* (New York: Simon & Schuster, 1990), pgs. 705–6.

2. Seth Mydans, "Poll Finds Tide of Immigration Brings Hostility," *New York Times*, June 27, 1993, pgs. 1, 16.

3. Frances Kellor "Americanization, an Opportunity," *Journal of the Association of College Alumnae*, September 1916, pg. 9, as cited in William Joseph Maxwell, "Frances Kellor in the Progressive Era: A Case Study in the Professionalization of Reform" (Ph.D. diss., Teachers College, Columbia University, 1968), pg. 214.

4. Arthur Herman, *The Idea of Decline in Western History* (New York: The Free Press, 1997), pg. 10.

5. Paul Kennedy, *The Rise and Fall of the Great Powers: Economic Change and Military Conflict from 1500 to 2000* (New York: Vintage Books, 1987), pg. 534.

6. Thomas Fleming, "Introduction," in *Immigration and the American Identity: Selections from Chronicles: A Magazine of American Culture, 1985–1995* (Rockford, Ill.: The Rockford Institute, 1995), pg. 11.

7. Abraham Lincoln, *Selected Speeches and Writings* (New York: The Library of America, 1992), pg. 364.

ACKNOWLEDGMENTS

This is my first book, and I learned two important things in writing it. First, as George Orwell noted half a century ago, "Writing a book is a horrible, exhausting struggle, like a long bout of some painful illness." Second, nothing can replace the generous and unwavering support of colleagues, friends, and family.

Dozens of people have my gratitude for aiding this project from the time of its conception to the moment of its delivery. Some helped in big ways, others in small ones. They all deserve thanks: Jonathan Adler, Jorge Amselle, Michael Barone, Tucker Carlson, Roger Clegg, Chad Conway, Glynn Custred, Rhett DeHart, Howard Dickman, Kara Driscoll, Dinesh D'Souza, John Fonte, Greg Forster, Lawrence Fuchs, Francis Fukuyama, Anita Garcia, Chris Garcia, Pablo Gersten, Greg Gourley, Anne Green, Andrew Hazlett, Rick Henderson, John Hood, Cynthia Inda, Brian Jendryka, Joe Loconte, Fred Lynch, Ying Ma, Sheila Maloney, David W. Miller, Larry Mone, Kathy Moffit, Joel Mowbray, Brendan O'Scannlain, Beth Persons, Noah Pickus, Rosalie Pedalino Porter, Matt Rees, Gerald A. Reynolds, Patrick Roberts, Peter Skerry, Jennifer Soinenen, Matthew Spalding, Dan Sutherland, Abigail Thernstrom, Gloria Matta Tuchman, Reed Ueda, and Dorothea Wolfson.

Lynne Munson deserves special mention. At times she seemed to take a greater interest in this book than its own author did, and I will always appreciate her diligence, friendship, and good advice.

David Bernstein was my friend before he became my editor at The Free Press. His creativity, determination, and loyalty helped turn a series of rambling conversations and meandering proposals into a genuine book. People inside the publishing industry say that nobody edits books anymore. David single-handedly proves them all wrong. Adam Bellow also deserves my thanks for important advice at several crucial junctures. Edith Lewis and Claire Wulker did a fine job of copyediting the manuscript.

Adam Meyerson had the kindness to offer me a one-year Bradley Fellowship at the Heritage Foundation, where I toiled away in Adam's fifth-floor "Ideaplex" alongside the staffs of *Policy Review* and Heritage's Educational Affairs department. I will always appreciate the confidence Adam showed in a young man who had previously never written anything longer than a magazine article, and the many friendships I made at Heritage. I am also grateful for the generous support of the Lynde and Harry Bradley Foundation, which made this project possible.

Long before I had even started to entertain thoughts of writing a book, Linda Chavez plucked me out of obscurity to become my boss, mentor, and friend. I doubt that I hold a single opinion about anything important that has not been influenced in some way by her sharp intelligence. Outside of my family, I owe more to her than anybody I've ever known.

Nothing would be possible without my family, especially my grandmother, to whom this book is dedicated, and my father. Together they are probably my most faithful readers. That honor used to belong to my mother, who passed away while this manuscript was only half written. Within two hours of her passing, however, I received a long-awaited phone call from New York and the offer of a book contract. My wife Amy likes to think that when Mom arrived in Heaven, she made taking care of me her first order of business. So do I.

Amy, of course, deserves the last word. The love and devotion she shows to her husband everyday—even when he is distracted by research, traveling away from home, or playing with the cats instead of changing Brendan's diapers—makes her contribution to this book rise above all others.

INDEX